The American Universe of English

アメリカの心と交わるリーディング

佐藤良明・栩木玲子 ── [編]
Yoshiaki Sato　　Reiko Tochigi

東京大学出版会

The American Universe of English
Yoshiaki Sato and Reiko Tochigi, Editors
University of Tokyo Press, 2010
ISBN 978-4-13-082141-4

Preface

　アメリカは欲望をむきだしにした強い人間たちが，抑圧的な社会を飛び出し，銃を頼みに，死ぬ気で荒野を開拓して作った国です．移民の流入は今なお止まず，アメリカ社会に若々しい粗っぽさをもたらしています．地縁社会の長い伝統のなかで，自分を引っ込める術に長けた人間が暮らす日本のような国とは大違い．権威に絡めとられない，独立独歩の表現者がうようよしています．

　それは一方で，傷つく機会も多いということでしょう．ということは，人々が求める慰安にも，またアメリカ的な特徴があるということです．

　『アメリカン・ユニバース』と称するテキストを編むにあたって，私たちはなによりも，アメリカ人の心の宇宙に焦点を合わせようと思いました．

　ハリウッドの，CNN や MTV の，基地やウォール街のアメリカなら，日本にも入ってきます．しかし暮らしの触感や文明の肌理といったものは，どんなに優れた映像やサウンドからも，すり落ちてしまう部分がある．それらは，他者の心に秘められた思いとして——つまりは，繊細な書き言葉によって，捉えるほかはありません．文字になった言葉こそ，昔から，相手の「思い」を読み取るための最良のメディアでした．

　ところが，文学作品に結実するような優れた文字表現というのは，一般に外国人学習者には敷居が高すぎるものです．口語ベースの読みやすいテクストを通して，知的で情感豊かなコミュニケーションの充実を図ることはできないだろうか．ぐんぐん読まされ，誰にとっても腑に落ちる文章．読むほどにアメリカの愛しい，エキサイティングな，わびしい，狂おしい，どうしようもない姿が滲んでくるような文章．それを見つけてきて，読者にやさしい分量（150 行程度）に編集して差し出すことに，私たちは十分な時間をかけました．考えてみれば編者ふたりは，1960 年代以来，ずっとアメリカを生き

て，観て，聴いてきました．自分たちが，心の柔らかいところで膨らませた，誰にでも通じるはずのアメリカがここに並んでいます．

　私たちの信じるところ，リーディングは滑走やダンスに似ています．母語でならスイスイ滑れる．でも外国語はどうしてもバタつく．ステップをふみ間違える．踊り方が十分わかっていないからです．ときにはずいぶんトリッキーな著者の動きに合わせてみなさんが踊れるよう，後押ししたい――

　そんな気持ちから，注のページでは，ずいぶん口を挟んでいます．原文と交わるために，知っていた方がいいことは，どんどん注に書き入れました．でも，「原文を滑走する」ことがないと，英語習得にはつながりません．左 (原文) ページを右 (注) ページのように還元して理解するのでは本末転倒．右から得たヒントを頼りに左のページを踊り進む――どうか，そのことを心がけていただきたいと思います．ところどころ [a. / b.] どちらかを選ぶ問いの形式を挟みましたが，これは「解説」によって読みを断ち切る代わりに，原文の思考の流れを補いたかったからです．流れに乗って読めていれば，おのずと正解が選べるはずなので，チェックしながら読んでいってください．

　The Universe of English という英語教材が，東京大学教養学部の統一英語教材として刊行されたのは，1993 年のことでした．数冊作って 2006 年春，*The Universe of English II* と *The Expanding Universe of English II* とが東大の教科書としては現役を引退しました．

　授業のために作った教材なのですが，高校生から高齢者まで，たくさんの一般読者の方々から「こういう教材なら読んで楽しい」という望外の反応をいただきました．

　学習者が「読んで楽しい」と思うためには，内容の充実と，平易な表現というふたつの要件を同時にクリアすることが必要です．10 年ぶりのシリーズ新作となった本編では，リキを込めて，鈍重な英文は一切入れない方針を徹底しました．収録した 16 章の内容は，エッセイ，創作，日記，雑誌記事，解説文，講演といろいろですが，どれも大学生以上の知的関心に耐える内容を持ち，かつ――ここが重要です――リズムのいい英語で書かれています．

　語学学習というと，文法的な規則を学び，単語と熟語を覚えていくという荒っぽいやり方に，どうしても走りがちになりますが，特別に調合したこれ

Preface

らの文章を通して，どうぞ，「英語の思い」に染まってみてください．この巻では，新機軸として，各章の最後に Comprehension Check の問いを設け，問題に答えるなかで，そのセッションの核となる内容を英語のまま，まとめ直す機会を設けています．またボキャブラリーの増強と，英語らしい表現の蓄積に目標を定め，巻末にそのためのページを割きました．Editors' Note と称する，英文・和文のコラムは，各セッション本文の楽しさをフォローアップすることだけを考えて書いたものです．

ここ 20 年ほど，日本の翻訳の質はずいぶんあがったようですが，外国の言葉の一つである「英語」で読む歓びは，なにものにも代えがたいと思っています．それを通して私たちは，単一言語による類型的な世界観を逃れ，そしてマスコミがますます煽りつつあるように思える紋切り型の視線から自由になることがされることができます．「発信型」の学習も必要．でも，英語を生きる人たちの心と交わる読書の場を用意することも大切です．両輪のバランスを上手にとっていくことが重要なのは，いうまでもありません．

東京大学出版会の後藤健介氏には，今回も信頼のチームづくりの要となっていただきました．平成ひとケタの時代から Universe を支えてこられた氏の活躍あればこその紙面の充実が，みなさまの読みの充実につながることをお祈りする次第です．

2010 年 3 月　　　編　者

凡　例

注に出てくる符合で *i.e.* は「すなわち」の意味．本文の表現の語義的な説明ではなく，別の角度から言い替えたケースなどで用いた．*e.g.* は「たとえば」，*cf.* は「参考までに」の意味である．

発音記号は，アメリカ人の代表的な発音を，ごく単純な表記システムによって，got [gɑt]，getting [gétiŋ]，easy [íːzi]，easier [íːziər] のように表記した．曖昧母音 [ə] は無音化する場合がよくあるが，それを特にイタリクス等で区別することはしなかった．

◆ Index と Morsels of the Universe のデータは http://www.utp.or.jp/download/ からダウンロードできます．

Table of Contents

Preface　佐藤良明・栩木玲子……………………………………………… i

PART I Taking a Stand

Introduction to Part I ……………………………………………… 2

Session 1　フライドポテト帝国の創立
The Great Potato Baron of Idaho　Eric Schlosser …………… 4

Session 2　臆病者は受動態を使え
Mr. King's Writing Class　Stephen King…………………… 18

Session 3　NYにダコタハウスが建った頃
He Called It the Dakota　Stephen Birmingham…………… 32

Session 4　立ちつくす孤高のコミック・ヒーロー
Charlie Brown: The Triumph of a Loser　David Michaelis … 46

PART II Dear Companions

Introduction to Part II ……………………………………………… 60

Session 5　新感覚な恋のはじまり
The Meeting　Aimee Bender……………………………………… 62

Session 6　イヌのおかげでヒトは喋れた？
The Early Man's Best Friend　Stanley Coren ……………… 72

Table of Contents

Session 7　神になっていた商品
The New Coke Story　Michael Bastedo Angela Davis 84

Session 8　脳死者のハートビート
Alive at Heart　Mary Roach 96

PART III There's No Stopping Us

Introduction to Part III 110

Session 9　多忙作家，女王様系シンガーに大変身
Mid-Life Confidential　Amy Tan 112

Session 10　戦場に生きる男と妻の肖像
Love Is a Battlefield　from *Newsweek* 126

Session 11　ゴシップがメディアを埋め尽くす
The Power of the Tabloids　Jane & Michael Sterns 138

Session 12　モンスターも時代の子
The Monster Is Born　David J. Skal 150

PART IV Let's Face It

Introduction to Part IV 166

Session 13　イラクでは今日も悲劇が
That Raid, That Boy　Zachary-Scott Singley 168

Session 14　ニューヨーク市のリアルな断片
Transported in NYC　Simi Linton / Robert Dumont 178

Session 15　痩せるも太るも哲学なり
The Philosopher's Diet　Richard Watson 190

Session 16　色即是空のユニバース
Nothing　Alan Watts 202

Index / Morsels of the Universe 215

Acknowledgment

Grateful acknowledge is made to for permission to reprint excerpts and figures from the following publications.

Session 1, "The Great Potato Baron of Idaho," by Eric Schlosser: From *Fast Food Nation: The Dark Side of the All-American Meal*, published by Harper Perennial, 2002. Reprinted by permission of Houghton Mifflin Company. Copyright © by Eric Schlosser.

Session 2, "Mr. King's Writing Class," by Stephen King: Reprinted by permission of Scribner, a Division of Simon & Schuster, Inc., from *On Writing: A Memoir of the Craft*, by Stephen King. Copyright © 2000 by Stephen King. All rights reserved.

Session 3, "He Called It the Dakota," by Stephen Birmingham: From *Life at the Dakota: New York's Most Unusual Address*, by Stephen Birmingham, published by Random House in 1979. Copyright © 1979 by Stephen Birmingham.

Session 4, "Charlie Brown: The Triumph of a Loser," by David Michaelis: From "The Life and Times of Charles M. Schulz," in *The Complete Peanuts by Charles M. Schulz*, edited by Gary Groth. Copyright © 2000 by David Michaelis. Reprinted by permission of Fantagraphics Books. All rights of cartoons cited in the chapter are reserved by United Feature Syndicate.

Acknowledgment

Session 5, "The Meeting," by Aimee Bender: From *Willful Creatures*, published in 2005 from Doubleday. Copyright © 2005 by Aimee Bender. Reprinted by permission of Knopf-Doubleday (Random House).

Session 6, "The Early Man's Best Friend," by Stanley Coren: From *How to Speak Dog*, by Stanley Coren. Reprinted and edited by permission of The Free Press, a Division of Simon & Schuster, Inc., from *How to Speak Dog: Mastering the Art of Dog-Human Communication*, by Stanley Coren. Copyright © by Stanley Coren. All rights reserved.

Session 7, "The New Coke Story," by Michael Bastedo Angela Davis: From "God, What a Blunder: The New Coke Story" by Michael Bastedo Angela Davis, included in the website "Cola Fountain" (http://members.lycos.co.uk/thomassheils/). Copyright © December 17, 1993, by Michale Bastedo Angela Davis. University of Tokyo Press made every attempt to reach the copyright holder of this material but in vain. Any information about the copyright of this material will be welcomed.

Session 8, "Alive at Heart," by Mary Roach: From *Stiff: The Curious Lives of Human Cadavers*, by Mary Roach. Reprinted by permission of W. W. Norton & Company. Copyright © 2003 by Mary Roach.

Session 9, "Mid-Life Confidential," by Amy Tan: From *Mid-Life Confidential: The Rock Bottom Remainders Tour America with Three Chords and an Attitude*, published by Plume (Penguin Books) in 1995. Copyright © 1997 by Amy Tan. Reprinted by permission of the author and the Sandra Dijkstra Literary Agency.

Session 10, "Love Is a Battlefield": From an article in *News-*

week, June 15, 2009, by Daniel Stone, Eve Conant, and John Barry. Reprinted by permission of the *Newsweek*, through PARS.

Session 11, "The Power of the Tabloids," by Jane & Michael Sterns: From "National Enquirer", in *Jane & Michael Stern's Encyclopedia of Pop Culture: An A to Z Guide of Who's Who and What's What, from Aerobics and Bubble Gum to Valley of the Doll*. Copyright © 1992 by Jane and Michael Stern. Reprinted by permission of HarperCollins.

Session 12, "The Monster Is Born," by David J. Skal: From *The Monster Show: A Cultural History of Horror*, by David J. Skal, published by Penguin Books, USA. Reprinted by permission of W. W. Norton. Copyright © 1993 by David J. Skal.

Session 13, "That Raid, That Boy," by Zachary-Scott Singley: From "Best American Excerpt from a Military Blog 21 from A Soldier's Thoughts," in *The Best American Non-Required Reading 2006*, Edited by Dave Eggers, published by Mariner Books (Houghton Mifflin Harcourt) in 2006. Copyright © 2006 by Zachary-Scott Singley. Reprinted by kind permission of the author.

Session 14   "Transported in NYC"
"TRANSPORTED" by Simi Linton: From "Transported," which appeared in the *New York Times*, Sunday, November 28, 2004, Section 14, The City Section, p. 3. All rights reserved. Used by permission and protected by the Copyright Laws of the United States. The Printing, copying redistribution or retransmission of the Material without written permission is prohibited.
"TIRED" by Robert Dumont: From *NYC Transit[s]*, published by Xlibris Corporation. Copyright © by Robert

Acknowledgment

Dumont.

Session 15, "The Philosopher's Diet," by Richard Watson: From *The Philosopher's Diet: How to Lose Weight & Change the World*, by Richard Watson. Reprinted by permission of David R. Godine, Publisher, Inc. Copyright © 1985 by Richard Watson.

Session 16, "Nothing," by Alan Watts: From *Nothingness*, by Alan Watts, published by Celestial Arts in 1974. Copyright © 1974 by Celestial Arts.

The American Universe of English

PART I
Taking a Stand

Introduction to Part I

　標題に選んだ take a stand という句は，「立場を明確にする」くらいの意味で広く使われるフレーズだが，ここでは少し大げさに，大陸の風に吹かれつつ独り地面を踏みしめる強い自我のイメージを読み込んでみよう．えり抜いた4編に登場するのは，みな，時の荒波のなかで「オレ流」を成功させたキャラクターばかりである．

　まず **Session 1** ではフライドポテトの帝王，J. R. シンプロット（1909–2008）に登場願う．開拓者の父親のもとを飛び出して芋農夫として自立し，忍耐と運によって成功の道を邁進し，ハンバーガー・チェーンとの提携を通して私たちの日々の食生活にまで関与するようになった経緯を，エリック・シュロッサーの快作 *Fast Food Nation*（2001）によって読む．ファストフード業界の暗部を暴いて話題となり，映画化（2006）もされた作品だが，収録部分のトーンは明るく，淡々とした語りになっている．

　かつては「ホラーの帝王」として知られたスティーヴン・キング（1947– ）だが，もはや「現代の偉大な物語作家」というほうがふさわしい．彼の書きつづる夥しいページ数の物語は，世界の夥しい数の魂をとりこにした．人の心をつかむという点で，彼の小説作法は，売れ筋の食品製法と通じるものがある——という言い方が適当かどうかは別として，そのシンプルで正直で力強い表現には，コミュニケーションの普遍的真実がこもっている．**Session 2** の出典は，キング自身のストレートな表現でつづったエッセイ集 *On Writing: A Memoir of the Craft*（2000）．聴衆を沸かせる講演そのもののような，パフォーマティブなメッセージを受け取ってみよう．

Introduction to Part I

　Session 3 の舞台は，19 世紀末のニューヨーク．「ダコタハウス」といえば，かつてジョン・レノンがヨーコと暮らし，その門の前で撃たれたという超高級アパートだが，まだ整備されていなかったセントラル・パークに面して，その特別な建造物が建つことになった時代のことに想像を走らせる．気品と風格と，どことなく霊気すらたたえるあの建造物が新しい時代の息吹だったころ，それを建てた男（とそこに住んだ人たち）は，どんな人生のスタンスを押しだそうとしたのだろう．アメリカの上流階級をルポし続けるスティーヴン・バーミンガム（1932– ）の *Life at the Dakota*（1979）から読み取ってほしい．

　追いかけた飛球をポトンと落としてグランドにたたずむチャーリー・ブラウンも，アメリカの孤高のヒーローの仲間に入れたい．1950 年に新聞の 4 コマ漫画として登場した『ピーナッツ』は，以後半世紀，作者チャールズ・シュルツの手で描き続けられ，作者の死をもって終了した．**Session 4** に収めたのは，その全集 *The Complete Peanuts* の第 1 巻 (2004) の序文．著者デヴィッド・マイケルスはこのあと *Schultz and Peanuts* という伝記本を出版した．

　4 つの章は，文体もさまざまだ．90 歳の成功者がしゃべる農夫英語も織り込んだ Session 1 の，きびきびとしたルポルタージュ．機知と批判精神に富んだキングの，俗悪すれすれの名言たち (Session 2)．覗き込んだ 19 世紀の社交界のちょっと気取った雰囲気を伝える，挿入と倒置の多い長文 (Session 3)．そしてコミック・キャラの悲哀から時代を読み解こうとする鋭利な分析文 (Session 4)．それぞれに活きのいい，ナマの英語の名文である．

Session

The Great Potato Baron of Idaho

Eric Schlosser

To reach the J. R. Simplot plant in Aberdeen, Idaho, you drive through downtown Aberdeen, population 2,000, and keep heading north, past the half dozen shops on Main Street. Then turn right at the Tiger Hut, an old hamburger stand named after a local high school team, cross the railroad tracks where freight cars are loaded with sugar beets, drive another quarter of a mile, and you're there. It smells like someone's cooking potatoes. The Simplot plant runs twenty-four hours a day, three hundred and ten days a year, turning potatoes into french fries. It's a small facility, by industry standards, built in the late 1950s. It processes about a million pounds of potatoes a day.

Inside the building, a maze of red conveyer belts crisscrosses in and out of machines that wash, sort, peel, slice, blanch, blow-dry, fry, and flash-freeze potatoes. Workers in white coats and hard hats keep everything running smoothly, monitoring the controls, checking the fries for imperfections. Streams of sliced potatoes pour from machines. The place has a cheerful, humble, Eisenhower-era feeling, as though someone's dream of technological progress, of better living through frozen food, has been fulfilled. Looming over the whole enterprise is the spirit of one man: John Richard Simplot, America's great potato baron, whose seemingly inexhaustible energy and willingness to take

The Great Potato Baron of Idaho

- [2] **downtown Aberdeen:**「アバディーンの町の中心」．downtown は，都市の中心部 (旧市街区) を指す (New York City は別，p. 41, 注 [130] 参照)．ここでは小さな田舎町に対してユーモラスに使われている．
- [3] **population 2,000:** この文章は全体に，てきぱきした語り口調で進む．より叙述的な文体なら，with the population of two thousand などとなるところ．
- [4] **(the) half dozen shops on Main Street:** 定冠詞に注意．通りに店が 6 つくらいしかないことが示され，Main Street が一本伸びるだけの小さな田舎町の光景が目に浮かぶ．
- [5] **(the) Tiger Hut . . . named after a local high school team:** 地元の高校のチーム (The Tigers と呼ばれるのだろう) に因んだ名前のタイガー・ハット
- [7] **sugar beets**：てんさい大根．アイダホ州の特産物．
- [11] **a small facility, by industry standards:** ポテト業界の水準からすると小さい施設．*She's a beauty by anyone's standards.*
- [13] **a maze of red conveyer belts crisscrosses:** 迷路 (maze) のような赤い運搬ベルトが交叉して
- [14] **wash, sort, peel, slice, blanch, blow-dry, fry, and flash-freeze:** 洗い，より分け，皮をむき，細切りにし，漂白し，熱風で乾かし，油で揚げ，瞬間冷凍する．*I had my hair blow-dried at the beauty salon.*
- [16] **hard hats:** ヘルメットのこと．
- [17] **the controls:** 制御装置

  checking . . . for imperfections: 出来具合の悪いものがないかチェックしている
- [19] **a cheerful, humble, Eisenhower-era feeling:**「アイゼンハワー時代の陽気で慎ましやかな感じ」．Dwight Eisenhower (1890–1969) が大統領を 2 期つとめた 1950 年代のアメリカは物質的な繁栄を極め，冷戦の脅威とあいまって，未来志向の科学万能主義が支配した．
- [20] **someone's dream of technological progress:** the dream ではなく，someone's dream ということで，みなに共有されているわけではない特異なテクノロジーの未来図が読者に印象づけられる．
- [22] **Looming over the whole enterprise:**「ここの営み全体の上に影を落としている」．この文は There is the spirit of one man looming over . . . と言い換えられる．loom: ボーッと威圧的にあらわれる．
- [23] **potato baron:**「芋男爵」はもちろん愛称．アメリカに爵位は存在しない．
- [24] **seemingly inexhaustible energy:** 無尽蔵のように見える精力

risks built an empire based on french fries. In a portrait that hangs above the reception desk at the Aberdeen plant, J. R. Simplot has the sly grin of a gambler who's scored big.

Simplot was born in 1909. His family left Dubuque, Iowa, the following year and eventually settled in Idaho. His father became a homesteader, obtaining land for free and clearing it with a steel rail dragged between two teams of horses. Simplot grew up working hard on the farm. He rebelled against his domineering father, dropped out of school at the age of fifteen, and left home. He found work at a potato warehouse in the small town of Declo, Idaho. He sorted potatoes with a "shaker sorter," a hand-held device, nine to ten hours a day for 30 cents an hour. With his earnings, Simplot bought a rifle, an old truck, and 600 hogs for $1 a head. He built a cooker in the desert, stoked it with sagebrush, shot wild horses, skinned them, sold their hides for $2 each, cooked their meat, and fed the horse meat to his hogs through the winter. That spring, J. R. Simplot sold the hogs for $12.50 a head and, at the age of sixteen, became a potato farmer.

The Idaho potato industry was just getting started in the 1920s. The state's altitude, warm days, cool nights, light volcanic soil, and abundance of irrigation water made it an ideal setting for growing Russet Burbank potatoes. Simplot leased 160 acres, then bought farm equipment and a team of horses. Then he got an electric potato sorter; it seemed a remarkable invention. Simplot sold all his farm equipment, and started his own business in a potato cellar in Declo. He traveled the Idaho countryside, plugging the rudimentary machine into the nearest available light socket and sorting potatoes for farmers. Soon he was buying and selling potatoes, opening warehouses, forming relationships with commodities brokers nationwide. When J. R. Simplot needed timber for a new warehouse, he and his men would just head down to Yellowstone and chop down some trees.

The Great Potato Baron of Idaho

[25] **built an empire:**「帝国を建設した」．built の主語は Simplot の資質．そういう人間だったからこそ「帝国を建設することが可能だった」と述べている．

[27] **sly grin:** ずる賢こそうなニタリ笑い．「してやったり」といったニュアンス．
scored big:「一山当てた」．とてもアメリカ的なフレーズ．

[28] **Dubuque, Iowa:** デビュークはウィスコンシン，イリノイ両州と接するアイオワ州東端のミシシッピー河沿いの町．このあたりは，the Midwest (中西部) のなかでも中心的な穀倉地帯で Heartland (深奥地帯) という言い方がピッタリ．

[30] **a homesteader:** ホームステッド法 (Homestead Act of 1862) による入植者．西部開拓の目的で作られたこの連邦法によって，フロンティアに (小屋程度の) 家を建てて 5 年以上住んだ成人男子は，160 エーカー分の土地の私有が認められた．
for free: [a. without charge / b. for his freedom]

[31] **a steel rail:** (横にわたした) 鋼材

[33] **domineering father:** 威張りまくる抑圧的な父親

[35] **Declo, Idaho:** 現在も農地のなかに道が何本か交叉するだけの小さな町です．

[39] **desert:** sagebrush などの灌木が茂る北米西部の乾いた土地もこう呼ばれる．
stoked it with sagebrush: ヨモギの草を (cooker の火に) くべた

[40] **hide(s):** 毛皮

[46] **altitude:** 標高 (が高いこと)
light volcanic soil: 弱い火山性の土壌．アイダホの西のワシントン州には St. Helens など大きな活火山がある．

[47] **abundance of irrigation water:** 灌漑用水がふんだんにあること
... made it an ideal setting: 〜のおかげで理想の場所となった

[48] **Russet Burbank potatoes:** 1870 年代に品種改良された大型ポテト．

[49] **160 acres:** 1 エーカーは約 0.4 ha．サッカーのフィールドの半分よりやや広い．それを 160 倍にした広さ．

[52] **potato cellar:** ポテトを貯蔵するための建物

[53] **rudimentary** [rùdəméntəri]: 原始的な；発明されてまもない

[54] **the nearest available light socket:**「一番手近な電球のソケット」．電気製品といえば電球がほとんどだった時代，電源をとるにはソケットの側面についたコンセントに差し込むのがふつうだった．

[56] **forming relationships with commodities brokers nationwide:** 各地の委託業者と契約し，全米規模での販売を展開していったということ．

[58] **his men:** 雇い人
just head down to: simply drive down to
Yellowstone: 有名な国立公園イェローストーンは，デクロの北東約 300 km．

Within a decade, Simplot was the largest shipper of potatoes in the West, operating thirty-three warehouses in Oregon and Idaho.

After the war, Simplot invested heavily in frozen food technology, betting that it would provide the meals of the future. The sales of refrigerators, freezers, and other kitchen appliances soared after World War II. The 1950s soon became the Golden Age of Food Processing, a decade in which one marvelous innovation after another promised to simplify the lives of American housewives: frozen orange juice, frozen TV dinners, the Chicken-of-Tomorrow, "Potato salad from a package!", Cheese Whiz, Jell-O salads, Jet-Puffed Marshmallows, Miracle Whip. Depression-era scarcity gave way to a cornucopia of new foods on the shelves of new suburban supermarkets. Ad campaigns made processed foods seem better than fresh ones, more space-age and up to date.

Postwar refrigerators came with freezer compartments, and J. R. Simplot thought about the foods that housewives might want to put in them. He assembled a team of chem-

The Great Potato Baron of Idaho

- [60] **the largest shipper:** 出荷量でトップの人，または会社
- [64] **bet(ting):** 賭ける；リスクを冒して決心する
- [66] **soared:** [a. rose / b. fell] sharply
- [68] **one marvelous innovation after another:** 次から次に登場する驚くべき新製品．*They told one funny joke after another.*
- [69] **frozen orange juice:** これをミキサーに入れ，水を加えてスイッチを入れる．以下「未来志向」の商品名やキャンペーンの惹句が並ぶ．
- [70] **TV dinner(s):** プラスチックのトレイにアルミホイルを被せた冷凍食品．熱するだけで，肉類，マッシュポテト，豆や野菜つきの "dinner" になる．
- [71] **Cheeze Whiz:** チーズ・スプレッドの商品名．驚きの発声 "Gee Whiz!" に引っかけている．*cf.* p. 143, [75]
  Jell-O: 上記と同じく Kraft 社発売の極彩色食品．学校のカフェテリアのデザートの定番ともなり，ゼリー食品の代名詞として使われる．
- [72] **Depression-era scarcity:** "The Great Depression"（大不況）の時代だった 1930 年代は scarcity（欠乏）の時代として記憶される．
- [73] 〈**A**〉 **gave way to** 〈**B**〉**:** A が終わって B が登場；A が下火になって B が栄えた
  a cornucopia of = an abundance of.　cornucopia の原意はギリシャ神話の「豊穣の角」．
- [75] **more space-age and up to date:** より宇宙時代的で現代風
- [77] **came with:**「一体型」ないし「おまけつき」の商品について使う表現．*The CD comes with a bonus track.*
- [79] **assembled:** gathered and organized

ists, led by Ray Dunlap, to develop a product that seemed to have enormous potential: the frozen french fry. Americans were eating more fries than ever before, and the Russet Burbank, with its large size and high starch content, was the perfect potato for frying. Simplot wanted to create an inexpensive frozen fry that tasted just as good as a fresh one. Although Thomas Jefferson had brought the Parisian recipe for *pommes frites* to the United States in 1802, french fries did not become well known in this country until the 1920s. Americans traditionally ate their potatoes boiled, mashed, or baked. French fries were popularized in the United States by World War I veterans who'd enjoyed them in Europe and by the drive-in restaurants that subsequently arose in the 1930s and 1940s. Fries could be served without a fork or a knife, and they were easy to eat behind the wheel. But they were extremely time-consuming to prepare. Simplot's chemists experimented with various methods for the mass production of french fries, enduring a number of setbacks, learning the hard way that fries will sink to the bottom of a potato chip fryer and then burn. One day Dunlap walked into J. R. Simplot's office with some frozen fries that had just been reheated. Simplot tasted them, realized the manufacturing problems had been solved, and said, "That's a helluva thing."

J. R. Simplot started selling frozen french fries in 1953. Sales were initially disappointing. Although the frozen fries were precooked and could be baked in an oven, they tasted best when heated in hot oil, limiting their appeal to busy homemakers. Simplot needed to find institutional customers, restaurant owners who'd recognize the tremendous labor-saving benefits of his frozen fries.

The success of Dick and Mac McDonald's hamburger stand had been based as much on the quality of their fries as on the taste of their burgers. The McDonald brothers had devised an elaborate system for making crisp french fries,

The Great Potato Baron of Idaho

- [81] **have enormous potential:** 非常に大きな可能性を秘めている
- [83] **high starch content:** 高いデンプン含有率
- [86] **had brought the Parisian recipe for *pommes frites*:**「パリ流揚芋」のレシピをアメリカに紹介した．*pommes frites* [pɔm frit] は，deep fried potatoes の意．第3代大統領ジェファソンは親仏家として知られ，フランス式に料理したポテトを来客にふるまったという．
- [90] **popularized ... by World War I veterans:** 第一次世界大戦の（欧州戦線の）帰還兵によって広まった
- [92] **subsequently:** later on
- [94] **behind the wheel:** while sitting in the driver's seat．the wheel = steering wheel（自動車の「ハンドル」というが，英語で handle は「取っ手」の意味）
- [95] **time-consuming:** 時間がかかる
- [97] **setbacks:** difficulties, holdups, disappointments ⇔ breakthroughs
- [98] **learning the hard way:** 失敗を通して学ぶ
  fries will sink to the bottom: 揚げ芋は（どうしても）底に沈んでしまう
- [102] **That's a helluva thing** = That's a hell of a thing.「こいつはすげえや」といった感じ．「紳士」であれば "hell" を避け，"That's great!" などというだろう．
- [107] **limiting their appeal to busy homemakers:** *i.e.* busy homemakers did not necessarily find it appealing. appeal: 訴える力＝魅力．homemakers は housewives の婉曲語．
- [108] **institutional customers:**（個人の消費者ではなく）大きな会社や団体の取引先
- [109] **the tremendous labor-saving benefits:** 労力がものすごく節約されるという利点
- [111] **The success ... had been based as much on ⟨A⟩ as on ⟨B⟩:** The secret of their success was not just ⟨B⟩．⟨A⟩ was equally important.
  Dick and Mac McDonald: カリフォルニア州でハンバーガー店を営んでいた Richard (Dick) McDonald と兄の Maurice (Mac) は 1948 年，最小限のメニューを最大限の効率で売る廉価迅速サービスを始めた．
  hamburger stand: 次にあるように，店内に座席をもつマクドナルドができるのは 60 年代に入ってから．当初は持ち帰り専門のスタンドだった．
- [114] **devised an elaborate system:** よく考え抜かれたシステムを作りあげた．devise [diváiz]（工夫する）の名詞形が device.

one that was later improved by the restaurant chain. McDonald's cooked thinly sliced Russet Burbanks in special fryers to keep the oil temperature above 325 degrees. In 1954, Ray Kroc took over McDonald's chain of hamburger stands. In 1962, the first McDonald's restaurant with seating opened in Denver, Colorado. As the number of shops mutiplied, it became more difficult and yet all the more important to maintain the consistency and quality of the fries. J. R. Simplot met with Ray Kroc in 1965. The idea of switching to frozen french fries appealed to Kroc, as a means of ensuring uniformity and cutting labor costs.

Simplot offered to build a new factory solely for the manufacture of McDonald's french fries. Kroc agreed to try Simplot's fries, but made no long-term commitment. The deal was sealed with a handshake.

McDonald's began to sell J. R. Simplot's frozen french fries the following year. Customers didn't notice any difference in taste. And the reduced cost of using a frozen product made french fries one of the most profitable items on the menu, far more profitable than hamburgers. Simplot quickly became the main supplier of french fries to McDonald's. At the time, McDonald's had about 725 restaurants in the United States. Within a decade, it had more than 3,000. Simplot sold his frozen fries to other restaurant chains, accelerating the growth of the fast food industry and changing the nation's eating habits. Americans have long consumed more potatoes than any other food except dairy products and wheat flour. In 1960, the typical American ate eighty-one pounds of fresh potatoes and about four pounds of frozen french fries. Today the typical American eats about forty-nine pounds of fresh potatoes every year and more than thirty pounds of frozen french fries. Ninety percent of those fries are purchased at fast food restaurants. Indeed, french fries have become the most widely sold food-service item in the United States.

The Great Potato Baron of Idaho

- [117] **325 degrees:** Fahrenheit（華氏）の値．Celsius（摂氏）では168度に相当．
- [118] **Ray Kroc:** (1902–1984) ミルクシェイク機器のセールスマンだったレイ・クロックは，最終的にマクドナルド兄弟からビジネスに関するすべての権利を270万ドルで買い取り，世界最大のファスト・フード・チェーンを築く．
- [121] **all the more important:** それだけいっそう重要
- [125] **ensuring uniformity:** 均質性を保証する (= maintaining consistency, *cf.* [122])
  cutting labor costs: 人件費を削減する
- [126] **offered to build a new factory solely for . . . :** （マクドナルド用に）特化した冷凍ポテト製造工場を新築すると申し出た．*I'm solely responsible for this. No one else is involved.*
- [132] **the reduced cost of using a frozen product made french fries one of the most . . . :** 原因を主語にして，make でつないでいく文型に注意．「～が～になったのは，～が原因」ということを表現するのに適している．
- [134] **profitable:** moneymaking
- [135] **the main supplier:** *i.e.* he sold more fries to McDonald's than anyone else
- [138] **accelerating:** speeding up
- [140] **have long consumed:** have consumed for a long time
  more potatoes than any other food except . . . : ～には及ばないものの，それ以外ではポテトをもっとも大量に
- [141] **dairy [déəri] products:** 乳製品 (milk, butter, cheese, yogurt, etc.)
- [142] **the typical American ate . . . :** 1人当たりの平均摂取量をいうときの定型表現．The average American もよく使われる．*The average Japanese watches nearly an hour more of television than an American does.*
- [148] **food-service item:** 食品業界用に流通するアイテム

J. R. Simplot, an eighth-grade dropout, is now one of the richest men in the United States. Despite being a multibillionaire, he has few pretensions. He wears cowboy boots and blue jeans, eats at McDonald's, and drives his own car, a Lincoln Continental with license plates that say "MR. SPUD." He seems to have little patience for abstractions, viewing religion as a bunch of "hocus-pocus" and describing his potato empire matter-of-factly: "It's big and it's real, it ain't bullshit." In 1999 he turned ninety and quit skiing. He stepped down as the chief executive of his company in 1994, but keeps buying more land and scouting new factories. "Hell, fellow, I'm just an old farmer got some luck," Simplot said, when I asked about the key to his success. "The only thing I did smart, and just remember this— ninety-nine percent of people would have sold out when they got their first twenty-five or thirty million. I didn't sell out. I just hung on."

The Great Potato Baron of Idaho

- [150] **an eighth-grade dropout:** 8年生（中学2年）で学校を中退した者
- [151] **a multibillionaire:** 数十億ドル以上の財をもつ資産家
- [152] **pretensions:** 仰々しいところ，気取ったところ
- [154] **Lincoln Continental:** 1939年以来の長い歴史をもつ大型セダン．2002年製造中止となった．

  license plates: 日本で言う「ナンバー・プレート」．州ごとにデザインがきまっているが，DMV (Department of Motor Vehicles) に有料の申請をして，このように「特注」のプレートをつけることができる．

  MR. SPUD: spudはpotatoの（ユーモラスな）俗語．
- [155] **seems to have little patience for ...:** is mostly [a. pleased with / b. annoyed by] ...

  abstractions: 抽象的な（小難しい）話
- [156] **a bunch of "hocus-pocus":** インチキだらけのもの．"hocus-pocus" は，元来「魔術師」がよく使った呪文．
- [157] **matter-of-factly:** サラリと，何ということはないというふうに
- [158] **it ain't bullshit:** It's not bullshit. bullshit は「口からでまかせの不誠実な言葉」を意味する乱暴な表現．
- [161] **I'm just an old farmer got some luck:**「正確な」英語にするには，gotの前にwhoを補う．"an old farmer whom I met yesterday" の whom の脱落は普通だが，主格の関係代名詞を落とすしゃべり方は文法的には破格で，Simplotの「田舎のオヤジ」らしさを強調している．
- [163] **The only thing I did smart:**「頭よくやった唯一のこと」．主語であるはずだが，以下構文が崩れている．
- [164] **would have sold out when they got their first twenty-five or thirty million:** 儲けが2500万か3000万ドル出たところで（事業を）売り払っていただろう
- [166] **I just hung on:** I just kept at it; I just stuck to it

[Session 1] Comprehension Check

1. **Put the following in chronological order.**

   ( ) → ( ) → ( ) → ( )

   a. French fries become popular at American drive-in restaurants.
   b. A typical American would eat 7 times more frozen french fries compared to about four decades ago.
   c. McDonald's starts business and grows into a big hamburger franchise.
   d. With the ideal environment, the Idaho potato industry takes off smoothly.

2. **How did Simplot's successful life develop? Fill in the blanks.**

   <u>1st stage: independent and hard-working</u>
   running away from home → ( ) → hunting wild horses and raising hogs
   <u>2nd stage:</u> ( )
   <u>3rd stage: into the world of business</u>
   an electric potato sorter → ( ) → increase in the number of warehouses → forming relations with commodities brokers nation wide
   <u>4th stage: the golden age of food processing</u>
   heavy investment in frozen food technology → ( )
   <u>5th stage: hand in hand with the fast food industry</u>
   wholesaling frozen french fries to McDonald's and other fast food restaurants

   > a. buying and selling potatoes
   > b. producing inexpensive french fries
   > c. working at a warehouse sorting potatoes
   > d. owning a potato farm

The Great Potato Baron of Idaho

Editors' Note

　1948 年，南カリフォルニアでドライブイン・バーガー店を経営していた Rick と Mac の McDonald 兄弟は，大々的なモデルチェンジを行って，「お持ち帰り専門」(for takeout only) の店として生まれ変わらせるとともに，メニューを数品に限定し，ウェイトレスも皿洗いも要らなければ，少年少女のたまり場にもならない "fast food" のサービスを実現した．それから，みるみる成長した．

　その店から 10 台目の注文が来たことに驚いた Multimixer (ミルクシェーク攪拌機) の販売人 Ray Kroc は，南カリフォルニアまで二人の店を見学にいった．そして，そのすべてが気に入った．1954 年，Kroc は，全米展開するためのフランチャイズ権を買い取る契約にこぎつける．だが収益の一定パーセントを兄弟に握られているのが気に入らなかった．

　ちなみに Kroc 経営の 1 号店がイリノイ州にオープンした 1955 年は，ディズニーランド開園とロックンロール始動の年としても記憶される．アメリカは「食」の変化も大きく巻き込みながら，次世代の資本主義へ向けて大きな前進を始めていたのだ．

　Kroc は未来を見ていた．自分が手にした権利は絶対に膨張すると思った．いくら利子がかさんでもかまわないと覚悟のうえで借り集めた 270 万ドルで，1961 年，ついに兄弟からマクドナルドのすべてを買い取った．それは後にまさしく「地上最強の事業の種」だったことが判明する．

　チェコからの移民の子 Kroc も，Simplot と同じく，事業のサイズと利益の膨張に興奮できる男だった．一方，Dick と Mac はいまの仕事の美学に生きた．「世紀のアイディア」を売り渡してなお，彼らはハンバーガーを作り続けた．もはや本名も名乗れず，店の名を The Big M として．ところが数年後，目の前に，金色の大きな M 字 (the golden arches) を掲げたバーガー店がオープンした．Kroc の新戦略のもと，世界展開を始めていたフランチャイズの威力には創始者といえどもひとたまりもなかった．1970 年兄弟はニュー・ハンプシャーに帰郷．翌年兄の Mac は 69 年の人生を閉じた．

[Answers for the a/b Questions]
[30] — a., [66] — a.

Session

Mr. King's Writing Class

Stephen King

Despite the brevity of his style manual, William Strunk found room to discuss his own dislikes in matters of grammar and usage. He hated the phrase "student body," for instance, insisting that "studentry" is both clearer and without the ghoulish connotations he saw in the former term.

I have my own dislikes. I believe that anyone using the phrase "That's so cool" should have to stand in the corner and those using the far more odious phrase "at this point in time" should be sent to bed without supper (or writing paper, for that matter.) Two of my other pet peeves have to do with this most basic level of writing, and I want to get them off my chest before we move along.

Verbs come in two types, active and passive. With an active verb, the subject of the sentence is doing something. With a passive verb, something is being done to the subject of the sentence. The subject is just letting it happen. *You should avoid the passive tense.* I'm not the only one who says so; you can find the same advice in *The Elements of Style*.

Messrs. Strunk and White don't speculate as to why so many writers are attracted to passive verbs, but I'm willing to; I think timid writers like them for the same reason timid lovers like passive partners. The passive voice is safe. There is no troublesome action to contend with; the subject just has

Mr. King's Writing Class

[1] **brevity:** 簡潔さ (< brief). *Brevity is the soul of wit.*
William Strunk: (1869–1946) コーネル大学英文科教授. 彼の著した *The Elements of Style* は 1918 年刊. Strunk の没後, *New Yorker* 誌の編集者 E. B. White が加筆編集した版 (1957 年刊) は, 正しい英語の書き方の標準教材として今日も使われている. 元々の版は http://www.bartleby.com/141 で読める.
[2] **found room to discuss:** 限られたスペースの中でわざわざ論じた
[4] **"student body":** 日本の「生徒会」「学生自治会」に相当.
[5] **the ghoulish connotations he saw in the former term:** 英語の body には「死体」という意味がある. ghoulish < ghoul [gu:l]: 墓を暴いて死体を食らう悪鬼
[8] **have to stand in the corner:** 日本では「廊下に立たされる」が, アメリカでは「教室の隅に立たされる」のが一般的.
[9] **odious:** awful; dreadful; unspeakable
"at this point in time":「現時点においては」という日本語と似た語感あり.
[10] **without ... writing paper, for that matter:**「ま, それをいうなら作文用紙ぬきで」. つまり書く資格はないということ.
[11] **pet peeves:**「いつもイヤだと思っていること」. いつも心に抱えているので pet という. *cf.* pet theory; pet project
have to do with: concern; are related to; are relevant to
[12] **get ... off my chest:** 〜を吐き出してすっきりする
[14] **come in two types:**「〜には 2 つのタイプある」. *The ice cream comes in three flavors—vanilla, green tea and red bean.*
[18] **tense:**「時制」の意味で用いられることが多いが, ここでは「態」の意味.「受動態」は the passive *voice* ともいう.
[20] **Messrs.:** (フランス語 *Messieurs* の短縮形) Mr. の複数形. 英語読みは [mésərz]
don't speculate as to why ... :「何故かについてはふれていない」. speculate は根拠なしにあれこれ考えること.
[24] **to contend with:** to cope with; to deal with; to struggle through

to close its eyes and think of England, to paraphrase Queen Victoria. I think unsure writers also feel the passive voice somehow lends their work authority; perhaps even a quality of majesty. If you find instruction manuals and lawyers' torts majestic, I guess it does.

The timid fellow writes **The meeting will be held at seven o'clock** because that somehow says to him, "Put it this way and people will believe *you really know*." Purge this quisling thought! Don't be a muggle! Throw back your shoulders, stick out your chin, and put that meeting in charge! Write **The meeting's at seven**. There, by God! Don't you feel better?

I won't say there's no place for the passive tense. Suppose, for instance, a fellow dies in the kitchen but ends up somewhere else. **The body was carried from the kitchen and placed on the parlor sofa** is a fair way to put this, although "was carried" and "was placed" still irk the shit out of me. I accept them but I don't embrace them. What I would embrace is **Freddy and Myra carried the body out of the kitchen and laid it on the parlor sofa**. Why does the body have to be the subject of the sentence, anyway? It's dead, for Christ's sake! Fuhgeddaboudit!

Over the first 35 years of his career, Stephen king has published more than 70 new works.

[25] **close its eyes and think of England:**「目を閉じてイングランドのことを思う」という言い回しは，気の進まぬ夫婦の行為に耐える女性の気持ちを述べた言葉として有名．ここでキングも言っているように，ヴィクトリア女王の言葉という説が流布しているが，これは単なる風説のようだ．
to paraphrase . . . : 〜の言葉を借りれば（もじって言えば）

[27] **lends their work authority:** 自分の仕事に権威（ハク）をつける
a quality of majesty: 一種堂々とした感じ

[28] **lawyers' torts:**「法律家たちのあくどい言い回し」．tort は「捻る」という意味のラテン語に由来し，不正行為の意味で使われる法律用語．マニュアル同様，受動態の宝庫なのだろう．

[29] **I guess it does:** [a. I guess the passive voice really does make one's writing majestic. / b. I guess you'd also find the passive voice majestic.]

[32] *you really know:* イタリックスの部分は「わーすごい」という気分を込めて，大げさに読むとよい．
Purge this quisling thought: そういう，売国奴の（表現者としての自分を売り渡してしまう）ような考えは捨て去れ

[33] **a muggle:** J. K. Rawling の Harry Potter シリーズで，wizzard でない並の人間を軽蔑的に指す言葉．以下，兵卒を叱咤する軍隊の上官の言葉遣いが続く．
Throw back your shoulders: 両肩をグイと後ろに引いて（胸を張れ）

[34] **put that meeting in charge:**「ミーティングの責任者が誰か見せてやれ」．つまり will be held などという弱々しい，受け身の言い方をするな．*i.e.* declare that *you* are in charge of that meeting.（ミーティングの責任者が誰か見せてやれ）

[35] **There, by God!:**「そうら，見ろよ」．by God は「神掛けて」．不敬な言葉遣い (swearing) によって，信念を臆せず吐き出していることが伝わってくる．

[37] **I won't say there's no place for the passive tense:** [a. I think / b. I don't think] that the passive tense is totally useless.
Suppose . . . : 仮に〜としてみよう；〜だと思ってごらん

[40] **is a fair way to put this:** この状況の表現としてまともだ

[41] **irk the shit out of me:** irritate me very much. 汚い言葉を使った下品な表現だが，「こっぴどくぶん殴る」(beat the shit out of him) など類例は多い．

[42] **don't embrace them:** don't particularly like them

[46] **for Christ's sake!:** For God's sake! とも．嫌なこと，変なことを「するなよ，たのむよ」という語感が（ここでは）ある．もちろん swearing なので使用は控えたい．
Fuhgeddaboudit!: Forget about it!（冗談じゃないぜ）

Two pages of the passive voice—just about any business documents ever written, in other words, not to mention reams of bad fiction—make me want to scream. It's weak, it's circuitous, and it's frequently tortuous, as well. How about this: **My first kiss will always be recalled by me as how my romance with Shayna was begun.** Oh, man! A simpler way to express this idea—sweeter and more forceful, as well—might be this: **My romance with Shayna began with our first kiss. I'll never forget it.** I'm not in love with this because it uses *with* twice in four words, but at least we're out of that awful passive voice.

The other piece of advice I want to give you is this: *The adverb is not your friend.*

Adverbs, you will remember, are words that modify verbs, adjectives, or other adverbs. They're the ones that usually end in -ly. Adverbs, like the passive voice, seem to have been created with the timid writer in mind. With the passive voice, the writer usually expresses fear of not being taken seriously; it is the voice of little boys wearing shoe polish mustaches and little girls clumping around in Mommy's high heels. With adverbs, the writer usually tells us he or she is afraid he/she isn't expressing himself/herself clearly, that he or she is not getting the point or the picture across.

Consider the sentence **He closed the door firmly.** It's by no means a terrible sentence (at least it's got an active verb going for it), but ask yourself if **firmly** really has to be there. You can argue that it expresses a degree of difference between **He closed the door** and **He slammed the door**, and you'll get no argument from me . . . but what about context? What about all the enlightening (not to say emotionally moving) prose which came *before* **He closed the door firmly**? Shouldn't this tell us how he closed the door? And if

Mr. King's Writing Class

- [47] **Two pages of . . . make me want to scream:** 〜を2ページも読まされたら（やめてくれ！と）叫びたくなる
  just about any business documents ever written, in other words: that is to say, almost all the business documents ever written
- [48] **not to mention reams of bad fiction:** 夥しい量のヘボな創作は言うに及ばず
- [50] **circuitous** [sə́ːrkwitəs]: まわりくどい
  tortuous: 拷問（torture）のよう
- [60] **modify verbs, adjectives, or other adverbs:** 動詞，形容詞，または他の副詞を修飾する
- [63] **created with the timid writer in mind:** 臆病な書き手を想定して創られた
- [64] **fear of not being taken seriously:** 自分の書くことなどまともに受け止められないのではないかという恐れ
- [65] **shoe polish mustaches:** 靴墨で描いた鼻髭. mustache [mústæʃ]
- [66] **clumping around in Mommy's high heels:**「ママのハイヒールをカタカタ鳴らして歩いている」．自分を一丁前に見せたがる書き手の心理の，意地悪なたとえ．
- [69] **getting the point or the picture across:** 要点や状況を伝える，解らせる．*If you want to be a good public speaker, try to get your feelings across to the audience.*
- [72] **at least it's got an active verb going for it:**「他動詞ががんばってるところは評価できる」ということ．it's got = it has. go for it は「いけいけ」というかけ声としても使われる．
- [74] **You can argue . . . and you'll get no argument from me:** 〜と論じてもけっこう，私に反論はありません
  expresses a degree of difference between . . . : 〜と〜との，ある中間段階を表現する
- [77] **enlightening:** insightful; illuminating; clear
  not to say emotionally moving: 心を揺さぶるような，とは言わないまでも

the foregoing prose does tell us, isn't **firmly** an extra word? Isn't it redundant?

In a way, adverbs are like dandelions. If you have one on your lawn, it looks pretty and unique. If you fail to root it out, however, you find five the next day . . . fifty the day after that . . . and then, my brothers and sisters, your lawn is **totally**, **completely**, and **profligately** covered with dandelions. By then you see them for the weeds they really are, but by then it's—*GASP!!*—too late.

I can be a good sport about adverbs, though. Yes I can. With one exception: dialogue attribution. I insist that you use the adverb in dialogue attribution only in the rarest and most special of occasions . . . and not even then, if you can avoid it. Just to make sure we all know what we're talking about, examine these three sentences:

> **"Put it down!' she shouted.**
> **"Give it back," he pleaded, "it's mine."**
> **"Don't be such a fool, Jekyll," Utterson said.**

In these sentences, **shouted**, **pleaded**, and **said** are verbs of dialogue attribution. Now look at these dubious revisions:

> **"Put it down!" she shouted menacingly.**
> **"Give it back." he pleaded abjectly, "it's mine."**
> **"Don't be such a fool, Jekyll," Utterson said contemptuously.**

The three latter sentences are all weaker than the three former ones, and most readers will see why immediately. **"Don't be such a fool, Jekyll," Utterson said contemptuously** is the best of the lot; it is only a cliché, while the other two are actively ludicrous. Such dialogue attributions are sometimes known as "Swifties," after Tom Swift, the brave

- [80] **foregoing:** その前にある
  extra: [a. unnecessary / b. special]
- [81] **redundant** [rid∧ndənt]: 言わずともすでにわかっている，冗長な
- [82] **dandelions:** この比喩を理解するには郊外の芝生付きの家に住んでいると思ってください．
- [86] **profligately** [práfləgitli]:「あふれんばかりに」「蕩尽と放縦のかぎりに」．副詞をわざと大げさに使ってユーモラスに表現している．
- [87] **see them for the weeds they really are:** そもそも雑草であるタンポポ本来の姿を見る
- [88] *GASP!!*: 息をのむときの擬声語的表現．漫画風に表記している．
- [89] **a good sport:** 話のわかる，いいやつ
  Yes I can:「ほんとです」．強く肯定して読者の疑念を吹き払おうとしている．
- [90] **With one exception:** しかしこういう場合は別だ
  I insist that you . . . :「ぜひとも～していただきたい」．次に来るのは動詞の原形．*I insisted that he come with us.*
- [91] **the rarest and most special of occasions:**「滅多にない特別な状況」．of があることで「えり抜きの」というイメージができる．*the most delicious of cakes*
- [92] **not even then:** even in those rare occasions, you should not use it
- [99] **dubious** [djú:biəs]: 疑わしい，信用ならない，粗悪な
- [101] **menacingly** [ménəsiŋli]: 脅すように (threateningly)
- [102] **abjectly:** 恥も外聞もかなぐりすてて (miserably)
- [103] **contemptuously:** 見下げたように (scornfully)
- [108] **is the best of the lot:** ならんだ中では一番ましだ
- [109] **actively ludicrous:** あほらしさが踊っているかのような，見るからにバカげた．
  ludicrous [lú:dəkrəs]: ridiculous; absurd; silly
- [110] **after:** ～に因んで
  Tom Swift . . . by Victor Appleton II: Tom Swift シリーズ（Victor Appleton 作，全 40 巻，1910–41）と次世代の Tom Swift, Jr. シリーズ（全 33 巻，1954–71）は，他の多数のシリーズとともに，ある連作物語制作企業の手になるもので，Victor Appleton という名の作家は一世も二世も実在しない．

inventor-hero in a series of boys' adventure novels written by Victor Appleton II. Appleton was fond of such sentences as **"Do your worst!" Tom cried bravely** and **"My father helped with the equations," Tom said modestly.** When I was a teenager there was a party-game based on one's ability to create witty (or half-witty) Swifties. **"You got a nice butt, lady," he said cheekily** is one I remember; another is **"I'm the plumber," he said, with a flush.** (In this case the modifier is an adverbial phrase.) When debating whether or not to make some pernicious dandelion of an adverb part of your dialogue attribution, I suggest you ask yourself if you really want to write the sort of prose that might wind up in a party-game.

Some writers try to evade the no-adverb rule by shooting the attribution verb full of steroids. The result is familiar to any reader of pulp fiction or paperback originals:

> **"Put down the gun, Utterson!" Jykyll grated.**
> **"Never stop kissing me!" Shayna gasped.**
> **"You damned tease!" Bill jerked out.**

Don't do these things. Please oh please.

- [114] **helped with the equations:** 式を解く（または立てる）のを手伝ってくれた
- [116] **witty (or half-witty):**「しゃれた（ないしは，トンマな）」．half-wit は「知恵のたりない者」．
- [117] **butt:**「尻」．尻のふくらみを頬のふくらみで受けて cheekily（小生意気に）といったところが witty（または half-witty）というわけ．
- [118] **with a flush:**「顔を赤らめて」——と同時に（水道屋さんなので）「トイレを流しながら」の含意がある．
- [119] **adverbial phrase:** 副詞句（全体で副詞の機能をもつ連語）
  When debating whether or not . . . :「以下のことの是非を論じるときは」．わざと大仰な言葉と構文を使ってユーモラスにいっている．
- [120] **pernicious dandelion of an adverb:** 有害なタンポポのごとき副詞
- [122] **that might wind up in a party-game:** パーティのおふざけのネタになってしまうような．wind up: end up
- [124] **evade the no-adverb rule:** 副詞を禁じる規則にひっかからないようにする
  evade: escape; elude; avoid
  shooting the attribution verb full of steroids:「話者の指示動詞（dialogue attribution verb）をパワーアップする」．ステロイド注射の比喩で述べている．
- [126] **pulp fiction or paperback originals:** 最初からハードカバーにならず，安物の娯楽本として消費されていく物語．
- [127] **grated:**（ドアがきしむような）しゃがれ声を出した
- [128] **gasped:** 喘いだ，息も荒々しく言った *cf.* [88]
- [129] **You damned tease!:**「その気にさせやがって！」tease は誘惑のそぶりだけ見せること．ここではそういう態度をとる女を指している．
  jerk(ed) out: いっぺんに荒々しく出すというイメージ．日本語の「吐き捨てる」は「ペッ」という感じだが，こちらは「グイ」と力のこもる感じがある．

The best form of dialogue attribution is **said**, as in **he said, she said, Bill said, Monica said.** If you want to see this put stringently into practice, I urge you to read or reread a novel by Larry McMurtry, the Shane of dialogue attribution. McMurtry has allowed few adverbial dandelions to grow on his lawn. He believes in he-said/she-said even in moments of emotional crisis (and in Larry McMurtry novels there are a lot of those). Go and do thou likewise.

Is this a case of "Do as I say, not as I do"? The reader has a perfect right to ask the question, and I have a duty to provide an honest answer. Yes. It is. You need only look back through some of my own fiction to know that I'm just another ordinary sinner. I've been pretty good about avoiding the passive tense, but I've spilled out my share of adverbs in my time, including some (it shames me to say it) in dialogue attribution. (I have never fallen so low as "he grated" or "Bill jerked out," though.) When I do it, it's usually for the same reason any writer does it: because I am afraid the reader won't understand me if I don't.

I'm convinced that fear is at the root of most bad writing. If one is writing for one's own pleasure, that fear may be mild—*timidity* is the word I've used here. If, however, one is working under deadline—a school paper, a newspaper article, the SAT writing sample—that fear may be intense. Dumbo got airborne with the help of a magic feather; you may feel the urge to grasp a passive verb or one of those nasty adverbs for the same reason. Just remember before you do that Dumbo didn't need the feather; the magic was in him.

- [131] **as in:** 〜の，の例のような．*Not P as in Paris, but T as in Tokyo.*
- [132] **see this put stringently into practice:** これが厳正に実践されているのを見る
- [134] **Larry McMurtry:** (1936–) 昔の西部や現代のテキサスを舞台に，半世紀近くも旺盛な作家活動を続けているピューリッツァ賞 / アカデミー賞作家.
  the Shane: 西部劇なら英雄シェーンに相当するような，最高の仕事人．
- [136] **believes in he-said/she-said even in moments of emotional crisis:** 心が張り裂けそうな感情的シーンでも，"he said" "she said" を信奉する．
- [138] **Go and do thou likewise:** 「あなたも行って同じようになさい」．聖書のなかのキリストの言葉．このあたり，作家の信念を一種の信仰として語っている．
- [141] **Yes. It is.:** It *is* a case of me advising you to "do as I say, not as I do."
  You need only . . . to know: 〜するだけでわかる
- [142] **I'm just another ordinary sinner:** 私も他の誰とも変わらぬふつうの罪人である
- [144] **I've spilled out my share of . . . :** 「私だって（みなと同様）〜をまき散らした」．spill は感情や秘密など，内に抑えているべきことを口に出してしまうこと．
- [145] **in my time:**「わしも若い頃は」．ユーモラスにいっている．
- [146] **never fallen so low as "he grated":** never written such a terrible phrase as "he grated"
- [152] *timidity* **is the word I've used here:** *cf.* "timid writers," [22] "timid lovers"
- [154] **the SAT writing sample:** SAT (Scholastic Assessment Test) は年に数回行われるアメリカの統一大学入試．そこで課される小論文のことをいっている．
- [155] **Dumbo got airborne with the help of a magic feather:** ディズニー映画でおなじみの子象ダンボは，本当は空に浮かぶ能力がありながら，怖くて飛べない．でもおまじないの魔法の羽根を持ってジャンプすると飛べる．この話を，どのように作文の心得に結びつけているのか，the magic was in him という最後の文意を読み取ろう．

[Session 2] Comprehension Check

1. **Which pieces of advice are from (or are likely to be from) Stephen King? Choose four.**

   ( ) ( ) ( ) ( )

   a. Verbs come in two types, active and passive. Good writers use both of them equally.
   b. There is a whole lot of difference between "You should avoid the passive tense" and "The passive tense should be avoided."
   c. Don't try to put on an air of authority by using difficult words or indirect statements.
   d. Adverbs are like dandelions. They make your sentences more colorfully expressive.
   e. Read Appleton's books and learn how to create witty Swifties.
   f. Keep your dialogue attribution as simple as possible.
   g. Be free from all restrictions. Forget grammar. Dive into the sea of chaos.
   h. Don't be timid. Always have confidence in what you write.

2. **Mr. King's lecture is funny. Mark a (☺) at where you laughed.**

   I have my own dislikes ( ). I believe that anyone using the phrase "That's so cool" should have to stand in the corner ( ) and those using the far more odious phrase "at this point in time" should be sent to bed without supper ( ), or writing paper for that matter ( ). Two of my other pet peeves have to do with this most basic level of writing ( ), and I want to get them off my chest before we move along ( ).

Mr. King's Writing Class

Editors' Note

Stephen King 原作の映画をチェックしたら，23 件ヒットした．*Carrie, Christine* から，*Stand By Me, The Green Mile, Hearts in Atlantic* ... 日本でもずいぶん多くの人が観ているはずだ．

リストのなかで，*Shining* だけは二つのバージョンある．Stanley Kubric が監督した映画版（1980）と，1997 年に ABC 系列で放映された TV ミニシリーズ．なぜ二本あるかというと，Kubric の作品に King が我慢できなかったからだ．作品の映画化の権利を買い取った Kubric は，「以後自分の作品を批判しない」ことを条件に，King 好みの"リメイク"制作を許可したのだという．

2001: A Space Odyssey（『2001 年宇宙の旅』）のシーンのいくつかを思い出すだけでわかるだろう．Kubric は，自分の映像世界を芸術的にコントロールせずにはいられない．世界をデザインする神のような視点をもち，極端に幾何学的な構成によって画面を作っていく．ハリウッドの喧噪が彼は大嫌いなのだろう，アメリカ人なのに仕事人生のほとんどをイギリスで過ごし，ゆったりとしたペースをついに崩すことなく，スクリーンの「構成」を練り上げた．バイオレンスやホラーを好んで扱いながら，つねに背後で秩序と調和を模索する．彼はヨハン・シュトラウスを愛していた．

約 20 歳年下の Stephen King はまったくタイプの違った想像力の持ち主だ．多作で猥雑，人のハートにぐいぐい組み込む直球を投げ続ける．生身の人間同士の間に生じるドロドロとした感情が恐怖のプロットを呼び込んでいくようすを，彼は小説 *Shining*（1977）に描き込んだ．King からみれば，Kubric の作った映画は，大切な物語を骨抜きにし，高踏な「視覚のよろこび」に遊ぶ鼻持ちならない映画に見えたのではないだろうか．30 年前の King はまだまだ，一介の大衆人気作家という扱いだった．世の文化人や大学教授が，「さすがは Kubric」との賛辞を送るたびに，Fuh-geddaboudit! と毒づいていたのではないだろうか．

[Answers for the a/b Questions]
[29] — a., [37] — b., [80] — a.

Session 3

He Called It the Dakota

Stephen Birmingham

By 1880, New York had passed beyond the Age of Innocence and had entered what James Truslow Adams called the "Age of Dinosaurs." In it, fortunes were being made on a scale that had never before been imagined and that were difficult even for the men who made them to comprehend. Twenty-five years earlier there had not been more than five men in the United States worth as much as five million dollars, and there were less than twenty who were worth a million. Now, however, the *New York Tribune* would report that there were several hundred in the City of New York alone who were worth at least a million and a number who were worth at least twenty million. The money, furthermore, was being made from sources never before heard of—from steel mills, steam engines, oil from the Pennsylvania hills, and all manner of mechanical inventions from machine guns to washing machines.

With money was supposed to come respectability, and all at once there was emphasis on being "in society." New York society was the subject of much attention in the newspapers, which fulsomely covered the banquets, fancy dress balls and quadrilles. There were no motion picture or television stars then to capture the imagination of the public, nor were there any stage actresses who were considered really "respectable," and so every new-rich parvenue—and every

He Called It the Dakota

[2] **(the) Age of Innocence**: 1870年代ニューヨークの上流階級の人間模様を描いた本のタイトル (Edith Wharton 著, 1920 年に出版). 次に出てくる the Age of Dinosaurs (恐竜＝大資本家による弱肉強食の時代) とは対照的に, お金より家柄が重視され, ある意味でおっとりしていた「無垢の時代」.

[3] **James Truslow Adams**: アダムズ (1878–1949) はアメリカの作家, 歴史家. *The Epic of America* (1931) で "American dream" という概念をポピュラーにした.
In it, fortunes were being made . . . never before been imagined: In the Age of Dinosaurs, a number of big-business people were making fortunes on a scale that people had never imagined before. この章は (前章のキング氏が嫌がりそうな) 受動態連発の文体です.

[5] **that were difficult even for . . . to comprehend**: 〜にとってさえ把握するのが難しい.
the men who made them: そんな財産を築き上げた当の本人たち

[6] **Twenty-five years earlier**: すなわち 1855 年 (南北戦争の始まる 6 年前). 南北戦争後に, アメリカの資本主義は飛躍的な発展段階に入った.

[7] **worth . . .**:「〜の価値がある」, つまり資産をもっている. こんなふうに人を主語にしてその「金銭価値」を口にするのは, アメリカでは珍しいことではない.

[9] **Now:** [a. 1855 / b. 1880]
the *New York Tribune*: 1841 年刊の新聞. 奴隷制反対の立場を貫き, 19 世紀末ニューヨークの他紙の多くが煽情主義に走るなかで「硬派」をめざし続けた.

[11] **in the City of New York alone**: ニューヨーク市だけで. *Love alone can heal broken hearts.*

[12] **a number who:** (there were) a number (of people) who

[14] **steel mill(s):** 製鉄所

[15] **all manner of:** all kinds of

[17] **With money was supposed to come respectability**: Respectability was supposed to come with money. 文の一部が前に出て主-述の順番が逆になった.

[18] **being "in society":** 社交界の一員であること

[20] **fulsomely covered . . . :** ふんだんに〜について報道した
fancy dress balls and quadrilles: 人々が華やかに着飾った舞踏会やカドリーユ (4 人が組んで踊るフランス起源の古風な舞踊) のパーティー

[22] **nor were there any . . . :** and there were no . . . either

[24] **"respectable":**「まともな」「だらしなくない」. 清教徒の伝統が支配していた過去のアメリカでは, 芝居を楽しむのは堕落だという考えが残っていた.
parvenue [pάːrvənjùː]:「成り上がり者」. 当時の新興富裕層は "the new rich" と呼ばれた.

shop girl—had her favorite society figure whose life she
longed to emulate, and whose perfumed circle she dreamed
of entering.

But entering society was not easy. Society in 1880 was
firmly delineated by Mrs. William Astor and her chief lieutenant, Ward McAlister, and her list of the "Four Hundred"
New Yorkers who, supposedly, were as many as she could
conveniently fit into her ballroom. (When Mrs. Astor's list
was eventually published, it turned out to contain only
three hundred and four names.)

To get into society, it seemed, required more than
money and the ability to surround oneself with the luxuries
bought by it. There was a new and important ingredient
called *taste*. Good birth, which was so important a standard
in England and European society, could not be purchased
by newly rich New Yorkers, but good taste could. In 1870,
Charles L. Tiffany had opened his splendid new store on
Union Square, which had quickly become the bellwether of
taste.

Good taste implied good breeding, which meant good
manners. In a popular play of the era called *Fashion*, a character with social pretensions named Mrs. Tiffany, a former
milliner whose husband had struck oil, declared, "Forget

Mrs. William Astor

- [26] **longed to emulate:**「まねたいと強く願った」．emulate は他動詞で目的語は her favorite social figure's life（お気に入りの社交界有名人の暮らし）．
  perfumed circle:「香水かおる仲間うち」．circle は文字通り「内輪」のニュアンスをもつ言葉．日本語でいう大学の「サークル」は英語では club.
- [28] **Society ... was firmly delineated:**（誰を仲間に入れて誰を入れないか）厳密な線引きが行われた．society は「上流階級」
- [29] **Mrs. William Astor:** 不動産王だった夫 William の死去後も，夫人（Caroline Webster Astor, 1830–1908）は社交界を牛耳るほどの力をふるった．
  chief lieutenant:「警部」もこう呼ぶが，ここでは「第一の側近」の意味．
- [30] **Ward McAlister:**（1827–1895）ウォード・マッカリスターは，ゴールドラッシュさなかのカリフォルニアで弁護士として活躍．ニューヨークの資産家の娘と結婚し，アスター家に取り入ってパーティの指南役をつとめた．
- [31] **were as many as she could conveniently fit:** 400 人もの人を苦労せず収められたということ．前に supposedly がつくことで，当時の人はそう思った（が事実は確かでない）ことが示されている．
- [37] **ingredient:** ここでは食品や薬のではなく，社交界に入る条件となる「成分」．
- [41] **Charles L. Tiffany:**（1812–1902）父親から借りた 1,000 ドルで 1837 年に小さなギフト・ショップを開いたのが始まり．その後「ティファニー」は銀製品やジュエリーを中心に制作・販売し現在に至る．
- [42] **Union Square:** 北に 17th St. 南に 14th St. 西に Broadway 東に Park Avenue が走る．1870 年前後はこの周辺がもっともファッショナブルだった．
  bellwether of taste: 高級趣味を主導する存在（または場所）
- [44] **... implied good breeding:** 〜からは育ちの良さがうかがえた
- [45] **a character with social pretensions:** 自分を上流層の人間だと見せたがる人物
- [47] **milliner:** 婦人帽のメーカーまたはショップ・オーナー
  struck oil: 石油を掘りあてた

what we *have* been, it is enough to remember that we *are* of the *upper ten thousand!*" But more than forgetting the past was involved; the past had to be covered by a new veneer of polish, and a flurry of books and manuals appeared—how-to books on "etiquette" and "proper social usage."

Where one lived and how one lived was also a matter of great importance. When in 1880 Edward Clark began the construction of a large luxury apartment house in the far reaches of the upper West Side, on West Seventy-second Street, people thought of his project as preposterous. The perimeters of Central Park had already been laid on the city's maps, but Eighth Avenue (not yet renamed Central Park West), the park's western border, was still a dirt road. Though Mr. Clark's expensive building would face the park, that section of the park had not yet been landscaped or developed. In the park, opposite and all around Mr. Clark's building site, lived squatters in shacks built of roofing paper and flattened tins—shanties without plumbing or heat, whose owners kept pigs, goats, cows and chickens that grazed and roamed among the rocky outcroppings. This was where, of all places, Mr. Clark chose to build the most lavish apartment houses ever built, far outdoing any that then existed anywhere in the country.

But things had been happening in New York that the highest reaches of society may not have noticed. For one thing, with all the new money that was pouring into the city, New York had become easily the most expensive American city to live in. A house in a respectable, if not affluent, neighborhood could not be rented for less than eighteen hundred dollars a year. Adding to the cost of everything was the fact that New York was becoming a very crowded city.

One of the first New Yorkers to realize that "nice" people of slender means might provide a market for a special sort of housing was Mr. Rutherford Stuyvesant. In the late

He Called It the Dakota

- [48] **of the *upper ten thousand***: 上位 1 万人（の金持ち）に属する
- [50] **a new veneer of polish**:（粗野な出自を隠すために）新たに上塗りされる見せかけの洗練
- [51] **a flurry of books and manuals appeared**:「書物や手引き書が突然，大量に現れた」．flurry は雪などが突風とともにさっと降ってくるイメージ．
- [52] **"proper social usage"**: その社会での適切な言葉づかい
- [54] **Edward Clark:** (1811–1882) シンガー・ミシン社の顧問弁護士から経営者へと転身，富を築いた．
- [55] **in the far reaches of the upper West Side, on West Seventy-second Street**: マンハッタンの 59th St. 以北は，中央を Central Park が占める．公園の西側，the Hudson River との間にある地区が upper West Side． the far reaches of（ずっと向こうの）という言葉が，当時の地理感覚を表している．
- [57] **preposterous**: ridiculous; absurd; outrageous
- [58] **(The) perimeters of Central Park had already been laid on the city's maps**: セントラル・パークはすでに地図に縁取られていた（区画として存在していた）
- [62] **landscape(d)**: 木を植えたりして公園らしくする
- [64] **lived squatters**:「無断居住者が暮らしていた」．squatters がこの文の主語．
  shacks:「掘っ立て小屋」，次の行の shanties も同じ意味．
  roofing paper: タールなどに浸して防水した厚紙．屋根のかわりに使った．
- [65] **flattened tins**: ブリキ製の容器（缶や箱）をつぶしたもの
  plumbing [plʌ́miŋ]:（上・下水の）配管
- [67] **grazed and roamed**: 草を食んだり歩き回ったりしていた
  among the rocky outcroppings:「露出した岩石のあいだを」．マンハッタンは，氷河の作用で表土が流れたため，固い岩盤で出来ている．
- [68] **of all places**:「よりによって，こんなところに」という驚きの響きがある．
- [69] **lavish**: luxurious; costly; splendid
  far outdoing any: much lavisher than any other apartment house
- [72] **(the) highest reaches of society**: 社交界でもっとも上流の人々
- [74] **easily**: [a. by far / b. barely]
- [75] **a respectable, if not affluent, neighborhood**: 富裕ではないがそれなりにきちんとした（つまり中産階級の）層が暮らす居住区
- [76] **eighteen hundred dollars a year**: 1800 ドルというのは，当時の住み込み家政婦の年間の給与のほぼ 10 倍にあたる．
- [80] **"nice" people of slender means**: それほどの財産 (means) があるわけではないけれどもそこそこ上品な（中流の）人々
- [82] **Rutherford Stuyvesant:** (1842–1909) 不動産業界の大物としてニューヨーク開発に力をふるった．スタイヴァサント家は，New York が New Amsterdam と呼ばれていたオランダ領時代の知事につらなる名家．

1860's he hired a famous architect to convert a row of town houses on Eighteenth Street into "French flats." The resulting apartment house was called the Stuyvesant, and to everyone's surprise, it was an immediate success. [85]

Such was the social climate when Edward Clark broke ground in 1880. His budget—an even million dollars—was unprecedented, and he had not gone far before he decided to pour yet another million into the project. From the beginning, such extravagance was denounced as foolishness by both his business associates and his friends. It would never work. The apartments would never rent. Many urged him to give up his concept of a residential building and to turn it into a hospital or an asylum. [90]
[95]

From Frank Leslie's *Illustrated Paper*, September 7, 1889

He Called It the Dakota

- [83] **town house(s):** 隣の家と共通の壁でつながった2階または3階建ての家．
- [84] **"French flats":** パリの高級ホテルを思わせるイメージから "French" と形容されたアパート．
  resulting: 結果として完成した
- [87] **Such was the social climate:** 社会の空気はこんな具合だった
  broke ground: 起工した
- [88] **an even million dollars:** even は「切れのいい」「半端でない」というイメージ．
- [89] **unprecedented:** never known before; more than ever before
  he had not gone far: the building was [a. almost finished / b. far from being finished]
- [90] **yet another million:** 追加の100万ドル
- [91] **extravagance** [ikstrǽvəgəns]: 浪費
  denounced: criticized; disapproved of; condemned
- [92] **business associates:** 仕事仲間
  It would never work: *i.e.* They thought it would never work.
- [93] **would never rent:**「借り手がつかないだろう」．*cf. His new album didn't sell much.*
- [94] **turn it into . . . an asylum:**「救護院に転用する」．当時，一つの建物内にいくつもの居住空間が存在するのは，病院か救護院，あとは監獄くらいのものだった．

Another friend of Clark's commented, with some sarcasm, that, in putting up a building so far north and so far west of civilization, Mr. Clark might just as well be building in Dakota, which was then still a territory and not yet a state. Clark, who was not without a sense of humor, rather enjoyed the metaphor. He instructed his architect to make the most of it, and the building's design was embellished with certain Wild West details—arrowheads, ears of corn and sheaves of wheat in bas-relief on the building's interior and exterior façades. Above the building's main portico, a carved stone Indian head in bas-relief would be placed. As the vast edifice slowly arose in the middle of what did indeed seem a prairie setting of great, untenanted plains, Clark announced that its name would be the Dakota.

Scale and massiveness were stressed throughout the building. Many apartments had drawing rooms of a glamorous size and scale. In the sixth-floor apartment, the architect designed the building's largest room—a ballroom-sized drawing room 24 feet wide and 49 feet long, with a fireplace at both ends and a ceiling graced by a pair of Baccarat crystal chandeliers. His interior design was innovative as well as efficient, and some have since become almost standard in the layouts of luxury apartment houses. There was his "stem" system of elevators, for example. Each of the four passenger elevators—placed just inside the four corners of the courtyard—was designed to service two, or no more than three, apartments to a floor. Elevator lobbies were therefore small and intimate, creating a sense of privacy, eliminating the feeling of being in a building that housed more than two hundred other people.

When the Dakota was at last completed on October 27, 1884, it was greeted with an article in the *New York Daily Graphic* headlined as such: "A Description of the Most Perfect Apartment Houses in the World." Throngs of people journeyed uptown to look at the new wonder of the city, and

- [96] **with some sarcasm:** いささか皮肉をこめて
- [98] **civilization:** 当時もっとも「文明的」だったのは 5 番街の 17 から 48 丁目．
  might just as well be building in Dakota: ダコタに建てているも同然
- [99] **a territory:**「準州」すなわち，State の資格を得ていない地方行政区
- [100] **who was not without a sense of humor:** who [a. *did* / b. did *not*] have a sense of humor
- [101] **make the most of it:**「最大限活用する」．the metaphor（ダコタへのなぞらえ）をできるだけ活かしたつくりにするということ．
- [102] **embellished:** decorated; adorned; ornamented
- [103] **certain Wild West details:** いくつかの開拓時代のアメリカ西部のモチーフ
  arrowheads, ears of corn and sheaves of wheat: 矢じり，トウモロコシの穂，麦の束
- [104] **in bas-relief** [bàːrilíːf]: 浅い浮き彫りの
- [105] **façade(s)** [fəsáːd]: 建物の前面
  main portico: メイン・ポーチ，玄関先の柱廊
- [107] **edifice:** building の意味だが，「建造物」といった立派な語感がある．
  what did indeed seem . . . : 実際に〜かと思えるような場所
- [108] **great, untenanted plains:**「広大な無人の大草原」というイメージに「テナントがいない」という言葉をかけた，洒落た表現．
- [110] **Scale and massiveness:** ともに「規模の大きさ」を示す．前出 fancy dress balls and quadrilles もそうだが，ほぼ同義の単語を重ねてリズムをとる文体．
- [114] **drawing room:**「客間」．縦横の数値から広さを想像してみよう．
- [115] **graced by a pair of Baccarat crystal chandeliers:** バカラ社（高級クリスタルの専門メーカー）のシャンデリアが優雅さを添えた
- [117] **some have since become:** since then, some have become
- [118] **his "stem" system of elevators:** クラーク考案の「茎(ステム)」方式のエレベーター
- [119] **the four passenger elevators:** 4 台の乗客用エレベーター．*cf.* freight elevator
- [121] **two, or no more than three, apartments to a floor:** 一つの階につき 2 軒，多くても 3 軒まで
- [124] **eliminating the feeling of being in a building . . . :** making you [a. aware / b. forget] that you are in a building . . .
- [127] **the *New York Daily Graphic*:** 1873 年発刊の米国初の挿絵入り日刊紙．1880 年に世界で初めて網目製版の写真を掲載した．
- [129] **Throngs of people:** large crowds of people
- [130] **journeyed uptown:** マンハッタンでは，"uptown," "downtown" が「町の北方」「南方」の意味になる．距離は大したことないが，心理的に遠かった時代の感じが "journeyed" という動詞で表現されている．

hundreds of requests for apartments in the Dakota poured in. But it was too late. The Dakota was fully rented. It had not even had to advertise. And taking their cues from the Dakota, many other apartments were built on the West Side, too, attracting the same kind of clientele—prosperous New York businessmen and their family, conveying a vaguely intellectual and artistic tone.

Socially, this set the early West Siders immediately apart from the members of Mrs. Astor's inner circle, where anything that smacked of intelligence and wit was actually frowned upon. In fact, the West Side was becoming a Mecca for those who were rich, yet preferred apartment living to a mansion, and a social life independent of the rules and rituals of the Four Hundred.

The atmosphere of airy independence still presides over the Dakota and its surroundings. It has always been assumed that the people who lived at the Dakota were somewhat different from other fashionable New Yorkers. To live in Dakota was almost like taking a stand.

- [133] **taking their cues from the Dakota:** ダコタの成功から指針を得て
- [135] **clientele** [klàiəntél]: clients; customers. 顧客全体を集合的に表すので単数表記.
  prosperous: wealthy; successful; flourishing
- [136] **conveying a vaguely intellectual and artistic tone:** なんとなく知的でアーティストっぽい雰囲気を漂わせている
- [138] **this set 〈A〉 immediately apart from 〈B〉:** この展開はAとBとをただちに分け隔てる結果となった
- [140] **anything that smacked of intelligence and wit:**「知性やウィットを匂わせるものは何でも」. *His attitude smacks (smells, stinks) of hypocrisy.*
  was actually frowned upon:「実のところ嫌われた，敬遠された」. frownは「眉をひそめる」,「渋い顔をする」.
- [141] **a Mecca:**「聖地」. *Northern Gunma is a Mecca for skiers and hot-spring lovers.*
- [142] **preferred apartment living to a mansion:**「一戸建ての大邸宅 (mansion) よりも集合住宅の暮らしを好んだ」. なお日本語の「マンション」にあたる英語は，condominium あるいは condo.
- [145] **The atmosphere . . . still presides:** 〜の雰囲気がいまだに支配的だ
  airy:（旧来の社交界が煮詰まって窮屈なのと対照的に）風通しのよい
- [147] **assumed:** thought; supposed; taken for granted
- [149] **taking a stand:** 信念を表明する；生き方の宣言をする

[Session 3] Comprehension Check

Complete the summary by choosing a, b or c.

In the "Age of Dinosaurs," being [a. in society / b. from a good family / c. an intellectual person] was the ultimate goal for those who had recently become rich.

Around this era, the city of New York was becoming crowded with newcomers, and the cost of everything was rising. Middle-class people who had enough money needed better places to live. At such a time, [a. Mrs. Astor would have a ball / b. Mr. Tiffany opened a jewelry store / c. Mr. Stuyvesant built an apartment house] for them and it became very popular.

Mr. Clark's apartment also aimed for the same type of people. It was to be a luxurious apartment with a huge budget. The place he had chosen was the upper West Side, right next to [a. the rich residential area / b. the French flats / c. the yet undeveloped park]. A friend teased him and said it was like building in Dakota. Mr. Clark liked the metaphor and added details that related to [a. the Old South / b. the Wild West / c. the Modern City].

The apartment was an instant success. It attracted those [a. who dreamed of joining / b. who were rich enough but different from / c. who could not afford to join] Mrs. Astor's inner circle. There was an intellectual tone to them. They also seemed [a. respectable and good-mannered / b. artistic and witty / c. pure and religious], which the Astors would never have liked. This particular atmosphere can still be sensed in the residents of the apartment and its surroundings.

Editors' Note

　悪魔映画の歴史に輝く『ローズマリーの赤ちゃん』(*Rosemary's Baby*, 1968). Roman Polanskii 監督による，さまざまないわく付きのこの映画は，ダコタの内部で撮ったように見せているが，それは見せかけで，実際に撮影許可が出たのは，中庭やエレベーターの入り口を含む，建物の外側だけだった．

　ニューヨークを訪れたら，あなたもその門の前に立つことだろう．1980年の12月8日の深夜，4, 5発の銃声が鳴ってジョン・レノンの血が流れた舗道の上に．僕も，過去30年，バカみたいに何度もそこを訪れている．門の外から，かすかに中庭をうかがうばかり．

　Birmingham の本を読むと，中のようすもかなりのところは書いてある．荘厳なお屋敷の中は，やはり相当無気味なようだ．館の造り自体が，幽霊を呼び寄せるみたいなところがあって(?)，"haunted" とのうわさも流れっぱなしだったようだ．

　ちなみに，最初にここに住んだ映画スターは「フランケンシュタインの怪物」氏．テキストの12章に登場する Boris Karloff その人だった．ギギーっとドアが開いて，燭台にうす明るく照らされ，毛並みの長い絨毯が敷かれている（と，いま僕が勝手に想像している）廊下に，背広姿の大柄中年紳士が出てくる．そしてエレベーターまで歩いていく．そんなようすを思い描くと，ちょっとおかしな気持ちになる．ある意味，微笑ましくもあるけれども，当時の住人の子供たちには，冗談抜きで会いたくないおじさんだったことだろう．子供好きのボリスは，毎年ハロウィーンの晩に，お菓子を用意して待っていた．なのにドアベルを鳴らし，Trick or treat. と大きな声で呼びかけてく威勢のいい子は，悲しいかな，一人もいなかったそうである．

[Answers for the a/b Questions]
[9] — b., [74] — a., [89] — b., [100] — a., [124] — b.

Session 4

Charlie Brown: The Triumph of a Loser

David Michaelis

On October 2, 1950, at the height of the American postwar celebration — an era when being unhappy was an antisocial rather than a personal emotion — a twenty-seven-year-old Minnesota cartoonist named Charles M. Schulz introduced to the funny papers a group of children who told one another the truth: "I have deep feelings of depression," a round-faced kid named Charlie Brown said to an imperious girl named Lucy in an early strip. "What can I do about it?" "Snap out of it," advised Lucy. This was something new in the newspaper comic strip.

Charlie Brown was a real person, with a real psyche and real problems. The reader knew him, knew his fears, sympathized with his sense of inferiority and alienation. When Charlie Brown first confessed, "I don't feel the way I'm supposed to feel," he was speaking for people everywhere in Eisenhower's America, especially for a generation of solemn, precociously cynical college students, who "inhabited a shadow area within the culture," the writer Frank Conroy recalled. They were the last generation to grow up, as Schulz had, without television, and they read Charlie Brown's utterances as existential statements—comic strip *koans* about the human condition.

The *Peanuts* characters spoke in plain language and at

Charlie Brown: The Triumph of a Loser

[1] **at the height of the American postwar celebration:**「第二次世界大戦の戦勝気分が最高潮だったとき」．これ以降は，朝鮮戦争の激化や核戦争の恐怖，赤狩りによる思想統制などで「祝祭気分」は冷え込んでいく．

[3] **being unhappy was an antisocial rather than a personal emotion:**「憂うつであることが単に個人の感情の問題におわらず社会にとけこめない (= 反社会的だ) として問題視された」．みんなと一緒に楽しくやっていないとつまはじきを食らうような社会を想像してみよう．

[5] **the funny papers:** 分冊になったアメリカの新聞の，日曜日に入っている漫画セクション（日曜日に配達される新聞は，とても分厚い）．

[7] **depression:** 落ち込み，うつ状態

[8] **imperious:** 傲慢な，横柄な (arrogant)

[9] **strip:**「四コマ漫画」(comic strip)．全体として細長いかたち (strip) なのでこう呼ばれる．

Snap out of it: wake up; get a hold of yourself. 催眠術師が指をならして (snap) 患者を現実に戻す身振りに由来する表現．

[12] **psyche** [sáiki]: 魂，心の内面

[13] **The reader knew him:** They knew him because they [a. had read about / b. recognized themselves in] Charlie Brown.

[14] **sympathized with:** 〜の気持ちをそのまま感じる

sense of inferiority and alienation: 劣等感と疎外感

[15] **I don't feel the way I'm supposed to feel:** 僕の感じ方はみんなの考える規範からずれている

[16] **speaking for:** 代弁している

[17] **Eisenhower's America:** p. 5, 注 [19] 参照．物質文明の繁栄と冷戦によって，画一化しつつある社会への順応の圧力が高まった時代でもある．

a generation of solemn, precociously cynical college students:「しかつめらしく，まだ若いのにシニカルな大学生世代」．60 年代のラディカルな学生とは対照的に silent generation と呼ばれた世代を指している．precocious [prikóuʃəs]

[20] **Frank Conroy:** (1936–2005) ジャズ・ピアニストとしても知られる．代表作 *Body and Soul*（邦題『マンハッタン物語』）．

[21] **read Charlie Brown's utterances as existential statements:**「チャーリー・ブラウンが口にすることを実存的な表明のように読んだ」．フランスの哲学者サルトル (Jean-Paul Sartre, 1905–80) らによって，いまここに生きている主体を重んじる実存主義 (existentialism) は，1950 年代，一世を風靡した．

[23] **koans:** 日本語の「公案」．公案とは，いわゆる「禅問答」の課題のこと．当時アメリカ知識人層には「東洋の奥深い思想」として禅が流行した．

the same time questioned the meaning of life itself. They were energized by a sense of the wrongness of things. The cruelty that exists among children was one of Schulz's first overt themes. Even Charlie Brown himself played the heavy at the start; in a 1951 strip, after prankishly insulting Patty to her face ("You don't look so hot to me"), Charlie Brown scampers away, relishing the trickster's leftovers: "I get my laughs!" But instead of merely depicting children tormenting each other, the cartoonist brilliantly used the theme of happiness—the warm and fuzzy happiness of puppies—as a stalking horse for the wrongness of things.

Peanuts depicted genuine pain and loss but somehow, as the cartoonist Art Spiegelman observed, "still kept everything warm and fuzzy." By fusing adult ideas with a world of small children, Schulz reminded us that although childhood wounds remain fresh, we have the power as adults to heal ourselves with humor. If we can laugh at the daily struggles of a bunch of funny-looking kids and in their worries recognize the adults we've become, we can free ourselves. This alchemy was the magic in Schulz's work, the mixture that fused the Before and After elements of his own life, and it remains the singular achievement of his strip, the source of its universal power, without which *Peanuts*

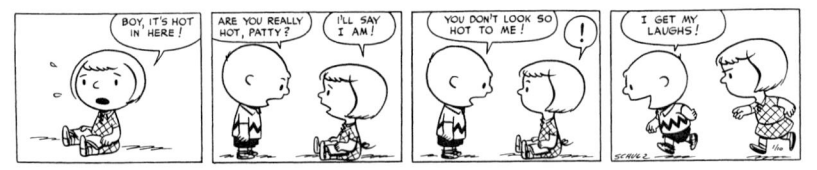

From *The Complete Peanuts* (2004), p. 29. Copyright © United Feature Syndicate, Inc.

Charlie Brown: The Triumph of a Loser

[26] **were energized by a sense of wrongess of things:** 物事が間違っているという思いをエネルギー源にして行動した

[28] **overt:** open; plain to see; not hidden (⇔ covert)
played the heavy: 悪役を演じた

[29] **after prankishly insulting Patty to her face:** 半分ふざけながらパティに侮辱の言葉を浴びせたあと

[30] **You don't look so hot to me:** hot に 2 つの意味（「暑い」と「かっこいい」）をかけている

[31] **scampers away, relishing the trickster's leftovers:** いたずらの余韻を楽しみながらそそくさと逃げる
I get my laughs: 僕だってこういう気分のいいことをやるときはやるさ

[32] **tormenting:** harassing; annoying; attacking

[34] **the warm and fuzzy happiness of puppies:** ぬくぬくふわふわした子犬的幸福感

[35] **stalking horse:**「隠れ蓑」．猟師がそれに隠れて獲物に近づく馬のことで，この場合，撃たれる獲物は wrongness of things ということになる．

[36] **depicted genuine pain and loss:** 本物の痛みや喪失感を描いた

[37] **Art Spiegelman:** アメリカの漫画家スピーゲルマン (1948–) は，父親が自分に語ったホロコーストの物語を，ネズミを主人公にして描いた *Maus* (1986) で知られる．

[38] **fusing ⟨A⟩ with ⟨B⟩:** combining (blending, mixing) ⟨A⟩ with ⟨B⟩

[39] **childhood wounds remain fresh:** 子供の時の傷は癒えない

[40] **the power...to heal ourselves:** 自らを癒す力

[42] **in their worries recognize the adults we've become:** 子供たちの悩みに接して，大人になった自分を認識する

[44] **alchemy:** 錬金術（魔法のような結果を生む化学反応）

[46] **singular:** unique; one-of-a-kind

[47] **the source of its universal power:** 世界の誰にも訴えかける力のもと
without which *Peanuts* would have come and gone in a flash: without this alchemy, *Peanuts* would have [a. disappeared instantly / b. shone brightly]

would have come and gone in a flash.

A generation before *Peanuts*, the comics parodied the world. Schulz *made* a world. He lured mainstream newspaper comics readers into a dystopia of cruelty and disappointment and hurt feelings. His characters demonstrated daily that we are all, closely examined, a bit peculiar, a little lonely, a lot lost in a lonely universe; and being aware of that and living with it is life's daily test.

"Nobody was saying this stuff, and it was the truth," said Jules Feiffer, whose drawings in the late '50s, like Schulz's, were steeped in a new humor of truth called "egghead" humor. "Nobody was doing this stuff. You didn't find it in *The New Yorker*. You found it in cellar clubs; and, on occasion, in the pages of *The Village Voice*. But not many other places. And then, with *Peanuts*, there it was on the economics page."

Feiffer, the melancholy Jewish intellectual striking at the heart of life as we knew it, saw in Schulz a fellow subversive. Their styles and audience could not have been more different. Feiffer aimed for an elite, urban audience; Schulz was drawing for everyone everywhere. But their territory overlapped. In a Feiffer cartoon of the late '50s, a teenager enumerates the horror of middle age: getting stuck in a marriage, living in the suburbs, dying of boredom. A man confronts the teenager: "Why don't you just grow up?" The teenager replies: "For our generation a refusal to grow up is a sign of maturity." That was the message of *Peanuts*, too. Schulz was drawing the "inner child" many years before the concept emerged in the popular culture.

The *Peanuts* gang was appealing but also strange. Were they children or adults? Or some kind of hybrid? What would push real children to the breaking point, Charlie Brown handled admirably and without self-pity or self-congratulation. What would reduce children to tears in the real world was routinely endured in *Peanuts*.

[50]	**lured . . . into a dystopia:** ディストピア (utopia と逆の暗黒郷) へ誘い込んだ	
[53]	**closely examined:** if we are closely examined	
	peculiar: strange. 50〜60年代のアメリカでは強く否定的な響きがあった単語．この辺り，a bit . . . a little . . . a lot と続く，l と t の音の戯れが楽しい．	
[54]	**being aware of that and living with it:** being aware of (your own peculiarity, loneliness and lostness) and living with (that awareness)	
[55]	**life's daily test:** 日々の暮らしに与えられた試練	
[56]	**this stuff:** such things	
	and it was the truth:「それこそが真実なのに」．この and は and yet に近い．	
[57]	***Jules Feiffer:*** (1929–) ファイファーは *The Village Voice* (注 [61] 参照) で漫画を42年間描き続け，1984年にピューリッツァー賞 (政治漫画部門) を受賞．	
[58]	**steeped in a new humor of truth:** 新手の「真実をつくユーモア」に溢れていた．**steeped in:** soaked up in, filled with	
	"egghead": インテリをからかっていう言葉．	
[60]	**cellar clubs:** 当時芸術家等の出入りが多かった (ヴィレッジ周辺の) 地下酒場	
	on occasion: sometimes	
[61]	***The Village Voice:*** 1955年創刊の，リベラル思想に彩られた無料週刊市民新聞．	
[62]	**with *Peanuts*, there it was on the economics page:** ピーナッツはというと (ひょいと) 新聞の経済欄なんかに載っていた	
[64]	**striking at the heart of life as we knew it:** 私たちが (身を以て) 知っている人生の，まさに核心をつく	
[65]	**saw in Schulz a fellow subversive:** saw a fellow subversive in Schulz. シュルツの内実は自分と同じく反体制的な人間だということ見いだした	
[66]	**could not have been more different:** were [a. very / b. not so] different	
[70]	**enumerate(s)** [injúːməreit]: 並べたてる	
	getting stuck in a marriage: 楽しくもない結婚生活に埋もれ	
[71]	**living in the suburbs:**「郊外の一戸建ての生活」はここでは退屈の象徴．	
[75]	**the "inner child":**「内なる子供」を大事にすることが人格の統合に必要だと，セラピー等で盛んに言われるようになるのは，70年代に入ってから．	
[77]	**gang:** ここでは「チビッコの仲間たち」といった語感．	
[78]	**What would push real children to the breaking point:**「実際の子供だったら耐えきれないことを」．break は「泣き崩れる」．これ全体が handled の目的節．	
[80]	**admirably** [ǽdmərəbli]: 立派に，みごとに	
	without self-pity or self-congratulation: 自己憐憫も自己賞揚もせずに	
[81]	**What would reduce children to tears:** 子供なら泣き出してしまうようなこと	
[82]	**routinely endured:** みんな当たり前のこととして耐えていた	

In their early years, the characters were volatile, combustible. They were angry. Coming home to relax, Charlie Brown sits down to a radio broadcast whose suave announcer is saying, "And what, in all this world, is more delightful than the gay wonderful laughter of little children?" Charlie Brown stands, sets his jaw, and kicks the radio set clear out of the room. Here was a comic strip hero, who, unlike his predecessors Li'l Abner, Dick Tracy, Joe Palooka, or Beetle Bailey, could take the restrained fury of the '50s and translate it into a harbinger of '60s activism.

On the one hand, the action in *Peanuts* conveyed an American sense that things could be changed, or at least modified, by sudden violence. By getting good and mad you could resolve things. But, on the other hand, Charlie Brown reminded people, as no other cartoon character had, of what it was to be vulnerable, to be human.

The experience of being an Everyman—a decent, caring person in a hostile world—is essential to Charlie Brown's character. The quality of fortitude (one of the seven cardinal virtues in Christianity) is at the heart of Charlie Brown. Humanity was created to be strong; yet, to be strong, and still to fail is one of the identifying things that it is to be human. Charlie Brown never quit. He is a fighter, but a fighter in terms of pure endurance, not in terms of working

From *The Complete Peanuts* (2004), p. 180. Copyright © United Feature Syndicate, Inc. [February, 1958]

- [83] **volatile, combustible:**「揮発性で燃えやすい」．ここは「すぐに怒り出す」の意．
- [85] **suave** [swɑːv]: 滑らかな語り口の
- [88] **sets his jaw:** グイと顎を固定して（奥歯をかみしめる感じ）
- [89] **clear:**「すっきり（なくなる）」というイメージを添える副詞．
- [90] **unlike his predecessors:** 前の時代の漫画主人公たちとは違って
  Li'l Abner, Dick Tracy, Joe Palooka, or Beetle Bailey: アメリカの漫画史を彩るこれらのヒーローを，画像検索でチェックしてみよう．
- [91] **the restrained fury of the '50s:** 1950年代の，内に抑え込んでいた怒り
- [92] **translate it into a harbinger of '60s activism:**「その怒りを60年代の反体制運動の先駆けへと変換する」．欺瞞的な言葉を「蹴る」行為が「先駆け」にあたる．
- [93] **conveyed an American sense that things could be changed:** 物事は変えられるというアメリカ的な感覚を伝えている
- [95] **By getting good and mad:**「しっかり怒ることによって」．good and ... は強調．
  I got good and tired, so I just jumped into bed.
- [97] **reminded people ... of what it was to be vulnerable, to be human:** 傷つきやすいこと，人間であることがどういうことかを人々に思い起こさせた
  as no other cartoon character had: [a. just like / b. unlike] any other cartoon character had reminded people before them の略．
- [99] **an Everyman:** どこにでもいる普通の人．15世紀イングランドの道徳劇に登場する人物の名前に由来する．
  a decent, caring person: それ相応の節度と思いやりがある人
- [101] **fortitude:**（逆境などに）堪える力，忍耐
  the seven cardinal virtues in Christianity: 初期のキリスト教の4つの美徳にパウロがさらに3つ加えて7つとした．最終的には，Faith 忠実，Hope 希望，Charity 愛，Fortitude 忍耐，Justice 正義，Temperance 節制，Prudence 慎重．
- [104] **the identifying things that it is to be human:** 人間とはどういう存在かを定義づける事柄
- [106] **(a) fighter in terms of pure endurance:** ひたすら堪えるという意味での闘争者
  working out strategically: 戦略的に考え出す

out strategically how he is going to win. He simply endures; he stays longer on the baseball field than all the other kids. When the field is flooded in a downpour and only the pitcher's mound is above water, he remains. His strategy is simple: hang on. He is ennobled by how well he handles being disappointed. He never cries.

The moment when *Peanuts* became *Peanuts* can probably be marked at several spots on Schulz's 1954 calendar, but nowhere more clearly than Monday, February 1: Charlie Brown is visiting Shermy. He looks on, bereft, as a smiling Shermy, seemingly unaware of Charlie Brown's presence, plays with a model train set whose tracks and junctions and crossings spead so elaborately far and wide in Shermy's family's living room, the railroad's complete dimensions cannot be shown in a single cartoon panel. Charlie Brown pulls on his coat and walks home. Finally, alone in his own living room, Charlie Brown sits down at his railroad: a single, closed circle of track, no bigger than a manhole cover. But there is no anger, no self-pity, no tears—no punch line— just silent acceptance. Here was the moment when Charlie Brown became a national symbol, the Everyman who survives life's slings and arrows simply by surviving himself.

From *The Complete Peanuts* (2004), p. 171. Copyright © United Feature Syndicate, Inc. [February, 1954]

- [109] **flooded in a downpoor:** どしゃぶりの雨で水浸しになる
- [111] **He is ennobled by how well he handles being disappointed:** *i.e.* The way he endures his disappointments is worthy of praise.
- [113] **The moment when *Peanuts* became *Peanuts*:** 初期段階を抜けて，真にピーナッツらしい漫画世界が誕生した時点
- [114] **Schulz's 1954 calendar:** calendar という言葉が出てくるのは，著者がシュルツの1年分の作品を日付とともに思い描いているから．
- [115] **nowhere more clearly than Monday, February 1:** *i.e.* the clearest moment is Monday, February 1
- [116] **looks on, bereft:** 所在なさそうにボ〜ッと見つめている
  as: while
- [118] **tracks and junctions and crossings:** 線路や分岐点や踏切
- [119] **spread so elaborately far and wide:**「とても複雑に広範に遠くまで広がっていて」．いわゆる so that 構文なので，the railroad's の前に that を補ってよい．
- [125] **punch line:** 最後のキメのセリフ
- [128] **life's slings and arrows:** 人生につきものの飛礫（つぶて）や矢（人を傷つけるもの）
  surviving himself:「自分自身を生き延びる」とは，自分の感情や利己心に溺れて破滅したりしないこと．

[Session 4] Comprehension Check

1. **Which word best describes Charlie Brown in the following situations?**

combustible	harsh	enduring
accepting	hurt	

   1) The radio announcer idealizes children and Charlie Brown kicks the radio set out of sight. He is (   )
   2) The baseball field is flooded in a downpour but Charlie Brown remains. He is (   )
   3) Charlie Brown insults Patty to her face and runs away, feeling great about what he did. He is (   )
   4) Charlie Brown quietly plays with his model train on a small decent railroad track. He is (   )

2. **Mark T for true, F for false.**
   1) In the American postwar era, people were expected to behave as if they were happy all the time. — (   )
   2) *Peanuts* allowed the adult audience to laugh at the troubles of the characters and free themselves. — (   )
   3) The world of *Peanuts* was rather cruel but it was wonderfully balanced with a sense of warmness. — (   )
   4) Feiffer and Schulz have the same elite, urban audience and they both depict the "inner child" in a very subversive way. — (   )
   5) Charlie Brown handles a cruel situation admirably, where in real life, a child would just start crying. — (   )
   6) From the beginning, Charlie Brown has always been the one we know today. — (   )

Charlie Brown: The Triumph of a Loser

> **Editors' Note**
>
> 『ピーナッツ』よりはチャーリー・ブラウン，チャーリー・ブラウンよりはスヌーピー．日本ではこんな順番で知名度が高い．そして漫画そのものよりもキャラクター商品の方がなじみ深い．でもこの作品がラッキーだったのは，谷川俊太郎という訳者によって日本に初紹介されたこと．そのセリフは子供でも十分楽しめるほどシンプルだが，シンプルなだけにそこからは深遠な意味を読み取ることもできる．それを訳すのはかなりの苦労だったろう．つまり単なる「子供騙し」ではないわけで，そのことはアニメ版のバックに流れる軽妙かつ本格的なジャズが巧みに象徴していた．
>
> 1950年からきっちり50年間も連載が続いたこの作品には，魅力的なキャラが大勢いる．個人的には Pigpen（直訳すると「豚小屋」）の登場が衝撃だった．
>
> 彼はいつも身汚くて，体のまわりに土ぼこりを舞い上がらせている．お風呂に入らないわけではないが，一歩外に出れば「ほこり磁石」の特殊技能をぞんぶんに発揮して，すぐにもとの汚れた姿に戻ってしまう．たとえ純白の雪の中を歩こうともしっかりババッチくなれる男の子，それが Pigpen なのである．
>
> なのに，あるいはそれゆえにか，彼はとてもほこり高い．幾星霜ものほこりを集め，その汚れっぷりには「文明」すら刻み込まれている（と彼は言う）．ジンギスカンや賢王ソロモンが踏んだ土が，今ここに舞っているのかもしれない，と Charlie Brown も手放しに賞賛(?)する．人は外見で判断してはいけません，と大人のモラルを導き出すことも可能だが，Pigpen にはそんなせこい解釈を超越するおもしろさがあった．
>
> 日曜日の朝，足の上に落としたらケガをしそうなほど分厚い新聞の中からコミック・セクションをえり抜き，ページを繰って *Peanuts* の4コマ漫画を探し出し，そこに Pigpen の姿を見つけると，その日は一日，子供ながらに幸せだった．彼には言うに言われぬ魅力があったのだ．

[Answers for the a/b Questions]
[13] — b., [47] — a., [66] — a., [97] — b.

PART II
Dear Companions

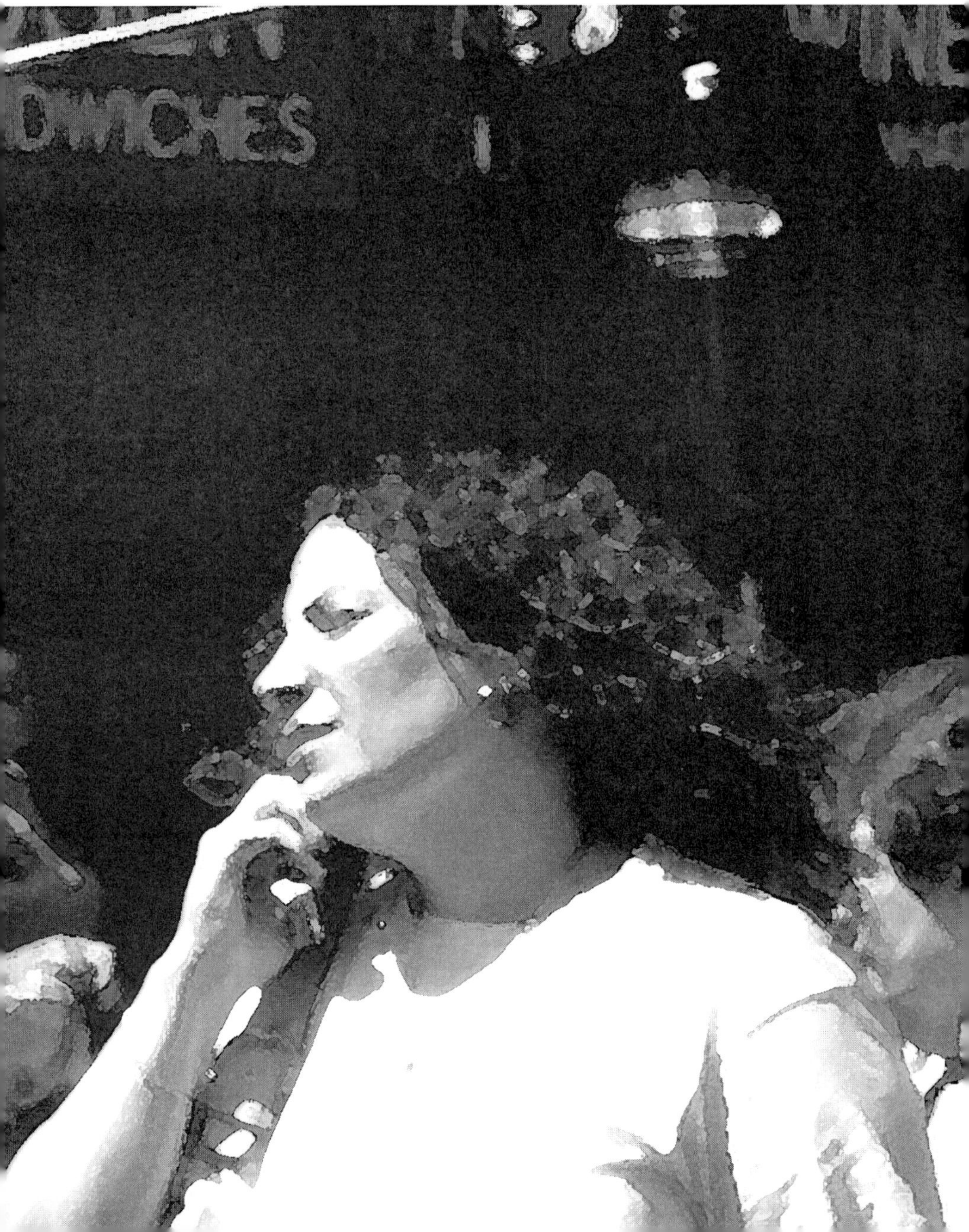

Introduction to Part II

〈大切な仲間 *dear companions*〉という章題のもとに，恋のはじまり，飼い犬のはじまり，清涼飲料との幸福な関係の終わり，人の生命の終わり，を描く4編の「ドラマ」を集めた．

Session 5 の著者エイミー・ベンダー（1969– ）は，アメリカの新世代作家を代表する一人．幻想的で不思議な，それでいて胸にヒリヒリくる作品を得意とする．2005年刊の短編集 *Willful Creatures*（『わがままなやつら』）所収の *"Meeting"* も，だれにでも想像ができる女と男の出来事を，独特の詩的口語文でつづっている．1音節か2音節の基本単語が——愛そのものがそうであるように——しばしば論理の制御を振り払い，強引に *and* でつながって先に進んでいくような文章は，最初のうちこそ読者のみなさんを戸惑わせるかもしれない．でも恋に落ちるときの心の動きに，難解なところがあろうはずはない．物語の大筋が把握できたら，その詩を，いっしょに声に出して詩ってみよう．この小さな珠玉篇がもし気に入ったら，*The Girl in the Flammable Skirt*（『燃えるスカートの少女』）や *An Invisible Sign of My Own*（『私自身の見えない徴』）などの作品（集）もどうぞ．

Man's best friend といえば昔から犬と相場が決まっているが，人類誕生の大昔からそうだった——という説を紹介するのは，犬のコミュニケーションの専門家で，ポピュラーな一般書もたくさん書いている心理学者のスタンリー・コーレン教授．**Session 6** で，ヒトが言語能力を獲得する上でイヌとの共生が重要な要因になったという大胆な仮説を紹介している．その説が正しいという保証はないが，複数の種が，互いに互いの変化をもたらしながら進化していくという「共進化 co-evolution」の考え方自体に慣れておくこと

Introduction to Part II

は有用だろう．どんな生物も，生きながらえていくには，いっしょに変化してくれる柔軟なコンパニオンが必要だ——という考えには，人生の寓意が潜んでいるように思われる．

世界で一番広く知られた英語が *Coca Cola* だというのはきっと本当だろう．あの印象的なロゴと特徴的なボトルとともに，コカコーラは，アメリカの，いや資本主義そのもののシンボルとして，地球の隅々へ浸透した．アメリカでは，お婆さんのそのまたお婆さんも，日曜午後の日だまりで，草野球の応援をしながらシュワーッと喉を潤した．そのドリンクが本国アメリカの一部国民に，神聖にして冒すべからざる意味を持ったとしても不思議はないだろう．1985年4月，誕生100周年を前にコカコーラ社が，大々的なキャンペーンとともに New Coke にモデルチェンジしたときに起こった国民的ブーイングは，新製品開発史の有名な事件となった．その事件を，センセーショナルな筆致で描く文章がネットに載っていたので **Session 7** で採用させていただいた．著者として Michael Bastedo Angela Davis の名があるが，どういう人（たち？）かは不詳．

臓器移植を必要とする人々にとって，脳死者こそ dearest companion だろう．まだ心臓がバクバク動いている「死体」から臓器が摘出される，ある意味で「えぐい」シーンを描きながら，**Session 8** の著者 Mary Roach は，文化や時代によって「魂の在りか」とされる場所が変化してきた事実に目を向ける．出典は彼女の単行本デビュー作となった *Stiff* (2003)．科学／医学のさまざまな領域で，死者がどれだけの貢献をしているかというテーマを，「不敬」と言われかねないような軽妙な文体で書きつづって話題を呼んだ本だ．口語体のノリによって，重い問題を，ユーモラスにアイロニカルに語る，現代のプロフェッショナルな文章の妙味を味わおう．

Session 5

The Meeting

Aimee Bender

The woman he met. He met a woman. This [1] woman was the woman he met. She was not the woman he expected to meet or planned to meet or had carved into his head in full dress with a particular nose and eyes and lips and a very particular brain. No, this was a dif- [5] ferent woman, the one he met. When he met her he could hardly stand her because she did not fit the shape in his brain of the woman he had planned so vigorously and extensively to meet. And the non-fit was uncomfortable and made his brain hurt. Go away woman, he said, and the [10] woman laughed, which helped for a second. He trailed the woman for a few days saying it was because he had nothing else to do, but in truth he did have plenty to do and he did not know why he was trailing her. His brain made a lot of

Aimee Bender, *Willful Creatures* (2005)

The Meeting

[2] **She was not the woman he . . . :** 以下 expected, planned, had carved into his head の 3 つの動詞 (句) が，冒頭で繰り返された met (事実として出会った) と対照されている．

[3] **had carved into his head:** 頭の中に刻み込んでいた；脳に刷り込んでいた

[4] **in full dress:**「バッチリ衣装を着せて」．男の夢想がそれだけ念入りであったということ．

a particular nose and eyes and lips:（彼の好みを反映した）独特な目鼻立ち．この文は最後までカンマがなく，一息に読まれることで，最初の短文の連続と対照的な，可笑しく軽妙なリズムをつくっている．

[6] **the one he met:** この文の主語．前行の this を言い替えている．

he could hardly stand her: For him, the woman was [a. attractive / b. awful].

[8] **vigorously:** strongly; powerfully; passionately

[9] **extensively:** in various ways; by various means

the non-fit:（自分が抱いていたイメージとの）不一致

[11] **helped:** helped him be a little more comfortable and painless

trailed: followed; pursued; stalked

[13] **in truth he did have plenty to do:** in fact he had a lot of things to do. had の代わりに did have とすることで直前の "had nothing else to do" が強く打ち消されている．

[14] **made a lot of shouts and static about his brain's own idea of hair color:** i.e. was noisy commenting about hair color saying it has to be like this or that. static はふつうは，通信障害の雑音をさす．

shouts and static about his brain's own idea of hair color and sense of humor and what animals the woman he met would like (mammals) and his brain's own idea of how to be a member of the world, and everything that was sort of like him and yet different enough and still: this woman he met was the woman he met and however you try, you cannot unmeet.

His brain was in an utter panic at changing. His brain was very pleased with its current shape and did not want to shift, not one bit. This woman liked *reptiles* and *fish*. What sort of decent human being could possibly like reptiles and fish?

He said, Go away woman. You go away, she said, shooing him with her hand. You're the one following me around all the time.

They went on a walk—or rather she went on a walk and he asked if he could join her—together over the small bridge which ran over a dry stream and looked down at rocks which jutted up like teeth. She talked significantly more than he expected the woman he met to talk and so while she was talking he thought she is surely, and clearly, not the woman for me. Blabbermouth, he thought. She paused at an oak tree and said, Did you stop listening? and so he started listening again and said some stuff himself, about this, about that. He liked talking to her. The woman said she did not know why she liked him, as he was being something of an irritation with all this static in his head and he said he was sorry, he liked her too, but his brain kept rejecting her and he did not know what to do about that. The woman said, Please, would you shut your brain down for five seconds and let the world participate a bit? No, said the man. I control the world. The woman's laughter bounced off the rocks below. The man laughed too but inside he still meant it.

The woman said goodbye and went to her cottage and

The Meeting

[16] **what animals the woman he met would like (mammals):** *i.e.* [a. He had planned to meet the kind of woman who would like mammals. / b. The woman he met liked mammals.]

[17] **how to be a member of the world:**「世の中の一員としての収まり方」．仕事や生き方のスタイルをさすのだろう．著者独特の言い回し．

[18] **everything that was sort of like him and yet different enough:**「自分と似ていなくもないのだが，しかし違うといえば違うすべての点」．made a lot of shouts and static about から続く．

[19] **and still:**「（ああだこうだとは言っても）でもやっぱり」．このコロンで，ある程度長いポーズをとる．次の文が，このパラグラフ全体の結論となります．

[20] **you cannot unmeet:** 出会いを取り消すことはできない

[22] **an utter panic:** a complete panic
His brain was very pleased with its current shape: [a. He liked the way people saw him. / b. He liked his own way of thinking about things.]

[24] **not one bit** = not at all
reptile(s): 爬虫類 (snakes, lizards, alligators, crocodiles, turtles, tortoises, etc.)
What sort of decent human being could possibly . . . :「まともな人間であれば〜などするはずがない」．decent: respectable; clean-living; pleasant

[27] **You go away:** あなたこそ消えなさい．（You に強勢）
shooing him with her hand: 手で「シッシッ」とやりながら

[33] **jutted up:**「突き出た」．続く like teeth はもちろん下あごの歯．
talked significantly more than he expected the woman he met to talk:「自分が会ったその女性は，思ったよりずっとお喋りだった」．significantly は量の違いが際立っているということ．

[36] **Blabbermouth:** おしゃべりなやつ

[38] **said some stuff himself, about this, about that:** 自分でもああだ，こうだとおしゃべりした

[40] **he was being something of an irritation:**「彼はいくぶんイライラの元になっていた」．being があるのは，彼の性格そのものではなく，そのときの状態をいっているから．something of: somewhat; a little bit of

[41] **and he said . . . :** 前にカンマがないことで独特な話法のリズムが生じている．

[44] **shut your brain down . . . and let the world participate:** 自分の脳のスイッチを切って，目の前の世界も参加させてあげたらどうなの

[47] **meant it:** honestly thought that he controlled the world

made some spaghetti and the next day guess who was at her door. Good afternoon. How are you, how are you. The spaghetti was fine-tuned and she was beautiful in the filtered sunlight and they made love that afternoon with the green sunlight through her green curtains. Her body was new to him and he did not like the way her shoulders were so broad and he very much liked the slope of her hips and he was scared because he did not know how to navigate the curves they made together. Later, when he would become a ship's captain on waves of the water of their bodies, it turned out that those broad shoulders were the thing he would think of with the most lust and the most tenderness. Those broad shoulders would be what he would recognize in a crowd if they all had paper bags on their heads. Those broad shoulders he could spot across an ocean.

The following day after the green-curtain day, he was back. They ate cold spaghetti out of paper cups on the stoop. He said, I just don't know if I want to marry you. She snorted. What? He said, I'm sorry but I'm just not certain that you are my future wife. She spit some spaghetti out on the stoop in a little red clump and he thought it was gross and she was laughing again, not with, definitely at. He said, I always thought the woman I'd marry would hit me easy in a bolt of lightning, and there is not lightning there is not even thunder there is not even rain. It all feels, well, foggy he said. And she said, What makes you so sure I want to marry you? and he said, Oh, hmmm, and she said, Why would I consider marrying a man whose brain is so bossy? I need a man with some *calm*, she said. He looked at her nose, thin and long and her eyes thin and long the other direction and her hair was straight and long and shone. He had a bite of spaghetti off her fork. They sat for a while on the stoop and watched the lizards skit and scat until the mailman came by and delivered some letters—two bills and a postcard from her cousin on an island. She made faces at the

The Meeting

- [50] **guess who was at her door:**「誰が来たか，当ててごらん」．びっくりするような来客があった，というニュアンス．
- [52] **fine-tuned:**「ファイン・チューニングされた」とは，ここでは細やかに気を配ってちょうどよい茹でかげんにしたということ．
- [55] **did not like the way her shoulders were so broad:**「肩幅が広すぎるところが嫌だった」．broad shoulders は「肩幅が広い」転じて「頼りになる」の意味も．
- [58] **(the) curves they made together:** 愛の行為の感覚的な表現．比喩は次の文へ発展していく．
- [59] **it turned out that ... :**「結局〜だった」．経験してみたら，蓋を開けてみたら〜だった，というときに使う．
- [61] **lust:** (sexual) desire; passion; urge
- [62] **would recognize in a crowd:** 群衆のなかでもきっと見分けられる
- [63] **had paper bags on their heads:** みな買物袋を被って(顔が見えなくて)も
  Those broad shoulders he could spot across an ocean: He could spot those broad shoulders even if she were faraway. 海や航海の比喩が続いている．spot: find; see; recognize
- [66] **the stoop:** 玄関前の階段
- [68] **snorted:** 鼻を鳴らした
- [70] **gross:** ugly; filthy; repulsive
- [71] **not with, definitely at:**「彼と」笑ったのではなく，明らかに「彼を」笑った．laugh at は誰かを笑いの標的にするということ．
- [72] **hit me easy:** あっという間に私を打つ (=虜にする)
  in a bolt of lightning:「雷に打たれるように」というのは恋愛感情の形容として珍しくないが，ポイントはそうした細部に文字通りこだわる男の脳の「うるささ」．それにもかかわらず「かわいい」ところが感じられますか？
- [74] **It all feels, well, foggy:** well を挟んだのは適切な言葉を探そうとしたから．
- [77] **bossy:** boss の形容詞形．「威張りちらして何でも言うとおりにさせようとする」．
- [79] **her eyes thin and long the other direction:**「(細長い鼻とは) 別な方向に伸びている細長い目」．この文も「構文」よりリズムに力点が置かれている．
- [82] **skit and scat:** トカゲが左右に体をくねらせながら素早く逃げていくさまを表す即興フレーズ．scat は「スキャッと逃げていく」という感じの動詞．
- [83] **bill(s):** 請求書
- [84] **made faces at:** しかめっ面をした，アカンベェの気持ちを顔にあらわした．

bills and laughed at the postcard and scrutinized the little type in the upper left-hand corner telling her where it was and then looked at the picture on the front for longer than he had ever looked at all the postcards of his entire life.

When they made love that day it was one step closer to making sense and she brought them some wine afterward and they sat and watched the sunset through the green curtains, naked, with deep-bellied glasses of wine. The green darkened into black. He let his hand trace each of her vertebrae and she did not say, That tickles, stop, like he thought she might. She just looked out the muted curtain and her hair swished at an angle. He moved his fingers down her whole spine, one by one by one, and during the time it took to do that, his brain remained absolutely quiet.

It is these empty spaces you have to watch out for, as they flood up with feeling before you even realize what's happened; before you find yourself, at the base of her spine, different.

The Meeting

[85] **scrutinized:** examined; looked closely at; probed
the little type in the upper left-hand corner: 観光ハガキにはたいてい「左上のすみに小さな活字」で絵柄の説明が書いてある．

[89] **one step closer to making sense:**「(二人の関係が) 腑に落ちるところへさらに一歩近づいた」．make love と make sense をつないだ会心の創作表現．

[92] **deep-bellied glasses:** とっぷり丸く膨らんだグラス

[93] **vertebrae** [vá:rtəbrèi, -bri:]: 椎骨 (単数形は vertebra)

[94] **did not say . . . like he thought she might:** 言うかと思ったが言わなかった
That tickles, stop: くすぐったい，やめて

[95] **the muted curtain:**「押し黙ったカーテン」．光の欠如を音の欠如になぞらえている．*cf.* [92] The green darkened into black
her hair swished at an angle: 彼女の髪が斜めにサラサラと揺れた

[97] **spine:** 脊椎 (the set of all the vertebrae)

[99] **have to watch out for:**（危いことが起こるので）注意していないといけない

[100] **they flood up with feeling:** その空虚なスペースに感情が満ちあふれてくる
before you even realize what's happened: 恋に落ちるときはいつもそんなものかもしれません．

[Session 5] Comprehension Check

1. **Images of the past are returning to the man. Rearrange them in order.**

   (a) → ( ) → ( ) → ( ) → ( ) → ( )

   a. her hand shooing him away
   b. the little red clump of spaghetti that she spit out on the stoop
   c. the base of her vertebrae
   d. the walk to the bridge overlooking a dry river
   e. the green-curtain day
   f. her face as she looked at the postcard from her cousin

2. **Complete the sentences by choosing a, b or c.**

   1) The woman the man met [a. was the very image of / b. was much prettier than / c. was quite different from] the one he had expected to meet.
   2) The man's brain rejected change, [a. so he stopped seeing her / b. although they were getting married / c. but it could not stop him from seeing her].
   3) At first the man thought the woman's [a. eyes were too big / b. shoulders were too broad / c. hair was too wavy], but later he came to love them all the more.
   4) The man was [a. very sweet / b. truly passionate / c. rather rude] when he first talked about their getting married.
   5) The man's brain was [a. finally calm / b. not working well / c. still making a lot of noise] as he ran his hand down her spine.

Editors' Note

Aimee Bender の短編集 *The Girl in the Flammable Skirt* (1998) の中に "The Healer" という作品があって，これはふたりの mutants——突然変異した女の子——の物語である．ふたりはそれぞれ「火の手」と「氷の手」を持っている．もう一人，カミソリの刃で皮膚に文字や模様を刻む男の子が出てきて，この子と「火の手」をした女の子とが仲良くなる．町の人は，二人の悪いうわさを流す……

現代の，ごくふつうの町や学校の教室を舞台にして，おとぎ話か古代神話のような物語が展開していく妙味．Aimee は今，USC (南カリフォルニア大学) の創作のクラスを担当している．以前には小学校の先生をしていた．長編小説 *An Invisible Sign of My Own* (2001) も，小学校の先生と子供たち，親と町の人たちの物語．日本では『燃えるスカートの少女』『私自身の見えない徴』『わがままなやつら』というタイトルで，三作品が角川書店から出ている．

その訳者の菅啓次郎さんといっしょに，私たち編者ふたりも，東京で Aimee に会ったことがある．やや大柄で，才能と余裕にあふれていそうな，笑みの絶えない表情が印象的だった．

Aimee 自身のウェブサイト (Flammableskirt.com) を訪ねてみよう．

エイミーを囲んで——編者ふたりと菅啓次郎氏 (中央)．写真：藤部明子

[Answers for the a/b Questions]
[7] — b., [16] — a., [22] — b.

Session 6

The Early Man's Best Friend

Stanley Coren

We will probably never have conclusive evidence to tell us how dogs and humans first formed their personal and working relationship with each other, but it is most likely the case that man did not initially choose dog; rather, dogs chose man. Dogs were likely attracted to human campsites because humans, like dogs, were hunters, and animal remains, such as bones, bits of skin, and other scraps of offal from the victims of recent hunts, were likely to be scattered around human campsites. The ancestors of today's dogs learned that by hanging around man's habitations, they could grab a quick bite to eat now and then, without all the exertion involved in actual hunting.

Although primitive man may not have been very concerned with health issues, it is still true that rotting food stuff does smell, and attracts insects that will make humans uncomfortable. Thus, it is likely that dogs were initially tolerated around the perimeter of the camps simply because they would dispose of the garbage. This waste-disposal function continued for countless centuries and is still being fulfilled by the pariah dogs in many less developed regions of the world. Anthropologists studying primitive tribes in the South Pacific have noticed that on those islands where people keep dogs, the villages and settlements are much

The Early Man's Best Friend

Stanley Coren, *How to Speak Dog* (2000)

- [1] **conclusive evidence:**「決定的な証拠」．conclusive < conclude: 終える，ケリをつける
- [4] **it is most likely the case that . . . :** 一番可能性が高そうなのは〜
  did not initially choose dog: イヌより先に相手を選んだのではない
- [6] **human campsites:**（移動を前提とした）人間の集落
- [8] **scraps of offal:** 臓物などの食べ残し
- [9] **be scattered around:** 散在している
- [10] **by hanging around man's habitations:** 人間の住処のまわりをうろつくことで
- [11] **grab a quick bite:** ぱっとお手軽に食べる
- [12] **all the exertion involved in . . . :** 〜に伴うあれやこれやの骨折り
- [14] **may not have been very concerned with health issues:** was probably [a. careful / b. thoughtless] about their own health
- [15] **rotting food stuff:**「腐りかけの食材」．food といってもいいのだが，「そのへんの口に入るもの」というイメージを持たせるために food stuff とした．
- [17] **tolerated around the perimeter of the camps:** 集落の周辺にいることを許されていた
- [19] **dispose of the garbage:**（肉片や皮などの）ゴミを片付け（＝食べてくれ）る
- [20] **is still being fulfilled by . . . :**（ゴミ処理機能を）いまも〜が果たしている
- [21] **the pariah dogs:** 野良犬．pariah [pəráɪə]: outcast
- [22] **Anthropologists:** 人類学者たち
- [23] **on those islands where . . . :** 著者はしばしば the に替えて those や that を用い，語りかけるような口調を生み出している．

73

more permanent. Villages without dogs have to move every year or so, simply to escape the environmental contamination caused by rotting refuse. This has even led to the suggestion that dogs may have been a vital element in the establishment of permanent cities in that bygone era before we learned the importance of public sanitation.

Once the wild canines that would eventually become dogs were attracted to human settlements, our ancestors noticed an added benefit. Remember, early humans lived in dangerous times. There were large animals around which looked on humans as potential source of fresh meat. There were also other bands of humans with hostile intensions. Since the canines around the village began to look upon the area as their territory, whenever a strange human or some wild beast approached, the dogs would sound the alarm. This would alert the residents in time to rally some form of defense if needed. As long as dogs were present, the human guards did not need to be as vigilant, thus allowing for more rest and a better lifestyle.

When we say that the canines of early man barked, we are not talking about the kind of barking that dogs exhibit now. The sounds originally made by these ancient dogs were probably much more like those of the wild canines of today. Wolves, jackals, foxes, and coyotes rarely bark, and the noise that they make is far from impressive. I remember the first time I heard a pack of wolves barking when we approached their den. I easily recognized the sound as barking, but was surprised at how restrained it was. Domestic dogs set up a continuous string of machine-gun-like bursts of barking. The wolves' bark was softer, sounding like a breathy "Woof." It never appeared in strings, but simply a single, monosyllabic bark, followed by a pause of two to five seconds, then perhaps another bark. Over a half-minute period I counted four modest barks, while a domestic dog may give thirty or more, very much louder barks

The Early Man's Best Friend

- [25] **permanent:** [a. staying at one place / b. always moving]
- [26] **the environmental contamination caused by rotting refuse:**「腐ったゴミによる環境汚染」．名詞 refuse [réfjùːs] の強勢の位置に注意．
- [27] **This has even led to the suggestion that . . . :** そこから〜という（大胆な）考えも出てきた
- [28] **a vital element in . . . :** 〜において欠かせない要因
- [29] **(the) establishment of permanent cities:** 定住都市の成立
  that bygone era: the past periods; the times gone by
- [30] **public sanitation:** 公衆衛生
- [31] **canine(s):**「イヌ科の動物」．発音が同じなので K9 と記されることも．
- [33] **noticed an added benefit:** *i.e.* found that there was another benefit besides public sanitation in having the canines around
- [34] **There were large animals around:** be around は日本語の「いる」に相当．*Is Jack around today?*
- [35] **looked on:** considered．[37] look upon も同義．
  potential source of fresh meat: something that [a. might eat them / b. they could eat]
- [36] **bands of humans with hostile intensions:** groups of people who were likely to [a. attack / b. trade with] them
- [39] **sound the alarm:**「警報を鳴らす」．この場合は激しく吠えること．
- [40] **alert the residents in time to rally some form of defense:** let the people know of the danger beforehand so that they have time to prepare for it
- [42] **vigilant** [vídʒələnt]: watchful; careful; alert
  allowing for more rest and a better lifestyle: より多くの休息と生活の向上を可能にする
- [45] **the kind of barking that dogs exhibit now:** 現代のイヌに見られる吠えかた
- [49] **the noise:** barking（吠え声）とも言えない「音」
  far from impressive: 立派とはとても言えない
- [51] **den:** 巣穴
- [52] **restrained:** held back; modest; weak
- [53] **set up a continuous string of machine-gun-like bursts of barking:** マシンガンの切れ目のない銃撃音のように続けざまに吠える．Bow-wow-wow-wow-wow!
- [55] **a breathy "Woof":**（声帯をほとんど震わせずに）息だけを発する「ワッフ」
  It never appeared in strings: *i.e.* the wolves never barked continuously
- [56] **a single, monosyllabic bark:** 一度きりの，一音節の吠え
- [57] **Over a half-minute period:** 30 秒間にわたって
- [59] **thirty or more, very much louder barks:** "thirty or more" は barks にかかる．

in the same time period when warning of the approach of a stranger.

The earliest "dog owners" at some point must have noticed some variations in the amount of vocalization among the various canines that shared their camps. It seems obvious that for personal and community security purposes, the most effective dog is one with a loud and persistent bark. Apparently, humans began a sort of primitive selective breeding program to create such dogs. A dog that barked was kept and bred with others that also barked. One that did not bark was simply disposed of as being useless. This seems to explain the eventual divergence in vocal tendencies between dogs and wild canines.

Specialists can tell you about the many shades of "meaning" conveyed by different ways dogs bark, growl, howl, whine, squeak, whimper, scream, pant and sigh. But we cannot teach them to speak as we humans do simply because they are not physically equipped for it. Humans and dogs are built differently and this limits the sounds that dogs can make in comparison to people. In dogs, there is only a slight bend in the airway as we go from the mouth to the windpipe. In human beings, because we stand vertically, there is a 90-degree bend in the airway; this leaves room for the larynx to lengthen, and for there to be additional sound-making accessories, such as two resonating cavities instead of dog's one. In addition, humans have room for a larger, rounder tongue in comparison to the shorter, flat tongue of dogs. Thus, a dog simply does not have the vocal apparatus and control to voluntarily and selectively produce various different speech sounds.

Don't let your dog develop an inferiority complex because of its limited ability to make certain sounds. This is a very modern evolutionary development. It seems that similar difficulties were experienced by some of our fairly recent human ancestors, such as Neanderthal man. The

The Early Man's Best Friend

[60] **the same time period:** [a. two to five seconds / b. half a minute]

[62] **at some point:** at some point in history; at some point in the evolution of man-dog relationship

[63] **noticed some variations in the amount of vocalization among the various canines:** イヌごとに発声の大きさが違っていることに気づいた．*i.e.* noticed that some canines' "voices" were stronger than others

[65] **for personal and community security purposes:** 個人を，また集団を守るという目的からすると

[66] **persistent:** continual; lasting; never-stopping

[67] **Apparently:** おそらくは，どうやら (It appears that . . .)

　a . . . primitive selective breeding program:「原始的な品種改良プログラム」．selective breeding とは，好ましい特徴をもった個体だけ選んで育てることを何世代にもわたって続けることで，好ましい遺伝子をもつ品種をつくる方法．

[69] **was kept and bred with others:** 飼われ，他の大声のイヌとの間に子をもうけさせられた．bred < breed:（家畜などを）交配させる

[70] **was simply disposed of:** was just killed or left to die

[71] **the eventual divergence in vocal tendencies:**「後に生じた吠え声の傾向の違い」．犬の発声が徐々に他の類とは異なったものへ分岐 (diverge) していくこと．

[73] **the many shades of "meaning" conveyed:** 伝わる内容の微妙で多様な違い

[74] **bark, growl, howl, whine, squeak, whimper, scream, pant and sigh:** p. 83, Editors' Note 参照．

[77] **not physically equipped for it:** そのための器官が備わっていない

[78] **built differently:** 体のつくりが違っている

[79] **there is only a slight bend in the airway as we go from the mouth to the windpipe:** 口から気管にかけて見ていくと，気道は少ししか曲がっていない

[81] **stand vertically:** 直立している

[82] **this leaves room for the larynx to lengthen, and for there to be additional sound-making accessories:** このおかげで喉頭 (larynx) が伸び，音を作るための付属品がそこ（＝気道，airway）につけ加わる余地が出る

[84] **resonating cavities:** 反響する腔

[87] **the vocal apparatus and control:** 音を出す器官 (apparatus) や調整する能力

[88] **voluntarily and selectively:** 自分の意志で選択的に

[90] **inferiority complex:** 劣等感

[93] **similar difficulties were experienced by . . . :** 〜も同じく，うまくできはしなかった

　our fairly recent human ancestors: 比較的最近の人間の祖先

evidence is that Neanderthals probably did not have speech, or only had limited speech abilities. Soft tissue such as a larynx doesn't survive well, so we have no fossilized vocal tracts from primitive humanoids. However, the cognitive scientist Phillip Lieberman has demonstrated that if you try to insert a human vocal tract directly into the skeleton of a Neanderthal, it simply doesn't fit. The modern larynx ends up in a weird and unlikely position inside the Neanderthal's chest; obviously, this is an impossible placement. We are left with the conclusion that Neanderthals probably lacked the more refined apparatus necessary to make complex speech sounds.

There is another aspect of human evolution which gives people an advantage over dogs in terms of speech production. Because humans walk upright, our hands are free to manipulate things so that we hunt and protect ourselves using weapons held in our hands. This means we don't need a strong muzzle full of teeth to do these jobs. We can have shorter snouts and muzzles, and can allow our lips more flexibility to shape sounds. Our more flexible faces also give us the apparatus to produce a broader range of voice sounds than is possible for dogs.

Actually, evolutionary concerns such as these have led to a marvelously speculative theory that dogs may be responsible for the development of human spoken language. To follow this argument, we need to point out that there is some new evidence, based upon DNA analyses, which suggests that dogs may have been domesticated by humans for far longer than scientists have previously imagined. It is possible that dogs may have been domesticated as long as 100,000 years ago. Pushing back the origins of the domestic dog into that distant past has allowed a new wave of thinking about how dogs and humans co-evolved.

It is well established that the primitive humans who survived to become our forefathers formed an early

The Early Man's Best Friend

- [95] **(The) evidence is that . . .**：根拠に基づいて発言するときの定型句．
- [96] **tissue:**（生体の）組織
- [97] **fossilized vocal tracts:** 化石になった声道
- [99] **Phillip Lieberman:** ブラウン大学のリーバーマン教授は，生物学的な言語起源の考察等で知られる認知科学者 (= cognitive scientist)．
- [101] **The modern larynx ends up in a weird and unlikely position inside the Neanderthal's chest:** 現代人の喉頭をネアンデルタール人にはめてみると，その胸郭の中（という奇妙な，ありそうにない場所）にまで届いてしまう
- [103] **We are left with the conclusion that . . . :** 〜と結論せざるをえない
- [105] **refined:** 精巧に発達した
- [107] **which gives people an advantage over dogs in terms of speech production:** which makes it easier for humans than dogs to speak
- [109] **walk upright:** 直立歩行する
- [110] **manipulate:** to use or control (by hands)
- [112] **a strong muzzle full of teeth:** 歯がぎっしり生えた強い鼻口部

  these jobs: hunting and protecting ourselves
- [113] **snout(s):**（動物の大きく突き出た）鼻

  can allow our lips more flexibility: can afford to have freer moving lips
- [115] **the apparatus:** 柔軟に動く頬，唇，舌などをさしている．
- [117] **evolutionary concerns such as these:** こうした進化論的な考察
- [118] **a marvelously speculative theory:**「すばらしい推論」．speculative は「頭の中で考えただけで検証を経ていない」．つまり以下の説はまだ実証されていない．

  may be responsible for . . . : may have caused (or have been helpful) in . . .
- [121] **analyses** [ənǽləsìːz]:「分析」．単数形は analysis [ənǽləsɪs]
- [122] **been domesticated . . . for far longer than scientists have previously imagined:** これまで科学者が想像していた時期よりずっと以前に家畜化された
- [125] **Pushing back the origins of the domestic dog into that distant past has allowed . . . :** 家畜犬の起源がそれほど古い時代にあったとすることで〜が可能になった
- [127] **co-evolved:** 共進化（連係進化）した．ここではイヌとヒトの全体がシステムとして進化してきたという考えが提示されているが，自然界では単体の種のみ進化することはありえない．進化とは常に，その種と環境（まわりの生物）とが連れだって進化する co-evolution の過程だと考えるべきだろう．
- [128] **It is well established that . . . :** 〜であるというのはもはや定説だ

  the primitive humans who survived to become our forefathers: 生き延びてわれわれの直接の祖先となった原始人

relationship with dogs. Compare our success to that of Neanderthals, who never got along with dogs, and who ultimately died out. Some evolutionary theorists have suggested that the survival of our ancestors had to do with the fact that our cooperative partnership with dogs made us more efficient hunters than Neanderthals. Dogs' exquisite sense of smell, combined with the adaptation of their airways to allow them to continue following a scent, even while running, made them proficient trackers. Finding game is clearly one of the most important tasks facing a hunting society.

Here is where the serious speculation begins. These theorists suggest that since these early humans now had dogs to do the tracking, they no longer needed the facial structures that would allow them to detect faint scents. This, then, allowed our early ancestors to evolve more flexible facial features, which were capable of shaping more complex sounds. In other words, our prehistoric association with dogs, who would do the smelling for us, gave us the ability to create speech.

The rival Neanderthal race, however, never formed a compact with dogs. This meant that they were left with less flexible facial features, since they still needed their better scenting abilities. Less flexibility means more limited voice control, which in turn would make speech far more difficult. Once early man had the ability to shape speech sounds, this permitted the development of spoken language. Language brings with it many advantages. It can help to organize a group, it can allow the passing on of knowledge and information, and it can provide us with a number of other survival advantages.

Think of it—if this theory is correct, then it may well be the case that human speech owes its very existence to our association with dogs!

The Early Man's Best Friend

- [131] **ultimately:** in the end
- [135] **exquisite:** refined; excellent; sensitive.
- [136] **the adaptation of their airways to allow them to . . . :** 〜できるように気道が適応したこと
- [138] **proficient trackers:** 非常にすぐれた追跡者
- [139] **game:** 獲物
- [141] **Here is where the serious speculation begins:** ここからの部分は大胆な想像に基づいた仮説である
- [142] **now had dogs to do the tracking:** [a. had to track the dogs / b. didn't have to do the tracking] now that they had dogs.
- [144] **detect faint scents:** かすかな臭いをかぎつける
- [145] **flexible facial features:** *cf.* p. 78, [112]–[116]
- [147] **our prehistoric association with dogs:** 犬との有史前のつきあい
- [151] **(a) compact:** 契約，盟約．ここでは「関係」「結びつき」くらいのニュアンス．
- [153] **Less flexibility means more limited voice control, which in turn would make speech far more difficult:** ここでは (a) facial flexibility, (b) voice control, (c) speech の三者の関係にふれている．a が小さくなると b も小さくなり，b が小さくなると今度は (in turn) c が成立しにくくなるということ．
- [158] **passing on:** conveying; spreading; sharing
- [161] **it may well be the case that . . . :** 〜ということも十分あり得る

[Session 6] Comprehension Check

Complete the sentences so as to match Prof. Coren's argument.

A) The Development of Man-Dog Relationship

<u>1st Stage:</u>
   Dogs came near humans for (1   ).
   Humans found that dogs functioned as (2   ).

<u>2nd Stage</u>
   Humans also found that dogs bark and provide a good (3   ).
   In order to improve the (3   ), humans began a sort of (4   ) program.

a. alarm system	b. food remains
c. garbage disposers	d. selective breeding
e. source of fresh meat	

B) A Marvelously Speculative Theory

Humans and dogs could have been hunting together for as long as 100,000 years. Since humans had dogs to do the tracking, they no longer needed an acute (1). This allowed them to lose the sturdy face front necessary to detect faint (2). Their (3) became flexible, and it became easier for them to make fine, controlled (4). This is the change that gradually led to the development of speech. The Neanderthals never got along well with dogs. This may have caused poorer (5) and even their extinction.

a. facial features	b. scents
c. sense of smell	d. sounds
e. hunting abilities	

The Early Man's Best Friend

Editors' Note

Dogs can't speak. Of course not! But does this mean they can't communicate? Not at all. As a matter of fact, they have wonderful ways to tell us exactly how they feel. Maybe that's one reason why dogs are said to be man's best friend. First of all, their tails. Just to see a dog eagerly wagging his tail makes people smile. If you take a look at their ears, you will be surprised at how expressive they are. But the most communicative of all would no doubt be their "vocals." Maybe dogs cannot speak, but they sure can ... well ... "talk!"

Unfriendly dogs—big, nasty ones—or any dog that is alarmed will growl at you in a threatening way (grrr ...) and eventually go "bow-wow-wow-wow!" On a lonely night from a distance, we sometimes hear a dog howl like a wolf. Some dogs love to howl together with the siren of a fire-engine or an ambulance. Do they think they are singing? Whining is also a type of crying but is sad and high-pitched, often telling you that the dog misses something he wants or needs. Whimpering is much lower and weaker, also conveying sadness or pain. You would hear a dog pant whenever he brings back the ball you just threw. He is quite excited! But have you heard a dog squeak, like a mouse? Try stepping on your pet's tail (oh, no!).

And if you want to hear a dog sigh, lie down with him and wait for the last moment before he comfortably goes to sleep. He would give out a soft sigh, shut his eyes and happily slip into his own doggy dream world.

[Answers for the a/b Questions]
[14] — b., [25] — a., [35] — b., [36] — a., [60] — b., [142] — b.

Session 7

The New Coke Story

Michael Bastedo Angela Davis

True Cokeaholics know the mystic ritual well. Only one source of the murky brown elixir is acceptable: the traditional, 6 ½-ounce bottle. No cans, please, and certainly none of those plastic jugs. The bottle is refrigerated for at least two hours and a wide-mouthed glass is filled with ice—preferably five full-sized cubes. The bottle is uncapped slowly, reverently, its contents allowed to trickle gently over the ice until the glass is filled: too much foam squanders carbonation. The glass is lifted and—eureka!—the tongue rejoices at the familiar, hearty, tingly, raspy, 99-year-old taste—neither sweet nor tart, a taste that is both complex and unique.

And all too soon, as the last desperately hoarded supplies of Old Coke disappear, it is a taste that will tickle American palates no more.

The introduction of New Coke represents one of the greatest marketing debacles of the 1980's. Pepsi Cola-USA president Roger Enrico called it "the Edsel of the 80's." How did this happen, and why?

Coke began with Dr. John Pemberton and his three-legged brass pot all the way back in 1886; by 1985, Coke was closing in fast on its centennial anniversary. There were some creeping problems, however. Most distressing of these

The New Coke Story

[1] **Cokeaholic(s)** [kòukəhálik]: コーク中毒者. *cf.* alcoholics, workaholics

[2] **Only one source ... the traditional, 6 ½-ounce bottle:** 秘儀 (the mystic ritual) に使うのは伝統的な 6 オンス半 (約 192 cc) の瓶に入っているものでないとダメだということ.

the murky brown elixir: ダークに淀んだ褐色の霊薬

[4] **certainly none of those plastic jugs:**「プラスチック容器などもってのほか」. アメリカでは取っ手付きの大型容器 (jug) に入った飲料をよく見かける.

New Coke

[6] **preferably five full-sized cubes:** できれば, 立方体の氷を砕かずに 5 つ

[7] **uncapped:** *cf.* undressed; unbottoned; untied
reverently: うやうやしく
its contents allowed to trickle:「中味が滴るのをゆるされ」. allowed の前に be 動詞の省略がある.

[8] **too much foam squanders carbonation:** アワが多すぎると炭酸 (のシュワシュワ感) を損ねる

[9] **eureka!** [ju:rí:kə]:「おお, これだ！」(古代ギリシャ語で I've found it! の意味)

[10] **rejoices at:**「〜を慶ぶ」. 日常的な enjoy に比べ, 文語的・宗教的な響き.
the familiar, hearty, tingly, raspy, 99-year-old taste: 馴染みの, たんまりとした, チクチク・ザワザワの, 99 年前からの味

[11] **tart:** sourish; lemony; acid in taste

[13] **all too soon:** 単なる very soon と比べ「残念！」という気持ちがこもる.
the last desperately hoarded supplies: 必死の思いでとっておいた最後の蓄え

[14] **will tickle American palates no more:** will never be enjoyed by the Americans.
palate: 食べ物を楽しむものとしての口

[18] **Roger Enrico:** (1944–) ペプシの社長就任は 1983 年.
Edsel [édzəl]: 1957 年に発表されたフォード社の車種部門で, 立ち上げに巨費を投じたものの販売不振のため 3 年で閉鎖. marketing debacle (マーケティングの大失敗) の代名詞となった.

[20] **Dr. John Pemberton and his three-legged brass pot:** アトランタの薬草研究家ペンバートンが最初にコーラの原液を調合したのは, (社の公式の伝説によれば) 自宅の裏庭に置いた三本脚の真鍮鍋.

[22] **closing in:** (目標地点に) にじり寄る
centennial: 百周年. cent は単位としての「百」. *cf.* centipede (百足)

[23] **creeping problems:**「這い進む問題」, つまり徐々に進行するいやらしい事態.

85

was the fact that Coke was losing market share to its biggest competitor, Pepsi. Coke's lead had dropped from a better than two to one margin to a mere 4.9 percent lead by 1984. In supermarkets, Coke was now trailing by 1.7 percent. Coke was clearly in danger of becoming the number two soft drink.

This was despite the fact that Coke was far outspending Pepsi on advertising, by upwards of $100 million per year. One major problem was that Pepsi's advertising was simply more effective. The Pepsi Challenge had been fabulously successful: Pepsi's share jumped 8 points almost immediately. Even worse, the tests were true: in blind taste-tests, Coke drinkers preferred Pepsi. At first Coke ads tried to laugh off the Challenge: "They called our product 'Q' and their product 'M' and you know people like the letter 'M' better." When that didn't work, the philosophy changed to, "One sip is not enough." Apparently, Coke tasted better only when you drank a full glassful. (The whole is greater than the sum of its parts in Cokeland.) Finally, Coke was forced to conduct taste-tests of its own, but here they clearly identified the two colas. Coke won.

Brian Dyson, president of Coca-Cola USA, was swayed. "Maybe the principal characteristics that made Coke distinctive, like its bite, consumers now describe as harsh. Maybe the way we quench our thirst has changed." By the fall of 1983, the top brass allowed Dyson "to explore the possibility of a reformulation."

Much of the market research conducted between 1983 and 1985 on the possibility of a new Coke was discouraging. One set of focus groups said that Pepsi could improve its formula, whereas the answer to a Coke reformulation was a resounding NO. But in September 1984, the technical division had brewed a formula of Coke that beat Pepsi in blind taste-tests, by as much as 6 to 8 points. Before, Pepsi had beaten Coke by anywhere from 10 to 15 points.

The New Coke Story

- [25] **competitor:** contender; challenger; rival
  a better than two to one margin: ダブルスコア以上の差．"better than two to one" が形容詞的に margin にかかっている．*We beat them by a wide margin.*
- [27] **trailing:** selling [a. more / b. less] than Pepsi
- [30] **far outspending Pepsi on advertising, by upwards of $100 million:** spending much more money on advertising, and the difference was more than $100 million.
- [33] **The Pepsi Challenge:** この宣伝作戦（第1期）は1975年に始まり80年代前半まで続いた．街頭のテーブルに2つのカップを並べ，目隠しをした被験者にどちらの味が好きか答えてもらう．この blind taste-test のCMはテレビで繰り返し流れた．
  fabulously successful: ウソみたい（おとぎ話みたい）な大成功を収める
- [35] **Even worse:** 長くいえば，What was even worse for Coca Cola was that . . .
- [36] **Coke ads tried to laugh off:** 笑って取り合わないような記事がコークの宣伝ページに載ったということ．
- [39] **When that didn't work:** それではだめだ（と分かる）と
  the philosophy: 会社のフィロソフィー，つまり組織としての考え方・姿勢
- [40] **Apparently:** 「きっと〜だったのだろう」と，社の苦しい抗弁を皮肉っている．
- [41] **The whole is greater than the sum of its parts:** 「全体は部分の寄せ集め以上のもの」とは，全体論哲学のおなじみの主張．一口一口の味と，全体の味わいとは違うといっているかのような Cokeland（コークの国）をからかっている．
- [43] **clearly identified . . . :** どっちがどっちか明示した
- [45] **was swayed:** became [a. more / b. less] confident of his company's product
- [46] **the principal characteristics that made Coke distinctive:** コークの一番はっきりとコークらしい特徴．describe の目的語．distinctive: unique; special; different
- [47] **bite:** （コーラの）刺激性，つまり苦みや酸味
- [48] **the way we quench our thirst:** 喉のうるおし方；喉が渇いたときのふるまい方
- [49] **the top brass:** 会社の幹部連中
- [52] **discouraging:** [a. favorable / b. unfavorable]
- [53] **focus groups:** 調査のために，年齢や職種によって分けたグループ
- [54] **reformulation:** formula（製法）を変えること
- [55] **resounding** [rizáundiŋ]: strong; loud; decisive
- [56] **had brewed a formula:**「新製法を完成させていた」．brew は「ビールを醸造する」「コーヒーを淹れる」というときに使う動詞．

On April 23, 1985, New Coke was released to a great deal of fanfare. By the middle of June, people were saying 'No' to New Coke. Reaction to New Coke was swift and humiliating. The taste of New Coke was likened to "sewer water," "furniture polish," "Coke for wimps," and, most disheartening to Coca-Cola management, "two-day-old Pepsi." [60]

Cokeaholics began stockpiling Old Coke in their homes. Black marketeers sold Old Coke for upwards of $30 a case and were looking for ways to import it from abroad. Some desperate addicts had the drink shipped to them from Montreal by FedEx. One Hollywood producer rented a $1,200 wine cellar to hold his 100 cases of Old Coke. The Old Coke Drinkers of America logged 60,000 calls to their national headquarters. [65] [70]

The mere idea of changing Coke provoked some of the more virulent responses. Here's a sample:

- "At first I was numb. Then I was shocked. Then I started to yell and scream and run up and down." [75]
- "Changing Coke is like God making the grass purple or putting toes on our ears or teeth on our knees."
- "There are only two things in my life: God and Coca-Cola. Now you have taken one of those things away from me." [80]
- "Next week, they'll be chiseling Teddy Roosevelt off the side of Mount Rushmore."

Coke Bottles

The New Coke Story

- [59] **to a great deal of fanfare:** たいへんな鳴り物入りで
- [62] **humiliating:** 屈辱的
  was likened to: was said to be like
  sewer water: 下水
- [63] **wimps:** cowards; chickens; crybabies
  disheartening: 心（やる気）をへこませる (dispiriting; demoralizing; discouraging)
- [65] **stockpiling** < stockpile: 買いだめ（する）
- [66] **black marketeers:** 闇取引を行う人
  upwards of $30 a case:「1ケース（24本入り）30ドル以上」．当時瓶コーラは自販機でだいたい1本25セントほどだったから，5倍以上になる．
- [68] **some desperate addicts:** 必死にコークを求める中毒者たち
- [69] **Montreal** [màntriɔ́:l]: モントリオール．
  FedEx: "The world on time" をスローガンとする空輸宅配便会社．社名が，それまでの Federal Express から FedEx に正式に変更されたのは1994年のこと．
- [70] **The Old Coke Drinkers of America:** 急遽結成された実在の団体で，Old Coke の復活を求める訴訟も起こしている．
- [71] **logged 60,000 calls:** 抗議の電話が6万本に達したということ．
- [73] **The mere idea of changing Coke provoked ... responses:** コークを変えるプランを出しただけで（こんな）反応が返ってきた
  some of the more virulent: いくつかの相当に激烈な．virulent [vírjulənt]: harsh; bitter; hostile
- [75] **I was numb:**「まるで感覚がなくなった」．茫然自失のたとえ．
- [82] **Next week, they'll be ... :** こんなひどいことが起こるなんて，この調子では「来週には〜みたいなことになってしまうかも」と言って嘆いている．
  chiseling Teddy Roosevelt off the side of Mount Rushmore:「ラシュモア山の山腹からセオドア・ルーズベルト像を削り落とす」．山腹の岩肌に彫った4人の大統領の巨大塑像は，ヒッチコックの映画等を通して世界中に知られている．

In a country dedicated to consumption, Coca-Cola had been the most successful product in history, the undisputed leader of the $25 billion soft-drink industry. A number of adjustments had been made in Coke's proportions of sugar and caffeine since 1886. But its secret flavoring formula never before had been changed. Unlike almost every other product ever built or bought, the one thing it never was was new.

The company took the gamble because Coke's market share fell from 24.3 in 1980 to 21.8 in 1984. The drop stemmed from the popularity of low-calorie drinks, including Diet Coke, and the "Pepsi Generation" campaigns made to America's youth. With aging baby boomers increasingly concerned about their weight and turning to nonsugar drinkers, Coke needed to increase its appeal to the young.

Coke decided to court teenagers by sweetening the recipe and calling it "new" Coke. Essentially, Coke got boxed in. Pepsi had positioned itself as the "leading edge" soft drink and called its consumers the "Pepsi Generation." As Pepsi USA President Roger Enrico explains, "For twenty years, we've used this Pepsi Generation campaign to reach out not just to the young but to all people who look forward, who are curious about the next thing, who want more out of life." Coke represented the past, nostalgia, small towns, parades, picnics, American values. The problem was that this image would not necessarily appeal to the younger constituency of soft drinkers who would dominate the market.

Were there less drastic alternatives? It could have simply changed its campaigns to give Coke a younger image. Image is probably more important than taste in selling soda pop. If Coke was determined to change the recipe, it could have done it without letting anyone know. Alternatively, a New Coke could have been introduced without knocking out Old Coke off the shelves. But the company considered,

The New Coke Story

- [85] **undisputed:** unquestioned; undeniable; acknowledged. *The undisputed heavyweight champion of the world*
- [86] **the $25 billion soft-drink industry:** 年商250億ドルのソフトドリンク業界
- [88] **its secret flavoring formula:** コカコーラに独特のフレーバーを与える原液の製法を知る人は世界に何人もいないといわれている．
- [89] **Unlike almost every other product ever built or bought:** これまでこの世に登場した他のほとんどの製品や商品とは違って
- [90] **the one thing it never was was new:** it always stayed the same; it never had been renewed.
- [94] **stemmed from:** originated in; was rooted in; came from
- [95] **the "Pepsi Generation" campaigns:** 1963年から67年まで，ペプシのCMは "Come alive, you're in the Pepsi Generation" という歌を伴った．以後，キャンペーンは数年に1度モデルチェンジをしたが，若い層に向けて「ペプシ世代」を強調するやり方は継続した．1984年には，Michael Jacksonを起用し "Billie Jean" の替え歌で，"You're a whole new generation." と連呼した．
- [96] **baby boomers:** 日本の団塊世代に重なるが年齢層は広い．アメリカ商務省センサス局の定義では，1946年から1964年生まれまでを含めている．
- [99] **court...:** 〜に愛を訴える，愛を求める
- [100] **got boxed in:** まわりから阻止された，身動きがとれなくなった
- [101] **"leading edge":**「進んでいるものの先端」．「時代の先端をゆく人たちがペプシを飲む」というのがPepsi Generation campaignの基本コンセプトだった．
- [105] **look forward:** この場合は「心待ちにする」というより「未来を見る」という日本語のほうが適切．
- [107] **small towns, parades, picnics:** アメリカの大部分を占める，だだっ広い田舎町の暮らしと風景を総称して，"small town America" と呼ぶ．ここでいうパレードには，マーチング・バンドの行進や，地元の高校で選ばれた「ホームカミング・クィーン」のカー・パレードなどが含まれる．
- [108] **American values:** 当然ながらAmerican（またはall-American）という言葉はこのように保守愛国的響きをもつ．
- [109] **constituency:** 消費者層
- [111] **less drastic alternatives:** これほど過激でない代替案
- [115] **Alternatively:** または（こういうやり方もとれたろう）
- [116] **(a) New Coke ... Old Coke:** Old Cokeは現に存在している固有のドリンクなので無冠詞．New Cokeはこの文脈ではいろいろなふうになりうる不定の存在なので，自然にaがついている．本文前出 [52] も同様．
- [116] **without knocking out Old Coke off the shelves:** *i.e.* [a. closing / b. continuing] the sales of Old Coke

and rejected, plans to keep the old-formula drink in circulation under the name Coke 100 or "original" Coke. Why did they make the most drastic move?

The one central mistake in Coca-Cola's decision to change the formula was maximization. When Goizueta became chairman in 1981, he was determined to be the chairman of change. He started shattering tradition early in his tenure. Putting the sacred Coke name on a new product for the first time, he introduced Diet Coke in 1982. In early 1985 he put the Coke name on another new product, Cherry Coke. Goizueta had moved the company aggressively and successfully into new fields, buying Columbia Pictures in 1982. He breathed new life into the company but perhaps he went too far. Goizueta and the other executives were getting caught up in the success of their previous changes and decided to make one grand decisive move to recapture the soft-drink market they were losing to Pepsi.

The taste question was crucial to Coke. But what Coca-Cola executives failed to realize was that there was more to marketing soft drinks than winning taste-tests. For most people, Coca-Cola was the quintessential representation of Americana. "Baseball, hamburgers, Coke—they're all the fabric of America." When Coca-Cola announced that it would bring back Old Coke, Democratic Senator David Pryor of Arkansas called Coke's capitulation "a very meaningful moment in the history of America. It shows that some national institutions cannot be changed."

"We did not understand the deep emotions of so many of our customers for Coca-Cola," said President Donald R. Keough. "It is not only a function of culture or upbringing or inherited brand loyalty. It is a wonderful American mystery. A lovely American enigma. And you cannot measure it any more than you can measure love, pride or patriotism."

The New Coke Story

[118] **keep . . . in circulation under the name Coke 100 or . . . :** Coke 100 などと改名して市場に出しておく

[122] **maximization:**（企業規模や収益の）最大化

Goizueta: ロベルト・C. ゴイスエタ (1931–1997). 革命以前のキューバ出身の実業家.

[125] **tenure:** 在職期間

Putting the sacred Coke name on a new product for the first time, he introduced Diet Coke: *i.e.* The name Coke had only been used for Coke. It had remained sacred, until Goizueta violated it and introduced Diet Coke.

[129] **Columbia Pictures:** たいまつを持つ女性のロゴで有名なハリウッドの老舗映画プロダクション. コカコーラのあと, ソニーに買収された.

[130] **breathed new life into . . . :** ～に新しい息吹を与えた

[131] **getting caught up in the success of their previous changes:** 最初のころに取った変化の路線がうまくいき, それにはまりつつあった

[133] **one grand decisive move:** 決定的に大きな一手

[136] **failed to realize:** [a. were aware of / b. were unaware of]

there was more to ⟨A⟩ than ⟨B⟩: A には B 以上のものがある, B だけのことではない. *There's more to it than mere nostalgia.*（ただ懐かしがっているだけじゃない）

[138] **the quintessential representation of Americana:**「アメリカの真髄のあらわれ」. Americana はアメリカの風物や文化の意味.

[140] **(the) fabric of America:** アメリカを織りなすもの

[141] **Democratic Senator David Pryor of Arkansas:** アーカンソー州選出の民主党上院議員デイヴィッド・プライアー. 同州の知事 (1975–79) も務めた.

[142] **capitulation:** 屈服

[144] **national institutions:** 国民の間にしっかりと打ち立てられたもの

[146] **Donald R. Keough** [kíːòu]: (1927–) 社長だったのは, 1981～93 年.

[147] **not only a function of . . . :** ～によって左右される問題というだけではない

[148] **inherited brand loyalty:** 世代間に受け継がれてゆくブランド信仰

[149] **cannot measure it any more than you can measure love, pride or patriotism:** それを測定しようとするのは, 愛やプライドや愛国心を測定しようとするようなもの（つまり測定不可能）

[Session 7] Comprehension Check

1. There were several reasons for the company's decision to change the sacred formula of Coke and introduce it as New Coke. Choose two from below that are NOT true.
   ( ) ( )
   a. More people were responding favorably to Pepsi in the blind taste-test.
   b. Coke had fallen to the number two soft drink.
   c. Coke was spending more money on advertisement than Pepsi, but with less effective results.
   d. Coke was approaching its 100th anniversary and there seemed to be a need to appeal to younger people.
   e. The company's technical division was experimenting with a new formula, and the result of the blind taste-tests were pretty favorable for the change.
   f. Until 1985, the company had not introduced any new products with the name Coke to it, and they thought it was about time.

2. What did the company executives FAIL to see?   Choose three.
   ( ) ( ) ( )
   a. That Coke had become an institution, something quintessentially American.
   b. That customers could respond with deep emotions to the commodities they love.
   c. That blind taste-tests were a reliable way of knowing what the consumers wanted.
   d. That there was more to the market than objective data could tell.
   e. That they needed to sweeten the recipe in order to appeal to the young.

The New Coke Story

> **Editors' Note**
>
> ここで扱ってきたコークへの熱狂が,「コーラは毒」と教えられて育った人たちに伝わったかどうか不安である.むかしの話をしよう.
>
> アメリカが眩しかった 1960 年代,日本の大衆市場で解禁された「スカッとさわやか」コカコーラは,赤い自動販売機で売られていた(当時のアメリカの宣伝文句は,"Things go better with Coke" で,その文字のついたマシンもよく見かけた).大きな四角いボタンを押すと,中のボトルがゴロゴロ動いて,ゴトンと一本,グラマラスな曲線を誇るダークグリーンのボトルが落ちる.ポテトチップスも,フライドチキンも,スヌーピーも,まだ日本人のほとんどが知らなかった時代の話である.
>
> その販売機に一緒に入っていたのが,FANTA グレープと FANTA オレンジ.最近は一部でしか見かけないこの FANTA が誕生したのが,ナチス・ドイツだったということは,あまり知られていない.
>
> ドイツ人ももちろんコークを愛したのだ.Coca-Cola GmbH の社長 Max Keith が,ヒトラー政権に接近して数々のキャンペーンをしかけ,コークは第三帝国下での地位を高めた.ところが 1941 年 12 月,日本軍の攻撃によってアメリカが敵国となり,原液の入荷が途絶えてしまった.
>
> この危機を救うために製造された代替ドリンクが,FANTA だったのである.砂糖の割り当てが制限されていた戦時下,砂糖の使用が特別に許された FANTA の需要はずいぶんと高かったらしく,おかげで会社は生き延びられた.もちろん用意周到なドイツ人のこと,消える前にコークのケースを各所に貯蔵していたらしい.負傷したナチスの兵士が病院で出された,懐かしのコカコーラに涙する,なんてこともあったのだろう.
>
> そういう話を聞くと,日本兵がかわいそうになる.大陸で犬死したわたしの伯父さんにも,コークを飲ませてあげたかった.(情報源: Mark Pendergrast, *For God, Country and Coca-Cola*)

[Answers for the a/b Questions]

[27] — b., [45] — b., [52] — b. [116] — b., [136] — b.

Session 8

Alive at Heart

Mary Roach

I have been standing around at the nurses' sta- [1]
tion on one of the surgery floors of a Medical
Center in San Francisco, waiting for a cadaver I will call H.
"There's your patient," says a nurse. H is being wheeled by,
calmly and with little notice, like a shopping cart. She is [5]
unique in that she is both a dead person and a patient on the
way to surgery. She is what is known as a "beating-heart
cadaver," alive and well everywhere but her brain. Up until
artificial respiration was developed, there was no such
entity; without a functioning brain, a body will not breathe [10]
on its own. But hook it up to a respirator and its heart will
beat, and the rest of its organs will, for a matter of days,
continue to thrive.

H doesn't look or smell or feel dead. If you leaned in
close over the gurney, you could see her pulse beating in the [15]
arteries of her neck. If you touched her arm, you would find
it warm and resilient, like your own. This is perhaps why
the nurses and doctors refer to H as a patient.

Since brain death is the legal definition of death in this
country, H the person is certifiably dead. But H the organs [20]
and tissues is very much alive. These two seemingly contradictory facts afford her an opportunity most corpses do not
have: that of extending the lives of two or three dying
strangers. Over the next four hours, H will surrender her

Alive at Heart

[3] **a cadaver** [kədǽvər]:（主に解剖や献体用の）死体．献体後は corpse となる．

[4] **your patient:** the patient you are [a. to cure / b. to write about]

H is being wheeled by: H が脇をごろごろと運ばれてゆく

[5] **with little notice:** [a. with a little note attached to the wheel / b. almost unnoticed]

[6] **unique in that . . . :** 〜という点で独特

[7] **what is known as:** いわゆる

[8] **Up until:** until と同義．ときどき思い切った口語表現に走る文体に注意．

[9] **artificial respiration:** 人工呼吸

there was no such entity:「そんな存在はありえなかった」．There's no such (thing) は，存在を強く否定する言い方．**an entity:** 一個の独立した存在者

[11] **on its own:** by itself

hook it up to a respirator and . . . :「そのボディを人工呼吸器につなげば〜」．わざと即物的な（罰当たりといえなくもない）表現を用いている．

[12] **for a matter of days:** for several days と同意．*The strange light lasted for a matter of seconds.*

[13] **thrive:** 活発な生命活動をする

[14] **feel . . . :** 触ったときに〜な感じがする．*This ball feels fluffy.*

If you leaned in close over . . . : に覆い被さるように近づけば

[15] **the gurney:** 台車付担架

[16] **arteries** < artery: 動脈

[17] **resilient** [rizíliənt]: ハリと弾力がある

[20] **H the person . . . H the organs and tissues:** 人としての H と，臓器や組織の集まりとしての H が対比されている．

certifiably: 正式なかたちでは

[21] **These two seemingly contradictory facts:** *i.e.* the facts that she is dead *and* that she is very much alive

[22] **afford her:** allow her to have; give her

[23] **that of:** the opportunity of

dying strangers: 死にかけている縁もゆかりもない人々

[24] **surrender her liver, kidney, and heart:** 肝臓，腎臓，そして心臓を譲り渡す

liver, kidney, and heart. One at a time, surgeons will come and go, taking an organ and returning in haste to their stricken patients. Until recently, the process was known among transplant professionals as an "organ harvest," which had a joyous, celebratory ring to it, perhaps a little too joyous, as it had been of late replaced by the more business-like "organ recovery."

H is cut open and her heart is connected to a monitor. The electric beat reinforces the impression that this is a living, breathing, thriving person. It is strange, almost impossible, really, to think of her as a corpse. When I tried to explain beating-heart cadavers to my step-daughter Phoebe yesterday, it didn't make sense to her. —But if their heart is beating, aren't they still a person? she wanted to know. In the end she decided they were "a kind of person you could play tricks on but they wouldn't know." Which, I think, is a pretty good way of summing up most donated cadavers. The things that happen to the dead in labs and ORs are like gossip passed behind one's back without their noticing. They are not felt or known and so they cause no pain.

The confusion people feel over beating-heart cadavers reflects centuries of confusion over how exactly to define death, to pin-point the precise moment when the spirit—the soul, the essence, whatever you wish to call it—has ceased to exist and all that remains is a corpse. Before brain activity could be measured, the stopping of the heart had long been considered the defining moment. The problem, for centuries, was that doctors couldn't tell for sure whether the heart had ceased to beat or whether they were merely having trouble hearing it. With improvements in stethoscopes and gains in medical knowledge, physicians began to trust themselves to be able to tell when a heart had stopped, and medical science came to agree that this was the best way to determine whether a patient had checked out for good or was merely down the hall getting ice.

- [25] **One at a time:** 一度にひとりずつ
- [26] **in haste:** in a hurry; hurriedly

  their stricken patients: stricken は strike の古い過去分詞の形．struck と違って病気，貧困，災難などに「打ちひしがれた」という特定のイメージをもつ．
- [29] **a joyous, celebratory ring:**「楽しそうな，祝祭的な響き」．「収穫，刈り入れ」という意味の harvest には，秋の収穫祭のイメージがこもっている．
- [30] **of late:** lately; recently; in recent years

  the more businesslike "organ recovery": より実務的な「臓器の回収」（という呼び名）
- [33] **The electric beat:** モニター画面にグラフとして現れる拍動のこと

  reinforces the impression: [a. makes you really feel / b. makes you doubt]
- [36] **step-daughter:** 実子でない娘
- [39] **decided:** 〜だということにした

  "a kind of person you could play tricks on but they wouldn't know":「いたずらされても気づかない種類の人」．臓器摘出を子供の目で tricks と言っている．
- [41] **(a) pretty good way of summing up most donated cadavers:** 献体された遺体を結構うまく（簡略に）説明する言い方
- [42] **labs and ORs:** laboratories and operating rooms
- [43] **gossip passed behind one's back without their noticing:** 本人に気付かれることなく，こっそり流されるうわさ話
- [46] **centuries of confusion over . . . :** 〜をめぐっての何世紀にもおよぶ混乱
- [47] **to pin-point the precise moment when . . . :** 〜の瞬間が厳密にどの時点なのかを指し示す
- [49] **all that remains is a corpse:** [a. there is nothing but / b. everything remains with] the dead body
- [50] **had long been considered the defining moment:** had been (for a long time) thought of as the very moment of death
- [52] **couldn't tell for sure:** 確実には判断できなかった
- [54] **stethoscopes:** 聴診器

  gains in medical knowledge: 医学的知識の蓄積
- [55] **trust themselves to be able to tell:** 自分たちに判別能力があると信じる；自信をもって判断する
- [58] **had checked out for good:** was gone forever. 以下，体をホテル，魂を宿泊客に喩えた比喩．

  merely down the hall getting ice:「単に氷を取りに廊下を歩いている」．生死の境目にある人間についての，著者らしいユーモア表現．

The concept of the beating-heart cadaver, grounded in a belief that the self resides in the brain and the brain alone, delivered a philosophical curveball. The notion of the heart as a fuel pump took some getting used to. It must be noted, however, that the seat-of-the-soul debate has been ongoing some four thousand years. It started out not as a heart-versus-brain debate, but as heart-versus-liver. The ancient Egyptians were the original heart guys. They believed that the ka resided in the heart. Ka was the essence of the person: spirit, intelligence, feelings and passions, humor, grudges, annoying television theme songs, all the things that make a person a person and not a nematode. The heart was the only organ left inside a mummified corpse, for a man needed his ka in the afterlife. The brain he clearly did not need.

The Babylonians were the original liver guys, believing the organ to be the source of human emotion and spirit. Living in the culture of Valentine's Day and I♥NY T-shirts, we might find it hard to imagine assigning spiritual or emotional sovereignty to the liver. But I've been marveling at H's liver, currently being prepped for its upcoming journey. The organs around it are amorphous and unappealing. But the liver gleams. It looks engineered and carefully wrought. Its flanks have a subtle curve, like the horizon seen from space. If I were an ancient Babylonian, I guess I might think God splashed down here too.

Of course, the modern medical community is on the whole quite unequivocal about the brain being the seat of the soul, the chief commander of life and death. It is similarly unequivocal about the fact that people like H are, despite the hoochy-koochy going on behind their sternums, dead. We now know that the heart keeps beating on its own not because the soul is in there, but because it contains its own bioelectric power source, independent of the brain.

Alive at Heart

[60] **grounded in a belief that the self resides in the brain:**「自己とは脳に宿るものという信条に基づいた」．resides in: lives in; lies in
[61] **in the brain and the brain alone:** in the brain and nowhere else but the brain
[62] **delivered a philosophical curveball:** 哲学的にやっかいな問題を投げつけた
The notion of the heart as a fuel pump: ハートは単なる燃料ポンプだとの見解
[63] **took some getting used to:** took some time and effort to get used to it
[64] **the seat-of-the-soul debate:** 魂の在処をめぐる論争．*cf. It's possible that the stomach is the seat of emotions.*
[67] **the original heart guys:** 初代心臓派
[70] **grudge(s):** 恨み
annoying television theme songs:「しつこく頭に取り憑いているテレビの主題歌」．現代ならば，冗談ではなくこういうものも心の構成要素だろう．
[71] **a nematode:** 線虫
[72] **a mummified corpse:** ミイラ化の処置を施された死体
[73] **The brain he clearly did not need:**「脳は明らかに必要ではなかった」．He clearly did not need the brain. が通常の語順だが，the brain を前へ持ってくることで the heart との対比が強まる．
[75] **The Babylonians:** メソポタミアの古代都市バビロンを中心に栄えた古バビロニア王国の人々のこと．
[78] **assigning spiritual or emotional sovereignty to the liver:** 肝臓に魂や感情の支配者としての地位を与える．sovereign [sávrən]: 専政君主
[79] **I've been marveling at:** marvel は自動詞で「驚嘆する」の意味．他動詞の surprise や amaze と違って I'm marveled at . . . とはいわない．
[81] **amorphous and unappealing:** グニャリとして見た目が悪い
[82] **gleam(s):**（反射して）ギラリと輝く
engineered and carefully wrought: 工学的にデザインされ精確に製造された
[83] **flank(s):** 側面
a subtle curve:（言葉で言い表しがたい）微妙な曲線
[84] **I guess I might think . . . too:** 私もまた〜と考えたりするんじゃないだろうか
[85] **God splashed down here:**「神はここに滴り落ちた」．肉のなかに（神に発する）霊的な要素が入り込んだことを，ユーモラスに擬声語 splash で表現した．
[86] **on the whole quite unequivocal [ʌnɪkwívəkəl]:** 全体として（一部の極端な論者を除いて）合意が成立している．対語の equivocal は「意見が割れた」．
[90] **despite the hoochy-koochy going on behind their sternums:** 胸骨の裏でクチャクチャした動きが続いているにもかかわらず
[93] **bioelectric power source:** 生体電気の動力源

Now, the doctor is ready for the organs' removal. The heart will go first—hearts remain viable only four to six hours; kidneys, by contrast, can be held in cold storage eighteen or even twenty-four hours.

The heart has been hidden until now behind the pericardium, a thick protective sac which the doctor now cuts away. There is her heart. I've never seen one beating. I had no idea they moved so much. You put your hand on your heart and you picture something pulsing slightly but basically still, like a hand on a desktop tapping Morse code. This thing is going wild in there. It's a mixing-machine part, a stoat squirming in its burrow, an alien life form that's just won a Pontiac on *The Price is Right*. If you were looking for the home of the human body's animating spirit, I could imagine believing it to be here, for the simple reason that it is the human body's most animated organ.

The doctor places clamps on the arteries of H's heart, stanching the flow of blood in preparation for the cuts. You can tell by the vital signs monitor that something monumental is happening to her body. The ECG has quit drawing barbed wire and begun to look like a toddler's Etch-a-Sketch scrawls. A quick geyser of blood splashes. If H weren't dead, she'd be dying now.

The rest of the organs to be taken, the liver and kidneys, are brought up and separated from the depths of her open torso. Finally, the doctor steps aside and an assistant sews H up. The incision is complete, a nurse washes H off and covers her with a blanket for the trip to the morgue. Out of habit or respect, he chooses a fresh one. The transplant coordinator and nurse lift H onto a gurney. The coordinator then wheels H into an elevator and down the hallway to the morgue. The workers are behind a set of swinging doors, in a back room. "Can we leave this here?" the coordinator shouts. H has become a "this." We are instructed to wheel the gurney into the cooler, where it joins

[95] **remain viable:** stay alive and usable
[98] **pericardium** [pèrəkáːrdiəm]: 心膜，心嚢
[99] **sac:** 袋，嚢
[100] **There is her heart:** *cf.* "There's your patient." (p. 96, [4])
      I've never seen one beating: I've never seen a beating heart before.
[103] **tapping Morse code:**（指先をトントン動かして）モールス信号を打つ
      This thing is going wild in there: そいつは狂ったように動いている
[104] **a mixing-machine part:** ミキサー（こね回す機械）の部品
[105] **(a) stoat squirming in its burrow:** 洞穴の中で体をくねらせているイタチ
      an alien life form: 宇宙から来た妙ちきりんな生命体
[106] **won a Pontiac on *The Price is Right*:**「テレビの値段あてクイズ番組で高級車ポンティアックを当てた」．興奮した心臓の，いかにも著者らしい喩え．
      If you were looking for . . . , I could imagine believing it to be here: 〜のありかが問われているときに，それはここだと本気で思っている自分が想像できる
[107] **the human body's animating spirit:** 人体の動きを司る魂
[110] **clamp(s):** 鉗子
[111] **stanching the flow of blood:**（その結果）血流を止める
[112] **the vital signs monitor:** 心拍，呼吸，血圧等の変化を表示する「命の徴のモニター」．
      something monumental: とてつもなく大変なこと
[113] **ECG** < **electrocardiogram:** 心電計
[114] **barbed wire:** 鉄条網のバラ線（のようなガギガギの波形）
      a toddler's Etch-a-Sketch scrawls:「幼児がお絵かき玩具に描きなぐった線」．心電図のギザギザがグチャグチャになった線をこう表現した．Etch-a-Sketch は1960年に発売され，描いては消せる仕掛けが大人気だった．
[115] **A quick geyser of blood:** 間欠的に短く吹き出す血．次の splashes は動詞．
[118] **from the depths of her open torso:** 切開された胴体部分の奥から
[120] **incision:** 切開手術
[121] **the morgue:** 遺体安置室
[122] **Out of habit or respect:** 慣例なのか（Hへの）敬意からか
      The transplant coordinator: 移植手術の全体を看視する専門家
[128] **the cooler:** 冷却室

five others. H appears no different from the corpses already here.

But H is different. She has made three sick people well. She has brought them extra time on earth. To be able as a dead person, to make a gift of this magnitude is phenomenal. Most people don't manage this sort of thing while they're alive. Cadavers like H are the dead's heroes.

It is astounding to me, and achingly sad, that with eighty thousand people on the waiting list for donated hearts and livers and kidneys, with sixteen a day dying there on that list, that more than half of the people in the position of H's family will say no, will choose to burn those organs or let them rot. On a rational level, most people are comfortable with the concept of brain death and organ donation. But on an emotional level, they may have a harder time accepting it, particularly when they are being asked to accept it by a transplant counselor who would like them to okay the removal of a family member's beating heart. We abide the surgeon's scalpel to save our own lives, our loved ones' lives, but not to save a stranger's life. H has no heart, but heartless is the last thing you'd call her.

[132] **brought them extra time on earth:** let them live longer
[133] **to make a gift of this magnitude:**「こんなにも大きな贈り物をする」. to be able から続く.
phenomenal: 驚くべき, すばらしい
[134] **don't manage this sort of thing:** aren't able to give extended lives to others
[136] **astounding:** greatly surprising
achingly: painfully
[138] **dying there on that list:**「待機者リストに載ったまま死んでいく」. there があることで,「そこに載っているのに」という無念さが強調される.
[141] **let them rot:** 腐るにまかせる
[145] **who would like them to okay . . . :** who are asking the family to agree to . . . この okay は「同意する」という意味の動詞.
[147] **abide:** 我慢する, 辛抱する
scalpel: メス
[149] **heartless is the last thing you'd call her:** You can [a. hardly / b. easily] call her heartless. the last は「到底〜でない」という強い否定の意味を含む. *He would be the last person to say such a thing.*

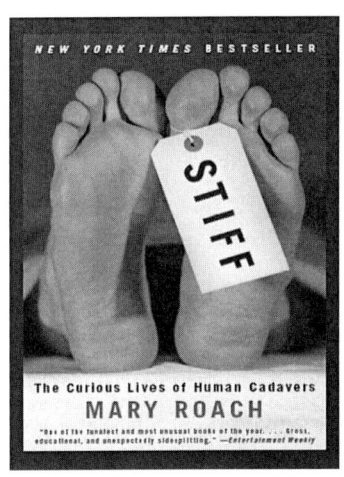

Mary Roach, *Stiff* (2003)

[Session 8] Comprehension Check

1. Mark T for true, F for false.

1) This is an objective report. Roach does not reveal her own view and states everything in a matter-of-fact way. — (   )
2) Roach is angry. She is an activist who claims that the practice of taking out organs from someone who is still alive must be stopped immediately. — (   )
3) At times, Roach seeks to write humorously on subjects that usually demand dead seriousness. — (   )
4) The author wishes that more families of the brain-dead would agree to donate the useful organs of their loved ones. — (   )

2. Complete the sentences so by choosing a, b or c.

1) [a. Brain death / b. The stopping of the heart / c. The disappearance of all activities of life] is the legal definition of death in the United States.
2) [a. A lung surgery / b. A functioning brain / c. A beating-heart cadaver] became possible only after the development of artificial respiration.
3) The author's step-daughter thought that taking out organs from a beating-heart cadaver was like [a. working a miracle on / b. playing tricks on / c. giving a great gift to] someone who wouldn't know.
4) In the 4,000-year-old debate about where the seat of the soul is, [a. the Mesopotamians / b. the Egyptians / c. the Romans] were the "original heart guys."
5) The author thinks that the idea of the liver being the seat of the soul is [a. quite believable / b. simply ridiculous / c. scientifically correct] after looking at the organ with her own eyes.
6) When the author first sees the beating heart, she is surprised at its [a. flashy colors / b. precise mechanism / c. wild movements].

Editors' Note

喜怒哀楽を司る「魂」についての考察は洋の東西を問わず枚挙に暇(いとま)がない．このセッションでは魂の在処として心臓派 vs. 肝臓派が紹介されたが，ならばたとえば魂に重さはあるのか？ これについては 1907 年にドクター・ダンカン・マクドゥーガルがおこなった，とある実験が有名だ（ちなみにこの話は原著 Stiff にも言及されているのでぜひご一読を！）．

彼はグラム単位の変化を記録する精巧な計りの上にベッドをしつらえ，そこに今しも死にそうな重症患者を寝かせ，死亡前と死亡後の体重を測定した．それによると 6 人の「被験者」に見られた体重差はいずれも約 21 グラム．

さらに興味深いことに，彼は同じ実験をイヌで行っている．瀕死のイヌ 15 匹を実験対象としたが，体重変化は見られなかったそうな．これはマクドゥーガル博士にとって好都合だった．というのも，これにて人間だけが魂を持つことが証明されたからだ．そう，マクドゥーガル医師は敬虔なカトリック信者でもあったのだ！

もちろんアバウトな計測技術や被験者の少なさを考えても，この実験はおよそ科学的ではない．そもそも 15 匹もの息もたえだえのイヌたちを博士はいったいどこから連れてきたのか．人間の被験者は養老院の肺炎患者だったそうだが……．いずれにしても博士の論文は医学専門誌 American Medicine に掲載され，The New York Times がその骨子を報道するや議論が巻き起こり，博士はいちやく時の人となった．そして「魂＝21 グラム」は俗説として広まってゆく．

バカバカしいと思われるかもしれないが，この俗説は耐用年数が意外と長く，今でも人々の無意識の底に沈潜しているらしい．2003 年には，タイトルもズバリ『21 グラム』という映画が公開され，主演のショーン・ペンはヴェネチア映画祭主演男優賞を受賞した．この映画もまた，臓器移植をきっかけに一見ばらばらな 3 つのストーリーが一体となってまとまる，重くて美しい映画だった．

[Answers for the a/b Questions]
[4] — b., [5] — b., [33] — a., [49] — a., [149] — a.

PART III | There's No Stopping Us

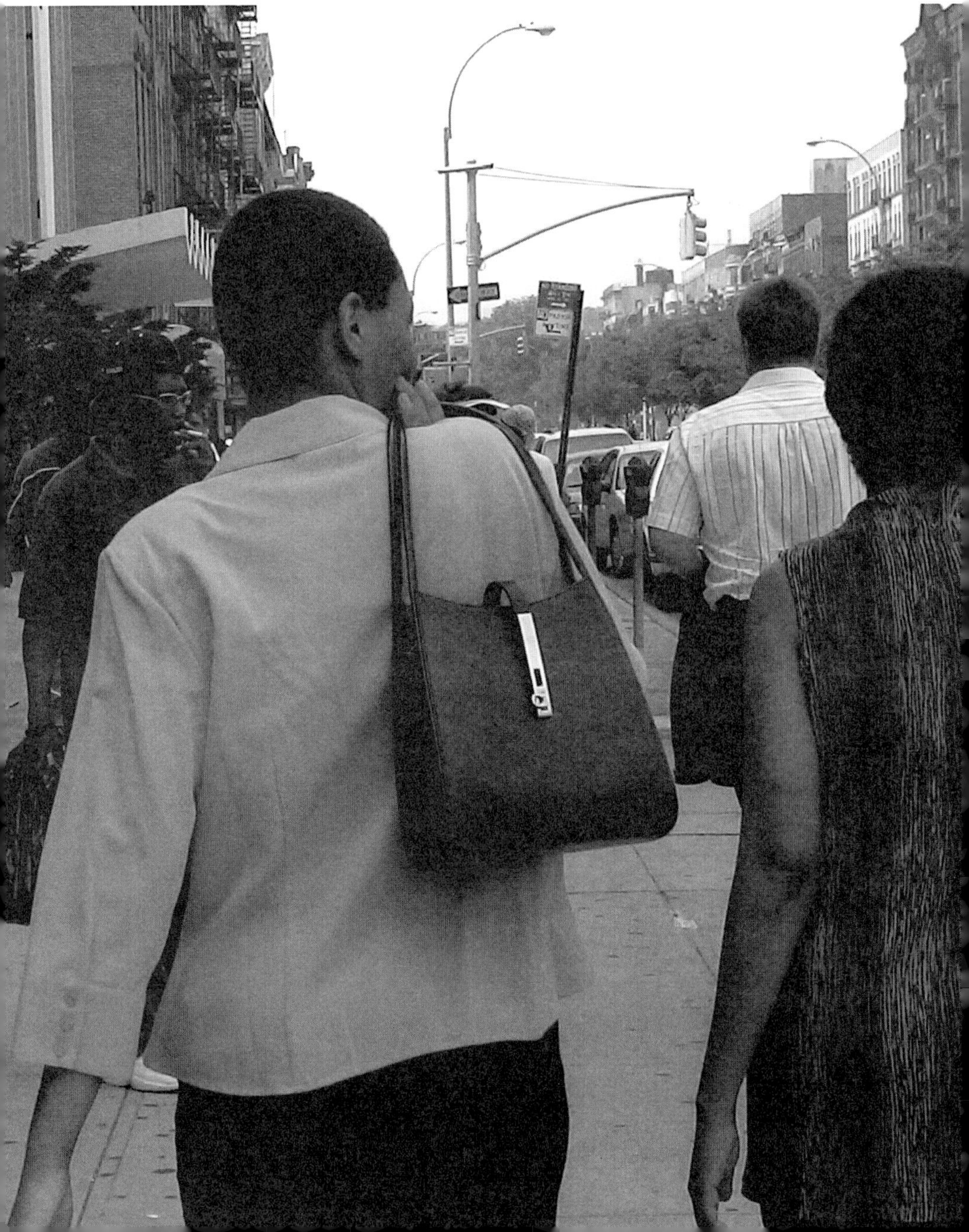

Introduction to Part III

　自由で奔放な社会は，人々の「思い」が走りやすい社会である．夢や幻想が，現実に引き留められずにあふれ出して文化を動かし，世間の常識を振り切った突飛な行動が，新しいビジネスを膨らませる．「走れ，走れ，いいぞ，いいぞ」というのは，昔から，世界の人がアメリカ映画を見るときの，基本の心の動きである．

　動き出したら止まらない，いいじゃん，このまま行っちゃえば——というアメリカらしい気分を捉えたフレーズを，Part III の標題に選んでみた．"There's No Stopping Us"「止められない」ものの内容は，しかし，それぞれ大きく違っている．

　ザ・ロック・ボトム・リメインダーズは小説家や音楽評論家によるロック・バンド．日本に当てはめていえば，村上龍，高橋源一郎，林真理子，みうらじゅん，柴田元幸，ピーター・バラカンに，音楽マネージャーとしてミッキー吉野がついたみたいなバンドだろうか（ちょっと違うな）．1992年にライブ・デビューしたこの文人バンド，ユーモア作家でメンバーのひとり，デイヴ・バリーの言を借りれば「メタリカが書いた小説のような音楽をやる」のだそうだ．だが問題は「質」ではない．60年代世代のアメリカ人にとって，ロックの意義は別のところにある．**Session 9** に抜粋したのは，ボーカルをとるエイミー・タン（1952–　　）による，バンド結成からツアーまでの回想記．しつけが厳しい中国系移民の家族で育った彼女が，アメリカ的快楽に身を委ねる，その（堕落ではなく）気高さを語るところが編者の胸を打った．一流作家の文章はやはり違う．歌っているし，踊っている．

　しかしアメリカから世界にあふれていったのは，8ビートの歓喜だけでは

なかった．朝鮮動乱からイラク戦争まで，国際紛争のほとんどに，アメリカは第一当事者国として荷担している．アメリカ社会の内側を覗き込めば，兵士として軍を支えた若者たちの歪んだ内面もまた見えてくるだろう．**Session 10** が取り上げるのは，危険地帯で軍務を果たすことにあたかも耽溺しているかのような兵士たちのリポートである．「戦うアメリカ」にも終わりは見えない．「暴力のアメリカ」も止まらない．平和主義者オバマのもとでも，アフガニスタン増兵の動きは進む．

ゴシップと扇情的なストーリーを売りにするメディアの蔓延も，現代の「歯止めのかからない」ものの一つだ．アメリカの場合「低俗ニュース」を担ってきたのは，長らく（一般紙の半分サイズの）タブロイド版の新聞だった．日本だとスポーツ新聞・芸能／女性週刊誌が取り上げてきた大衆ネタが，アメリカではどのように扱われてきたか．そのなかで，下品な印象をぬぐい去った一紙がどのように浮上して1990年代のジャーナリズムの主流の一角を担うようになったか．**Session 11** ではポップ・カルチャーの百科事典を執筆した博識カップル，ジェーン＆マイケル・スターンに語ってもらおう．

Session 12 にはトーンを変えて，ホラー映画研究書の一節を載せた．ハリウッドが生んだ怪物のなかでも特に有名な「フランケンシュタインのモンスター」がいかにしてあのような姿で誕生したのかを，文化史的側面から語る文章だ．それを読む私たちは，1930年代という時代の精神——電化・機械化といった変化に夢や恐怖をもって反応する集合的な心の深み——について考えさせられる．テクノロジーとは，私達に止められない力のなかでも最たるものだ．テクノロジーが生んだ怪物を，テクノロジーを駆使した映画に定着させようとした人々の，生身の心に感情移入してみたい．

Session 9

Mid-Life Confidential

Amy Tan

A few months before my fortieth birthday, I [1]
heard the fax machine churning out what
was sure to be yet another request to author appearance. I
had been on the road nationally and overseas for the better
half of the year. But this one was different. [5]

It was from Kathi Karmen Goldmark, the media escort who'd taken me to numerous book-related publicity events around the Bay Area. As I can best recall, her fax said something to this effect: "Hey, Amy, a bunch of authors and I are putting together a rock 'n' roll band to play at the ABA in [10] Anaheim. Wanna jam with us? I think you'd have a lot of fun."

I pondered the fax. Do I look like the kind of writer who has time for a lot of fun? As to singing in public, could there possibly be anything more similar to a public execu- [15] tion? Furthermore, how could I, the author of poignant mother-daughter tales, do something as ludicrous and career-damaging as playing in a rock 'n' roll band? Amend that to a *mediocre* rock 'n' roll band.

Two minutes later, I faxed Kathi back my answer: [20] "What should I wear?"

Being a rock 'n' roll singer presented only one small obstacle: namely, the fact that I couldn't *sing*. I had to do something about it.

Mid-Life Confidential

Mid-Life Confidential:「中年秘話」．confidential のスタンプが書類に押されていたらはそれは「極秘」という意味．

[2] **churning out:**（ファックス機が紙を）吐き出す．churn はもともと（ミルクを）攪拌すること．グルグル作動させて何かを生み出すことを churn out という．

[3] **yet another request:** またまたやってきた依頼
author appearance: 作家本人が書店などへ出向いて行うサイン会や朗読会

[4] **on the road ... for the better half of the year:** 1 年の半分以上旅回りを続けて

[6] **the media escort:** メディア宣伝担当者

[7] **numerous book-related publicity events:** さまざまな書籍関係の宣伝イベント

[8] **the Bay Area:** カリフォルニア湾一帯の人口密集地帯．サンフランシスコ，バークレー，オークランド，サンノゼなどの市を含む．
As I can best recall: 記憶の限りで言えば
something to this effect:「要するにこんな感じのこと」．*cf. The boss said something to the effect that he no longer needed George to work for him.*

[10] **the ABA:** アメリカ書店協会 (American Booksellers Association)．1900 年の創立以来，独立系書店を支援してきた．

[11] **Anaheim:** アナハイムは大ロサンジェルス圏の南東部にある都市．1955 年，ここに世界初のディズニーランドが開園した．
Wanna jam with us?: バンドの演奏への参加を促すときの決まり文句．wanna はとてもカジュアルな表現なので TPO に注意．

[13] **pondered the fax:** ファックスの内容についてじっくり考えた

[14] **As to singing in public, could there possibly be anything more similar to ... :** Isn't singing in public exactly like ... ?

[16] **poignant:** 痛切な，胸にじんと来る

[17] **ludicrous:** ばかばかしい，冷笑に値いする (*cf.* p. 25, 注 [109])

[18] **Amend that to ... :** 〜に訂正してください

[19] *mediocre* [mìːdióukər]: 冴えない，凡庸な

[21] **What should I wear?:** The author is already [a. willing / b. afraid] to sing in public.

[23] **obstacle:** something that stands in the way
namely: すなわち (that is to say)

The following week, I left for my vacation in Hawaii. For five hours a day, I sat on the beaches of Kona, wearing headphones while singing to the background instrumentals that my new band friend Ridley Pearson had recorded for the benefit of the musically disadvantaged. To an audience of porpoises and turtles frolicking in the waves, I sang my heart out, loud and strong. My husband later reported that whenever beachcombers came within earshot of me, they retreated with the same deft haste people employ for avoiding sidewalk hell-and-brimstone preachers.

When I was a child, I used to go the beach to recruit kids for Christ. I'm the daughter of hardworking Christian immigrants. In our family "fun" was a bad f-word, as bad as another f-word "freedom," as in "So, you want American freedom to go wild and bring shame on your family?" Which brings me to yet another f-word, "friends," those purveyors of corruption and shame whose sole purpose in life was to encourage me to talk back to my mother and make her long to go back to China, where there were millions of girls my age who would be only too happy to obey their parents without question. The good f-word, of course, was "family" as in "go to church with family," or "do homework with family," or "give your toys to your poor family in Taiwan."

My parents did allow certain versions of *family* fun, like walking around the campus of Stanford University, a form of entertainment that served to remind me of a destination and a reward second only to getting into heaven. Both rewards could be attained only if I listened carefully to my parents, meaning no boys, no pizza, and of course, no rock 'n' roll.

Editor's Note: Kathi had also written to Stephen King, asking him to join in. By then, the group already had quite a few famous members, such as Dave Barry, Barbara Kingsolver and Matt

Mid-Life Confidential

- [26] **Kona:** ハワイ島 ("the Big Island" と呼ばれるハワイ諸島中最大の島) の西岸域
- [28] **Ridley Pearson:** 以下, バンドメンバーは Editors' Note のコーナーで.
- [29] **the musically disadvantaged:** 生来音楽的センスがない者. *cf.* the hearing impaired (聴覚障害者), the visually impaired (視覚障害者), the physically challenged (身体障害者)
- [30] **porpoise(s)** [pɔ́ːrpəs]: イルカ. 生物学的には dolphin と別の属名だが, 日常的には混同されている.
  frolicking: 遊び戯れ, 飛んだり跳ねたりしている
  I sang my heart out: 大声で思い切り歌った. *cf. I laughed my head off.*
- [32] **beachcomber(s):** 海辺を散歩しながら貝殻などを拾う人たち
  within earshot of me: 私の (歌) 声が届く範囲内
- [33] **retreated:** moved back; withdrew; ran off
  with ... deft haste: さりげない早足で **deft:** skillful and quick
- [34] **sidewalk hell-and-brimstone preachers:** 街の舗道に立って地獄の恐ろしさを説く伝道者たち. brimstone (硫黄) は「地獄」の言い替え. hell and brimstone で成句.
- [37] **a bad f-word:** 例の f で始まる 4 文字言葉を思い浮かべて笑ってください.
- [38] **as in ... :** 以下の例にあるような. *cf.* p. 29, [131]
  So, you want American freedom to go wild and bring shame on your family?:「つまり好き放題やるためにアメリカ的自由をくださいと, それで家族に恥をかかせたいというわけね?」. この一文に移民しつつもお中国人としてのアイデンティティを保とうとする両親のスタンスが滲んでいる.
- [40] **those purveyors of corruption and shame:**「堕落と恥辱をもたらす者」. friends の説明.
- [41] **sole:** one and only
- [42] **talk back:** 口答えをする
  make her long to: make her want to
- [44] **be only too happy to ... :**「大喜びで〜する」. only too が happy を強調.
- [50] **Stanford University:** 1885 年創立の, ベイエリアきっての私立エリート大学.
- [51] **served to remind me of ... :** 〜を思い出させる役目を果たした
- [52] **second only to ... :** 〜の次にくる; これを上回るのは〜しかない
  Both rewards could be attained only if ... my parents: I wouldn't be able to get into Stanford nor heaven if I didn't listen carefully to my parents.
- [54] **meaning ... :** ということはつまり〜

Groening. It had a name: the Rock Bottom Remainders. Famed rock critics Greil Marcus and Dave Marsh came in, and as musical director the band had none other than the legendary Al Kooper.

Al was actually the one who suggested I sing lead on "These Boots Are Made for Walkin'." When I first saw my name written on the song list next to this Nancy Sinatra classic, I called up Kathi. "Tell Al to forget it. Of all the songs in the world, I hate that one the most."

Kathi, ever so diplomatic, broke things to me gently: "Actually, I think this could be a great song for you. You know how you always worry about whether you can really sing? Well, with 'Boots,' you don't need a great voice, just a lot of attitude."

"Attitude?"

"Yeah—you know, a bad-girl attitude. You could look cheap and sexy. You could smoke cigarettes and have all the guys fall all over you. "

For my "Boots" outfit, I carefully combed through a Frederick's of Hollywood catalogue and found a pair of zip-up patent-leather booties that would transform an ordinary pair of black business pumps into awesome, man-stomping, thigh-high intimidators. At a local S&M shop, I bought a biker's cap and a leather dog leash, as well as studded cuffs, collar, and belt. Like any girl vying to be prom queen, I fretted over which of three outfits I should actually wear. The see-through leopard? The tawdry fishnet lace? Or how about the classically simple little black bustier?

At the risk of sounding maudlin, I must confess I felt just like Cinderella going to the ball.

At school I was not a popular girl. I was not the kind who got invited to after-school garage parties where 45s were played at top volume and 7-Up was laced with vodka. I hated myself for being perceived as the "good girl," unlike the

[59] *the Rock Bottom Remainders*: 訳せば「ロックのいちばんカスな野郎たち」．remainder には「売れ残った返品本」の意味も．

[61] *none other than*:「他でもない」．有名な人物を紹介するときの決まり文句の一つ．

[62] **sing lead**: メイン・ボーカルを担当する
"These Boots Are Made for Walkin'": 1966 年にヒットした女王様系ポップスの古典．♪ "One of these days my boots are gonna walk all over you..."

[65] **Tell Al to forget it**: 絶対にムリってアルに伝えて

[67] **ever so diplomatic:** very very diplomatic. とても人の扱いがうまい
broke things to me gently: （いいにくいことを）優しく伝えてくれた

[71] **(a) lot of attitude:** 特に反抗的な若者が自分を誇示するような態度を，(an) attitude という．「あいつ生意気だ」は，*She has an attitude*.

[74] **have all the guys fall all over you:**「男たちはみんなあなたにイチコロよ」．fall all over... は「（魅力的な人に）デレデレになる」．

[76] **"Boots" outfit:** "These Boots Are Made for Walkin'" を歌うときの衣装
combed through...: 〜の隅から隅まで目を通した

[77] **Frederick's of Hollywood:** 1946 年創業の大手ランジェリー・ブランド．
zip-up patent-leather booties: パテントレザーのジッパー式オーバーシューズ

[78] **transform ⟨A⟩ into ⟨B⟩:** A を（見違えるように）変えて B にする

[79] **awesome, man-stomping, thigh-high intimidators:** 息をのむほどステキな，男を踏みつけるにも怖気づかせるにもピッタリの太ももまであるブーツ

[81] **biker's cap:** バイク乗りがよくかぶる帽子
a leather dog leash: 犬をつなぐ革ひも
studded: 飾り鋲つきの

[82] **vying to be...:** 〜になろうと（ほかの女の子たちと）張り合っている
prom queen: 大学や高校などで卒業記念に開かれるダンスパーティのクイーン．この座をめぐって悲喜劇が繰り広げられる．
fretted over...: kept worrying about...

[84] **(The) see-through leopard:**「ヒョウ柄のシースルー」．次ページの写真で，実際に Amy が着ているのを確認してください．
The tawdry fishnet lace: 安っぽくてけばけばしいアミアミレース

[85] **bustier:** ビスチェ

[86] **At the risk of sounding maudlin:** うっとりしすぎていると思われてしまうかもしれないけれど．maudlin: foolishly sentimental

[87] **ball:** a formal dance party

[89] **45(s):** 毎分 45 回転のシングル盤レコード

[90] **laced with vodka:** ちょっぴりウォッカを垂らした．*coffee laced with brandy*

"bad girls" who ratted their hair, slouched around in their father's white dress shirts, and stole nail polish from Kmart.

As freshman class secretary, I had to help organize the dances. I argued persuasively with my mother about the necessity of my going to the dances as well: "Come on, I have to be there to make sure that everything goes like planned. Like, you know, what if someone doesn't pay to get in? That's like stealing. Of *course*, I'm not interested in actually dancing with a stupid boy. Of *course*, I'll get my Ph.D. before I even *think* about dating. Duh, I'm not *that* dumb."

Before going to the dance, I used masking tape to shorten my dress and I asked my girlfriend Terry to lend me her tube of white lipstick. Neither measure had any effect on the boys. At the dance, I stood near the punchbowl, mortified as Terry, then Janice, then Dottie were asked to dance.

I stood alone, unasked. Well, a girl can go to the bath-

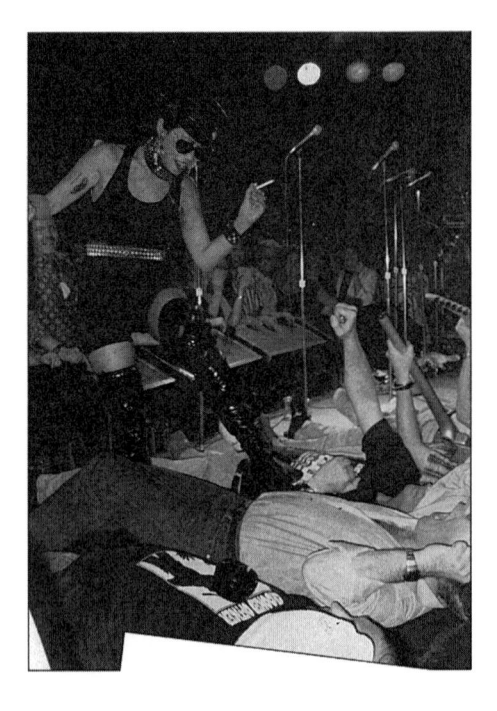

- [92] **ratted their hair:** 人工の毛を入れて，結った髪にボリュームを出した
  slouched around：かったるそうにしていた
- [93] **dress shirts:** ぶかぶかの男物のワイシャツを着ることが，著者がティーンだった頃に流行っていた．
  nail polish: マニキュア
- [94] **Kmart:** 1962年創業の大手ディスカウント・デパート
- [95] **freshman class secretary:** 1年生の生徒会 (student council) 書記
  help organize the dances: ダンスパーティの企画準備を手伝う
- [96] **persuasively:** effectively; forcefully; logically
  about the necessity of my going to the dances as well: that I needed to go to the dances as well as organize it
- [97] **Come on:**「分かるでしょ」．反対者に同意を求める間投詞．
- [98] **like planned:** the way we planned it
- [99] **Like, you know:**「たとえば，ほら」．Likeで文を始めるのは，若者の「乱れた」言葉づかいの典型．
  what if . . . ?: 〜だったらどうするの？
- [100] **not interested in actually dancing with a stupid boy :**「下らない男子なんかと踊りたいわけない」．stupidの一語がつくことで「まさか，そんなバカなこと」という気分が強調される．「賢い子となら踊ってもいい」という意味ではない．
- [101] **Of *course*:**「もーちろん」．続くthinkやthatの強調と同様，気持ちと裏はらなことを熱っぽく主張しているおかしみが伝わってくる．
  Ph.D. [píːèitʃdíː]**:** Doctor of Philosophy, 博士号 (法学, 医学系を除く)
- [102] **Duh** [dɚː]**:** ここでは「バカバカしい」とちょっと呆れた（フリをするための）ニュアンスを演出している．強く発音する．
- [103] **masking tape:** 塗装用マスキングテープは，スカートの一時的な裾上げに便利
- [105] **her tube of white lipstick:** lipstickを数える単位はtube. 白のパール系口紅は1960年代の女の子たちのあいだで流行した．
  Neither measure had any effect on the boys: Neither the shortened skirt nor the white lipstick made me look more attractive to the boys.
- [106] **the punchbowl:** ダンスパーティの定番飲物は，大きなガラスの鉢に入ったフルーツ・パンチ．
  mortified as Terry, then Janice, then Dottie were asked to dance: thenを繰り返すことで，一人また一人と「売れ残り」が減っていく恐怖を表現している．
  mortified: embarrassed; ashamed; humiliated
- [108] **can go to the bathroom only so many times before she has to . . . :** そう何度も（恥をさらさないよう）トイレに逃れるわけにもいかず，いずれは〜せざるをえない．*There are only so many times friends will help you move.*（引越社の宣伝）

room only so many times before she has to make up another reason why she's not dancing and otherwise thoroughly occupied. I pretended to be fascinated with the band. I fantasized that the lead singer would finally spot me and beckon me with his surly lips—"Yeah, you, the Chinese girl with the moon face. Come up here and do primitive movements with me on stage."

That would show them, all those guys who asked the other girls to dance instead.

And then reality would set in. That would never happen, not in a million trillion years. The lead singer? Singing to me? Get real.

But suddenly I *was* the lead singer. I growled, "Are you ready, boots? Start walking!" and the Remainder boys would fall supine and quake. Dave Marsh was especially sweet. As I started to stomp on him, he begged me—to no avail—not to stub out my burning cigarette on his chest; the hotel ashtray he had stolen and strategically placed was not visible to the audience.

"It's just not fair," Stephen King blurted one night after the show. "Dave Barry got the whip jammed into his mouth *two* nights in a row! When's it going to be *my* turn?"

Right about now, I can hear my parents lecturing me: "You see? Having fun is bad. More important is family." And in a way, I discovered they were right. Because ultimately, the best part about being a Remainder was the fact that we became a family. We had family fun . . .

Our life together on the road included getting neck cramps while sleeping on the bus. Waking up and seeing how haggard we looked without coffee, without makeup. Popping food into Ridley's half-open mouth while he was sleeping. Swearing on an oath of death to never reveal to each other's spouses who among us had taken up smoking again. Opening up our laptops, then not writing a single

Mid-Life Confidential

- [110] **why she's not dancing and otherwise thoroughly occupied:** なぜ踊ってもいないのに他のことに夢中になっていないのか. otherwise: in a different way
- [112] **spot me and beckon me:** 私に目を留めて招いてくれる
- [113] **with his surly lips:**「無愛想な唇で」. ロックバンドにありがちな, カッコつけてる苦み走った表情をほのめかしている.
- [114] **the moon face:**(「三日月顔」もありうるが, ここは満月のような) 丸顔
  do primitive movements:(腰をうねらすなど) 原始的な動きをする
- [116] **That would show them:** *i.e.* (If that happened,) they would realize my true values. これに続く all those guys... は them の具体的な説明.
- [118] **set in:** 舞い戻ってくる
- [119] **not in a million trillion years:** 何百万, 何兆年たっても無理
- [120] **Get real:** 目を覚ませ, 現実に戻れ
- [121] **"Are you ready, boots? Start walking!":** "These Boots..." の歌詞の最終行.
- [123] **fall supine and quake:** あお向けに寝ころんで震える
- [124] **stomp on him:** 彼を踏みつける
  to no avail: 効果はなかったが (= in vain)
- [125] **stub out my burning cigarette:** 火のついたタバコをもみ消す
- [126] **strategically placed:** *i.e.* cleverly held on his chest
- [128] **"It's just not fair":** Stephen was complaining that Amy was [a. harassing him too much / b. not harassing him enough].
  blurted: suddenly said
- [129] **got the whip jammed into his mouth:** 口の中にムチを突っ込まれた
- [131] **Right about now, I can hear...:** 今ごろきっと〜と言ってるだろう, 声が聞こえるようだ, ということ.
- [134] **being a Remainder:** being a member of the Rock Bottom Remainders
- [136] **Our life together on the road included...:** 以下, 共同の巡業生活のうちに繰り広げられた出来事が, パラグラフ全体に列挙される.
  neck cramps: 首筋のけいれん
- [138] **haggard:** やつれた, げっそりした
- [140] **Swearing on an oath of death:** 死の誓いを立てて
  reveal to each other's spouses: 互いの連れ合いにバラす

word. Buying postcards of road kill and other trucker paraphernalia. Standing in line to go to the movies and noting how many people thought Steve almost looked like Stephen King. Reading outrageous stories aloud from the *Weekly World News*, including the one that said illegal Chinese aliens were digging tunnels through the center of the earth. [145]

To all those people who've been asking me why I joined a rock 'n' roll band, I've been telling them this: I wanted to have fun. I simply wanted to have fun. And I finally learned how. [150]

(still younger than keith)
FIFTEENTH ANNIVERSARY TOUR
With special guest Roger McGuinn
Friday, June 1, 2007
Webster Hall, NYC
→ TICKET INFO ←
presented by: verizon

- [143] **postcards of road kill:** 道路でひき殺された動物の絵ハガキ
  trucker paraphernalia:「長距離トラック運転手向けの品々」．かなりエグイものも含まれる．
- [144] **Standing in line:** 列に並ぶ
- [145] **Steve almost looked like Stephen King:** 実際，本人です．
- [146] **outrageous stories:** とんでもない記事
- [147] **the *Weekly World News*:**「世界で唯一信頼できる新聞」をキャッチフレーズに，悪魔の骨が発掘されたニュースや鼠サイズのバッタの襲来などを伝えるトンデモ系タブロイド紙．http://weeklyworldnews.com/
  illegal Chinese aliens:「中国からの不法移民」．このトンネル掘りの冗談ネタは，19世紀に清国から渡ってきた移民たちが，アメリカ西部山中の鉄道敷設の苦役に耐えた歴史的事実をほのめかしているのかもしれない．

[Session 9] Comprehension Check

1. Mark T for true, F for false.

1) For a short while, Amy was negative about joining the band for a variety of reasons, including the fact that she couldn't sing. — (   )
2) While Amy was practicing singing on the beach of Hawaii, a preacher came up to her. — (   )
3) The Remainder boys fell all over Amy when she sang the "Boots" song, just as Kathi had told her. — (   )
4) Some of the members of the band started to smoke again and were caught by their spouses. — (   )

2. Fill in the blanks with either "good," "bad" or "cool."

At first, I thought my singing the "Boots" song was a (   ) idea, but once I made up my mind and started choosing my outfit, I felt so (   ). It eventually reminded me of how unpopular I was when I was a schoolgirl. Everybody thought I was a "(   ) girl," but in fact, I had a secret longing to be (   ). I remember once persuading my mother to let me go to the dance. I did everything to look (   ) but ended up not being asked to dance at all.

3. Choose one sentence that can NOT be implied from lines [40]-[45] on page 114. — (   )

a. Friends were thought of as sinful and dishonest, a very bad influence on the author's attitude.
b. Whenever the author denied her mother, she would grieve and say they shouldn't have come to America in the first place.
c. The author's friends were corrupt and shameful enough to force her to talk back to her mother.
d. Daughters in China were generally very obedient and would never talk back to their parents.

Editors' Note

　The Rock Bottom Remaindersのメンバーから人気小説家を並べてみるとこんなぐあいになる．
　・デイブ・バリー (lead guitar, vocals)：ユーモア作家．邦訳された『デイブ・バリーの日本を笑う』は噴飯物．
　・スティーブン・キング (rhythm guitar, vocals)：紹介不要．
　・リドリー・ピアスン (bass guitar, vocals)：音楽の腕は本物．ミステリー小説の邦訳多数．最近は子供向けの本も．
　・バーバラ・キングソルヴァー (keyboard, vocals)：アフリカの宣教師一家を描いた『ポイズンウッド・バイブル』等の邦訳あり．
　・エイミー・タン：映画化されたデビュー作『ジョイ・ラック・クラブ』のほかに，『私は生まれる見知らぬ大地で』などの邦訳もあり．リードをとるのは一曲だけか．
　彼らと共に気になるのは，『ザ・シンプソンズ』で有名な漫画家のマット・グレーニング，そしてロック批評界の大物，グリール・マーカスとデイブ・マーシュがメンバーに含まれることだ．マーカスは1975年に『ミステリー・トレイン』を出版して，ロック批評を文化研究の地位に引き上げた．マーシュはブルース・スプリングスティンについての権威だが，他にもロック，フォーク，ポップに関する多数の著書がある．
　もう一人，本文に "legendary" という形容つきで紹介した Al Kooper だが，Bob Dylan のヒット曲 "Like a Rolling Stone" での，ゴスペル風味たっぷりのオルガン演奏を聞かせているのが彼である．
　ちなみに，メンバー全体で著書の数が約150点，総売り上げは1億冊くらいいくのではないだろうか．ライブ以外で人気はないようだけど，今年2010年4月にもツアーを組んではしゃいでいるようである．
（参考 URL: http://www.dqydj.com/rbr.htm）

[Answers for the a/b Questions]
[21] — a., [128] — b.

Session 10

Love Is a Battlefield

from *Newsweek*

Staff Sgt. Shaun McBride would rather be in a war zone than at home. He likes the adrenaline, he says, even the "fear someone can shoot you." He hates the petty responsibilities of home life, the bills and family issues.

He's clocked 43 months in Afghanistan and Iraq. His first wife of three years sent him divorce papers while he was fighting Taliban militants—she wanted to marry a friend of his. (She couldn't be reached for comment.) "Whatever," says McBride, 32, with a shrug. Now he's remarried—to Evangeline (Star) McBride, a 27-year-old divorced mother of one—and getting ready for his fifth deployment with the Third Brigade combat team of the 101st Airborne Division.

When asked in front of Star what he misses most when he's overseas, he doesn't hesitate: his souped-up Mustang. He likes to drive it fast, and "show what's what" when another flashy car pulls up next to him at a stoplight. But even the driving is better in Iraq. There, you "do whatever you want on the road. You own the road. You can go into people's houses without being invited in. It's like you own their house."

Sergeant McBride is a soldier's soldier. He knows his job, and loves it above all else. At a time when the military desperately needs trained fighting men and women, he's

[1]

[5]

[10]

[15]

[20]

Love Is a Battlefield

Love Is a Battlefield: これは引っかけのタイトル．読んでみると，「戦場と化した愛」の話ではなく，「愛するは戦場」という意味だとわかる．

[1] **Staff Sgt.:** 職業軍人の士官または将校 (officers) と兵卒 (soldiers) の間に，ふつう兵卒上がりの下士官 (noncommissioned officers) がいる．米陸軍では squad (兵士10名ほどの隊) を指揮する下士官が Staff Sergeant．Sgt. は Sergeant の略．

[2] **likes the adrenaline** [ədrénələn]: 戦場の緊迫の中で，アドレナリンが分泌されているその興奮がたまらない，ということ．

[4] **petty:** small; trivial; insignificant

the bills and family issues: 請求書の支払いや家庭内のあれこれ

[6] **He's clocked 43 months in Afghanistan and Iraq:** clock は動詞で「記録を出す」．危険な地域で連続43ヶ月も軍役についていたことが強調されている．

His first wife of three years: 3年間続いた (3年で離婚した) 最初の妻

[8] **Taliban militants:** タリバンの戦闘員

[9] **couldn't be reached for comment:** コメントを求めたが連絡がとれなかった

Whatever: まぁいいけど

[10] **with a shrug:**「肩をすくめて」．しょうがないな，という気持ちの表現．

[11] **a ... divorced mother of one:** 離婚歴があり子供が1人いる女性

[12] **his fifth deployment:** 5回目の戦地派遣

[13] **(the) Third Brigade combat team of the 101st Airborne Division:** 第101空挺師団第3旅団の戦闘チーム．合衆国陸軍 (US Army) の Division には，通常 Brigade (3000〜5000人の兵士団) が3つ含まれる．

[15] **his souped-up Mustang:**「パワーアップしたムスタング」．動詞 "soup up" は，車の改造に関して使う．「ムスタング」はフォード社を代表するスポーツカー．

[16] **"show what's what":** 示しをつけてやる，という語感．*He doesn't know what's what.* (あいつは物事がわかってない)

[17] **flashy:** 派手にかっこつけた

[19] **You own the road:** The road is all yours; you are free to do anything there. 自分のことを言っているのだが，「俺でなくても誰だって」という気持ちがこもっているので you が使われる．

always ready to go. But there's also something disturbing about a young man who thrives on conflict and doesn't really feel at ease with his family. Asked the hardest part of coming home, he responds: "Having to live with other people. Having to deal." He doesn't like having to rush to pick up his stepdaughter from day care, or to get the groceries. Where is the line between the highly valued fighting man and the guy who's loving it too much, and been too long in the war zone?

A tiny fraction of Americans are doing the bulk of the country's fighting and policing in far-off lands. Less than 5 percent of Americans are in the active military at any time. Of those, a much smaller number of officers and enlisted men have done multiple tours. Most are in the Army, and less than 15 percent of Army soldiers have done three or more deployments.

Some of those men and women answer the call because they think it's their duty, whether they like it or not. Some go because it's a good way to advance their careers, or because they like the extra money they get with combat duty. Others just like it. "Soldiers want to fight," says retired Gen. Barry McCaffrey, who was the youngest and most decorated Army general when he retired in 1996. "That's why they signed up."

First Sgt. Jason Dodge is that kind of soldier, an extreme guy in every respect. He gets to his office between 0425 and 0428. A few hours later, he's on his morning run—usually 10 to 15 miles. He can climb a 30-foot rope using just his arms in 10 seconds. He works best in a room without direct sunlight, he says, and doesn't like to eat more than one meal a day—"and that's dinner with my wife, but only because she makes me." His job: to engineer explosives to blow down doors and walls.

It doesn't seem to really bother Sergeant Dodge, 36, that most of his Army buddies have moved on, either transfer-

Love Is a Battlefield

- [25] **there's . . . something disturbing about . . . :** 〜にはどこか不穏な（人の気持ちをかき乱すような）ところがある
- [26] **thrives on conflict:** 闘争を餌にして繁茂する；戦闘があると輝く
- [27] **Asked the hardest part of . . . :** (When he is) asked (about) the hardest part of . . .
- [29] **deal:** （さまざまな現実に）対応する
  rush to pick up his stepdaughter: 義理の娘を急いで車で迎えにいく
- [30] **day care:** 託児所
  get the groceries:「スーパーへ買い出しに行く」という語感．
- [31] **Where is the line between . . . ?:** What's the difference between . . . ?
- [32] **the guy who's loving it too much:**「（単に有能な兵士であることを越えて）すっかり戦場にのめり込んでしまった男」．who loves it too much でもよいのだが，進行形にすると，そのようすが顔や態度にありありと出ている感じが加わる．
- [34] **A tiny fraction:**「ほんの一部」．次の bulk (a big volume) と対比されている．
- [35] **(the) country's fighting and policing:** 米国が担っている治安維持の仕事
- [36] **the active military:** 戦闘下の軍
- [37] **officers and enlisted men:**「職業軍人とその下の兵士」．両者で軍全体が構成される．
- [38] **have done multiple tours:** 2度以上の海外派遣を経験した
  Most are in the Army: アメリカで軍は，Army, Navy, Air Force からなるほか，海兵隊 (Marine Corps [mərí:n kɔ̀:r]) が，Navy から半ば独立して存在する．
- [41] **answer the call:** [a. go to a war zone / b. stay in the US camps] as ordered
- [43] **because it's a good way to advance their careers:**（履歴書の箔付けとなり）キャリア・アップにつながるから
- [46] **Gen. Barry McCafferey:** Gen. は General の略で「軍司令官，将官」
  most decorated: もっとも多くの勲章を受けた
- [48] **signed up:** enlisted; enrolled; joined up with the Army
- [49] **First Sgt.:**「曹長」に相当．下士官のなかでトップ・クラス．
  that kind of soldier: a soldier who [a. signed up / b. just wants to fight]
  an extreme guy in every respect: あらゆる点において過激な男
- [50] **between 0425 and 0428:** 数字は zero-four-two-five などと読む．軍隊式の時間の表し方で，ドッジ曹長がオフィスに入る時間の正確さが強調されている．
- [55] **and that's dinner . . . :** *i.e.* the only meal I eat is dinner . . .
  only because she makes me: I eat dinner only because she forces me to
- [56] **to engineer explosives:** 爆弾を設計すること．engineer は動詞．
- [59] **have moved on:** are no longer with him
  transferring to a non-deploying base: 戦闘態勢にない軍事基地へ移動になる

ring to a non-deploying base or leaving the military altogether. He'll miss the old tradition of going to an Outback Steakhouse with his Army friends and their wives before and after each deployment. ("No one was authorized to go while we were gone," he says.) But the way he sees it, he's got a job to do, and it's in Iraq or Afghanistan.

Dodge's wife, Dana, 31, says he's always himself when he gets back from a deployment, but she does handle him carefully at first. "Maybe his temper is a bit short when he first comes home," she says. "If he gets that look, I can just tell and walk away for a while." She's learned not to call him and make one request, then tack on others. She also knows he doesn't like crowds.

Does Dodge like the war zone? "I don't look at it like that, sir, I really don't," he says. He enjoys "playing with explosives," and shooting his gun, and forming the tight bonds that can be forged in a hostile setting. But he also feels professional satisfaction. "I haven't lost a single soldier... and I consider that my biggest accomplishment," says Dodge, whose brother died in a training accident in 1995. "If I wasn't there, I don't know who would do my job. But what I do know is that I would do it better."

Everyone likes doing what they're good at. But soldiers have to weigh the benefits and costs in ways that others don't. The more time soldiers do in war zones, the more likely they are to suffer post-traumatic stress disorder. A mental-health survey conducted by the Army has quantified the psychological wear and tear of repeated tours. As of spring 2008, 27 percent of noncommissioned officers with three or four deployments had shown symptoms of PTSD, compared with 12 percent of those with one tour.

An optimist reading the data might point out that nearly three quarters of NCOs don't suffer any such mental-health symptoms. But in worst-case scenarios, a stressed soldier can be lethal. In early May, 44-year-old Army Sgt.

Love Is a Battlefield

- [60] **altogether:** [a. completely / b. together with him]
- [61] **He'll miss the old tradition of . . . :**（以前はいつもやっていた）〜がもうできなくなってさびしく思うことになるだろう
  Outback Steakhouse: 1988年フロリダで創業した世界展開のステーキ・チェーン店．
- [63] **No one was authorized to go while we were gone:**（そのステーキ店へは）自分たちが戦地にいるあいだは，行ってはいけないことになっていた．authorize: give permission
- [64] **the way he sees it:** 彼の見方によれば；彼に言わせれば
- [66] **always himself:** ふだんのまま，変わった点はない
- [68] **his temper is a bit short:** he is easily [a. offended / b. calmed down]
- [69] **If he gets that look, I can just tell and walk away for a while:** あの表情が浮かんだらすぐ分かるからしばらく離れていればいいの
- [70] **She's learned not to . . . :**（失敗から学んだので）いまでは〜しない．to は call だけでなく，make と tack にもかかる．
- [71] **tack on others:** ほかの用事も（ついでに）言いつける
- [73] **I don't look at it like that:** そうは考えてない；好きか嫌いかの問題ではない
- [76] **be forged in a hostile setting:** 敵に囲まれた厳しい環境の中で強められる
- [80] **If I wasn't there:** 自分が戦地任務についていなかったとしたら
- [83] **weigh the benefits and costs:** 利益とコストを秤にかける
  in ways that others don't: 他の者とはちがったやり方で
- [84] **The more time soldiers do in war zones:**「戦闘地域での勤めが長くなればなるほど」．do time で「兵役期間を過ごす」．
- [85] **post-traumatic stress disorder:** 心的外傷性ストレス障害，略して PTSD．とても大きなショックを受けた後の憂うつ感，恐怖，性格変化などの障害．
- [86] **(A) . . . survey . . . has quantified:** 調査によって（数量的に）明らかになった
- [87] **the psychological wear and tear:** 精神的な消耗やダメージ．wear and tear で成句．
  As of . . . : 〜の時点で
- [88] **noncommissioned officers:** 下士官，略して NCO
- [91] **An optimist . . . might point out . . . :** 楽観主義者ならばこう指摘するだろう
- [94] **can be lethal:** [a. can be killed / b. can kill people]

John M. Russell went berserk in a military stress center in Baghdad, killing five fellow soldiers. Russell was weeks away from finishing his third tour in Iraq, and apparently thought the military was trying to get rid of him.

Sergeant McBride and his wife know he has some PTSD-like symptoms. It's always tough when he first comes home from overseas. After his last deployment, she recalls, she suddenly dropped a laundry basket. He started screaming at her never to do that again. "He was about ready to hit the floor," she says—as if he were taking cover from an incoming round. "After three months, he gets normal again."

Star understands what bugs him about home life. "There are bills; you're getting nickeled-and-dimed all the time here," she says. "Everyday life, errands and all that." She handles the mundane duties—including the phone calls to banks or the cable-TV service. "He's kind of antisocial," she says. "It's a hassle for him." The sergeant objects: "I'm not antisocial, I just don't like dealing with strangers."

He may always have been a bit that way. McBride joined the Army in 1996, when he was just 18. That was after he'd dropped out of high school and his mother had kicked him out of the house, he says. Mom was glad when he signed up: she thought he could use the discipline. He did an early stint in Korea and had a child with his first wife. But he was back in the United States on 9/11, taking his wife for surgery that day. He dropped her at the clinic and went to breakfast at a McDonald's, where he saw the towers falling on television. He then picked up his wife, dropped her at home and said, "Sorry, I'm going to work." At the base, everyone was buzzing. "We all knew we were going to war," he says. "We were all excited about it."

Now he's in his fifth year of marriage to Star, and headed into his fifth deployment. Star knows how to handle his mood, and tries not to surprise him with much. She likes

Love Is a Battlefield

- [95] **went berserk:** とつぜん凶暴化した
- [96] **was weeks away from finishing . . . :** 〜を終えるまで数週間を残すばかりだった
- [100] **PTSD-like symptoms:** PTSD と思われるような症状
  when he first comes home: 帰郷したてのうちは
- [103] **was about ready to hit the floor:** ほとんど床に身を伏せんばかりだった
- [104] **taking cover from an incoming round:** 屋内への一斉射撃から身を守る
- [107] **bugs him:** annoys him; irritates him; bothers him
- [108] **getting nickeled-and-dimed:** 細かなことで（原意は「5セント10セントのことで」）神経をすり減らす
- [109] **Everyday life, errands and all that:** 日常でも，買い物でも，なんでも
- [110] **the mundane duties:** こまごまとした毎日の用事
- [111] **antisocial:** 人と交わりたがらない，社交的ではない
- [112] **a hassle:** a bother; a problem; a nuisance. *Parking around here is such a hassle.*
- [114] **a bit that way:** somewhat like that
- [118] **he could use the discipline:**「軍隊の規律正しさは彼にとって必要なことだ」. could use は need という動詞に伴う断定調を避けた，やや婉曲な言い方．*You could use a haircut.*
  did an early stint in Korea:「年若くして韓国での外地勤務をした」．"do a stint" は一定期間の任務を行うこと．
- [120] **9/11:** 2001年9月11日．読み方は nine eleven.
- [124] **At the base:** 軍隊基地では
- [125] **buzzing:** noisy; excited; in commotion
  We all knew we were going to war: We were all sure that this was the beginning of a war
- [129] **likes that he's an authority figure:** 彼が自分や娘に対して権威をもって強くふるまうところが気に入っている

that he's an authority figure who can tell her "no," which she "missed out on growing up." When she bought a puppy during one deployment, and it chewed up a carpet, Star e-mailed a photo with a caption: "Don't kill the dog." Shaun says he was "pissed," but he's come to love the dog.

Star knows her husband is less warm than other men, those who show lots of affection to their wives. "I meet them all the time and I'm like—you exist?" she says. "He's kind of emotionally closed. Sometimes it's lonelier when he's here than when he's gone."

Over several interviews with *Newsweek*, there were two moments when Sergeant McBride let down his tough-guy guard. The first was when he teared up recalling 9/11. The second came when he mentioned that on his upcoming tour he'd be in a desk job, orchestrating the positions of soldiers "outside the wire." To the pleasant surprise of his wife, he offered that he was "ready to take a break" from the real action.

Still, McBride insists the deployments don't wear him down psychologically. "If you want help, you can go and get help," he says. "We do suicide-prevention briefings every two months or so." But he scoffs at the suicides: "It's just a bunch of weak people." Has he ever been to a psychologist? "No. Never seen a psychologist one-on-one," he says. Star intervenes, in her usual plain-spoken manner. "He needs to. Write that down." Shaun laughs: "Whatever."

- [131] **"missed out on growing up"**:「自分の成長過程には欠けていた」．Star の家にはきちんと No と言える大人がいなかったということ．
- [133] **caption:** 映画の字幕だけでなく，写真やイラストなどにつける短い説明書きも caption という．
- [134] **"pissed"**:「コンチクショウと思った」．pissed は angry の口汚い言い方．
  he's come to love the dog: [a. he came and petted the dog / b. he grew fond of the dog]
- [137] **you exist?**:「あなたみたいな（妻にやさしい）人ってこの世にいたんだ」．（その前の I'm like はここでは I say something like と同じことで，きわめて口語的な表現）
- [138] **kind of emotionally closed:**「他人と心を通わせない（うちとけない）みたいなところがある」．kind of は somewhat と同じ意味の口語表現．
- [141] **let down his tough-guy guard:** *i.e.* stopped being a tough guy and opened up his heart
- [142] **teared up:** 涙を浮かべた
- [143] **on his upcoming tour:** 次に派遣されるときには
- [144] **orchestrating the positions of soldiers "outside the wire":**「戦闘地域外から兵士たちに位置取りを指令する」．orchestrate という動詞を使うことで，全体の配置を統括するイメージが出ている．
- [148] **wear him down:** 彼を参らせる，消耗させる．*cf.* wear and tear (p. 130, [87])
- [150] **do suicide-prevention briefings:** 自殺予防のための説明会をやる
- [151] **scoffs at the suicides:**「自殺する人間を軽蔑する」．次の just a bunch of weak people は「どいつもこいつも弱虫なんだ」という語感．
- [153] **Never seen a psychologist:** 心理カウンセリングなど受けたことがない
  one-on-one: 一対一で
- [154] **intervenes:** 間に入る
  in her usual plain-spoken manner: いつものストレートな言い方で
- [155] **Write that down.:**（忘れないように）メモしておきなさい
  "Whatever": Shaun の口癖であるこの言葉 (*cf.* p. 126, [9]) は，"Okay" とはちがって，納得しているのかいないのか，ともかく争わないという態度表明である．言い方がやさしければ「まあ，いいか」といった感じ．What を強く ever を思い切り下げたイントネーションでいうと，「しったことかよ」と突き放したニュアンスも出る．

[Session 10] **Comprehension Check**

1. **Choose two statements that best represent the general idea of the text.** — (   ) (   )
   a. the contribution of the professional soldiers in an American combat team
   b. the difficulty of coming back from a war zone to a mundane, everyday life
   c. the healing of the psychological wear and tear of repeated deployments
   d. the danger of doing more time in war zones and loving it
   e. the importance of well-trained military men and women after 9/11

2. **Fill in the blanks with a sentence that best completes each statement.**
   1) On his Mustang, Sgt. McBride is very competitive. (   )
   2) Sgt. Dodge easily gets angry. (   )
   3) Sgt. McBride knows his job and loves it. (   )
   4) Star's husband is less warm than other men. (   )
   5) Sgt. McBride dropped out of high school and signed up for the Army. (   )

   a. He is somewhat emotionally closed.
   b. His temper is a bit short.
   c. He could use the discipline.
   d. He likes to show what's what.
   e. He is a soldier's soldier.

3. **Back home, what would Sgt. McBride NOT mind doing? Choose two.** — (   ) (   )
   a. going back to the battlefield
   b. taking care of the unpaid bills
   c. visiting an Outback Steakhouse with his Army friends
   d. riding his tuned-up sports car

Editors' Note

　世界の国は，20世紀のどこかの時点で，アメリカにあこがれた経験をもっている．♪「右のポッケにゃ夢がある，左のポッケにゃチューインガム……」．占領下の日本で，12歳の美空ひばりがスローなタップを踏みながら歌ったこの歌には，大げさにいうと，20世紀の地球の歴史がこもっているのだ．瓦礫のなかで，アメリカ軍兵士をまぶしく眺めたのは「東京キッド」だけではない．ロンドンでもローマでも同じだった．冷戦終結後はブカレストの若者たちも，ステージを跳梁するマイケル・ジャクソンに，純粋な目の輝きをもって反応した．

　20世紀に，5つの大陸を順ぐりに席巻していったアメリカの吸引力．その興奮を一度も味わったことのない珍しい人々が，アメリカの内奥に暮らしている．銃とバイブルを手放さず，自業自得の貧者を救う福祉も，健康保険も間違っていると感じ，「ワシントン」のエリートを敵視してブッシュやマケインに投票する人たちだ．

　彼らの祖父やそのまた祖父は，いろんな国の田舎から，食えなくなってこの国にきた．そして広大な国土に散らばり，人里離れた場所に小さくかたまり，厳しい自然と闘ってきた．だが，いまだもって浮かばれない．そのうちに自動車文明と，ファストフードと，ケーブルTVがやってきた．

　ジャンクな車とジャンクな番組が，彼らの日常を構成する．

　この章で描かれた兵士とその妻の住む町は特定されていないが，彼らの集う Outback Steakhouse の近くのショッピング・センターの光景は，なんとなく目に浮かぶ．マーケットからカートを押して駐車場に出てきた，パーマ頭のお母ちゃん．カートの上には，トイレット・ロールの山と，原色ドリンク入りの巨大ペットボトルと，小さな子供が乗っている．ママの胴回りは50インチほどあるだろうか．腹一杯食べなければ満足感の得られない廉価低質の加工食品をもりもり消費して，食品業界を繁栄させることはできても，フィットネスにお金を注ぎ込むことができるほど豊かではない．そんな彼らの日々の不満が，大統領選の票のゆくえを——すなわち世界政治を——左右する．アメリカを深く知ろう．

[Answers for the a/b Questions]
[41] — a., [49] — b., [60] — a., [68] — a., [94] — b., [134] — b.

Session 11

The Power of the Tabloids

Jane & Michael Sterns

The *National Enquirer* of the early 1960s was a fifteen-cent-per-copy weekly weirdo's delight filled with what one critic called "all the news that's *un*fit to print." In ugly black-and-white, it regularly featured photos of mangled corpses, deformed faces, and grisly crime scenes alongside articles that told foul and horrid melodramas about the dregs of society. "If a story is good," said the paper's editor in 1965, "no matter how vile, we'll run it." As of 1965 it had a circulation of 1.1 million, with virtually all copies sold at city newsstands alongside nudie magazines. (The fifteen-thousand-odd subscribers received their issues through the mail in plain brown wrappers.)

It hadn't been always so scummy. Founded as a Hearst publication in 1926 as the *New York Enquirer*, it took a relatively high road among tabloids, in contrast to the city's *Daily Mirror*, *Daily News* and *Graphic*, all of which fought with each other with the most scandalous stories and shocking pictures (including the *Daily News'* notorious, illicitly snapped page-one photo of Mrs. Ruth Snyder, who had been convicted of murdering her husband, frying in Sing-Sing's electric chair in 1928). It was their no-holds-barred circulation war in the twenties that gave tabloids the reputation for sensationalism; but the *Enquirer* soon became known as much for its thorough sports coverage as for its cheesecake

The Power of the Tabloids

[2] **fifteen-cent-per-copy:** 1 部 50 セントの．copy は本など印刷物を数える単位．
weirdo's delight: 変な趣味のやつが目を輝かせるようなもの

[3] **unfit to print:**「活字にするには不適切な」．"all the news that's fit to print" という *The New York Times* のスローガンのもじり．

[5] **mangled corpses:** めった切りにされた死体
deformed: 形が崩れた
grisly: gruesome; horrid; macabre. より口語的に言い換えるなら，awful; terrible; horrible.

[6] **foul and horrid melodramas:** 薄汚くて忌まわしい煽情的ストーリー

[7] **dreg(s):** おり，かす，取るに足らないもの

[8] **vile:** unpleasant; morally bad; low
we'll run it: 私たちは（その記事を）掲載します

[9] **circulation:** the number of copies sold
virtually all copies: almost (nearly, practically, just about) all copies

[11] **The fifteen-thousand-odd subscribers:** 15,000 人あまりの定期購読者．
cf. twenty odd years ago

[13] **scummy:** 気色悪い，汚くて軽蔑すべき
a Hearst publication: 新聞王ウィリアム・ハースト (1863–1951) が築いたメディア財閥の出版物

[14] **took a relatively high road among tabloids:** was [a. more / b. less] respectable than most tabloids

[18] **notorious:** well-known for something bad
illicitly snapped: 不法に撮影した

[19] **had been convicted of murdering:** 殺人で有罪になった

[20] **frying:**「フライになる」というのは「電気で焦げる」ということ．言い換えると，electrocuted (= electricly executed).
Sing-Sing: 1826 年に完成した，歴史的に悪名高いニューヨーク州刑務所

[21] **no-holds-barred:**「何でもありの」，「どんな組み方も反則にならない」という意味の，レスリングに由来するフレーズ．
circulation war: 発行部数（拡張）戦争

[24] **cheesecake pictures:** セクシーな写真

pictures of pinup girls. Still, by 1952 its prurience seemed a remnant of another era, and circulation had dropped to 17,000 when it was sold by the Hearst Corporation to Generoso Pope for the bargain of $75,000.

Mr. Pope was well prepared to take the *Enquirer* to a new level of success. He already had experience in the newspaper business, having boosted the circulation of *Il Progresso*, an Italian-language daily founded by his father. How? By livening it up with maudlin editorials, goggle-eyed features about fashion extremes and eccentric personalities, and stunts staged hand in hand with press-hungry celebrities. Before that, after graduating from MIT at age nineteen, Pope had worked as an employee of the Central Intelligence Agency in the psychological warfare division. Obviously, he was well-trained in the inner trickeries of the human mind.

Mr. Pope, who said he was inspired by auto accidents' uncanny ability to draw crowds, sought "something jazzy" for the *New York Enquirer*. His publishing vision was described by *The New York Times* in his 1988 obituary (he died at age sixty-one, of a heart attack) as "a showcase of the bizarre, with tales of mutilation, sadism, murder, and gory accidents." This formula made circulation skyrocket. *New York Enquirer*, soon renamed the *National Enquirer* to reflect its growing readership, hired some of the cleverest writers away from legitimate papers by offering them double their usual salary, and had them use their talents to transform humdrum wire-service copy and freelance writers' perfunctory stories into juicy melodrama. Word went out to newspapers in cities throughout the world that whenever they had an item or photo too gross and disgusting to print themselves, a hefty fee could be earned by selling it to the *Enquirer*.

By the late 1960s, the porno-violence magazine business was getting very competitive. Censorship had all but van-

The Power of the Tabloids

- [25] **prurience** [prúriəns]: お色気路線
- [26] **(a) remnant of another era:** 過去の遺物
- [31] *Il Progresso*: 英語の *The Progress* にあたるイタリア語．daily は「日刊紙」．
- [33] **livening it up:** (*Il Progresso*) に生気を吹き込む，活気づける
  maudlin: 安っぽい感情に身を任せるような (*cf.* p. 117, [86])
  editorial(s): 新聞・雑誌のエディター自身によるオピニオン・コラム
  goggle-eyed features:（目玉が飛び出すほどの）たまげた特集
- [34] **fashion extremes:** 極端なファッション
- [35] **stunts staged hand in hand with press-hungry celebrities:** メディアに注目されたい有名人と共謀して仕掛けられたやらせ
- [36] **MIT:** Massachusetts Institute of Technology. マサチューセッツ工科大学
- [37] **the Central Intelligence Agency:** 米国中央情報局 (CIA)
- [38] **the psychological warfare division:** 敵の情報収集と士気低下を図る研究・立案を担当した部署
- [39] **the inner trickeries of the human mind:** 人の心の複雑で不可思議な動き
- [42] **uncanny ability to draw crowds:** 野次馬を引き寄せる無気味な力
  jazzy: spirited; exciting（感傷的なポップスに比べて，ジャズが景気のいい，心躍らせる音楽だった時代のスラング）
- [44] **his 1988 obituary:** 彼が 1988 年に死んだときの死亡記事
- [45] **died ... of a heart attack:** 心臓発作で亡くなった
  a showcase of the bizarre: 奇異なる物の展示ケース
- [46] **mutilation:**（体部を損傷させるような）激しい暴力
  gory: bloody; blood-soaked; grisly
- [47] **made circulation skyrocket:** 販売数を飛躍的に伸ばした
- [48] **to reflect its growing readership:** because of the increase in the number of its readers
- [50] **legitimate papers:** 世間一般に認知された新聞
  double their usual salary:「ふつうの給料の 2 倍」．double の使い方に注意．
- [51] **transform humdrum wire-service copy and freelance writers' perfunctory stories into juicy melodrama:** 通信社から入ってくる退屈な記事や，外注で書かせていた通り一遍のストーリーを，みずみずしいメロドラマに仕立てる
- [53] **Word went out:**「うわさが広まった」．次行の that 以下がうわさの内容．
- [55] **print themselves:** 自社の新聞に載せる
- [56] **a hefty fee could be earned:** 多額の謝礼が得られる
- [58] **porno-violence:** porno- は英語では接頭語．pornography の略語は porn.
- [59] **was getting very competitive:** 競争がとても激しくなっていた
  Censorship had all but vanished: 検閲はなくなったも同然になった

141

ished, and so the marketplace was crowded with periodicals every bit as repulsive as the *Enquirer,* and some (like the *National Tattler*) even more so. To make matters worse, city newsstands were dying off; magazine sales were shifting into supermarkets, where the brutal old *Enquirer* would never fit. In 1968 Generoso Pope performed a miracle: he regained the soul of his newspaper and made it fit for supermarket shoppers. He hired an all-new staff and completely cut out gore and crime in favor of higher-weight features about aliens from outer space, test-tube babies, dogs with ESP, children's essay contests, marvelous hemorrhoid cures, evangelistic columns by no less than Billy Graham, predictions by psychics, appeals to help the handicapped, and spy photos of Jackie Onassis—what one critic called "soft core sensationalism," or what was known during tabloid wars of the 1920s as "gee-whiz journalism." Pope explained the source of his new publishing philosophy: "I went back and read some old *Reader's Digests* of the 1930s, when the *Digest* was having its greatest growth. Most of the stories were about triumphs over adversity, breakthroughs in medicine, UFOs, and nutrition. The most important element was that most of it was *uplifting.*"

The *Enquirer* was still no competition for *The New York Times,* but its publisher didn't want it to be: "What you see on page one of *The New York Times* does not really interest most people," he said. In particular the *Enquirer* began to specialize in what is known as *human* interest—stories about weird, lucky, heroic, and pitiful people, and always so successful that Rupert Murdock copied it in 1974 when he began publishing the *Star,* which became the first of the tabloids to use color pictures on the cover.

About the time of its editorial change in direction, *Enquirer* offices were moved to New Jersey; then in 1971, they were relocated in the small town of Lantana, Florida, where the born-again newspaper sponsored a Little League

The Power of the Tabloids

- [61] **every bit as repulsive as:** repulsive な（不快な気持ちをかき立てる）ことにかけては，まったくひけをとらない

    some ... even more so: some were even more repulsive. その代表として名前が挙がっている *National Tattler* の tattler は「悪口媒体」といった意味．
- [62] **To make matters worse:** さらに悪いことに
- [64] **the brutal old *Enquirer* would never fit:** かつての粗野な路上販売紙が，主婦の夢を商う新時代の消費空間に合うはずはない，ということ．
- [65] **he regained the soul of his newspaper:** *Il Progresso* の魂を取り戻した（具体的には p. 140, [33] から始まる文を参照）．
- [68] **cut out gore and crime in favor of ...:** 残忍さと犯罪物をなくして〜を容れた

    higher-weight: 分厚い，読みがある
- [70] **ESP:** extra-sensory perception　いわゆる「第六感」や「霊視」を通した知覚

    hemorrhoid cures: 痔の治療法．「痔」の発音は [hémrɔ̀id]．
- [71] **evangelistic columns by no less than Billy Graham:**「なんとビリー・グラハム本人による宗教コラム」．Billy Graham は，野球場を満杯にする人気を長年保った大御所の説教師．**no less than:** none other than (*cf.* p. 117, [61])

    predictions by psychics: 霊媒による予言
- [73] **Jackie Onassis:** ジョン・F・ケネディ大統領の妻ジャクリーン（愛称ジャッキー）は，後にギリシャの大富豪オナシスと再婚した．
- [75] **gee-whiz:**「おやまあ」「こいつぁたまげた」という語感．発音は [dʒíːwíz]．
- [79] **adversity:** difficulties; hardship; misfortune

    breakthroughs in medicine:（壁をつきやぶっての）医学の躍進
- [80] **nutrition:** 栄養，食と健康
- [81] *uplifting*: 心を高揚させる，元気にさせる
- [82] **no competition for ...:** 〜とわたり合う存在では全然なかった
- [88] **Rupert Murdoch:** ルパート・マードック (1931–) はオーストラリア出身のメディア王．のちに Fox TV でアメリカの三大ネットワーク体制 (ABC, CBS, NBC) を食い破る．
- [93] **were relocated in:** moved again to

    Lantana, Florida: マイアミの北約 100 km の海辺に位置する人口 1 万ほどの町
- [94] **the born-again newspaper:**（保守層に受け入れられるべく）生まれ変わった *Enquirer* のこと．born-again の原意は「キリストの信仰に目覚めた」．

    sponsored a Little League team: 少年野球をバックアップするということは，アメリカの保守的・感情的な核心に切り込んだということ．

team. In 1972, circulation was up to 2.6 million copies every week.

More and more since the move to Florida, the *National Enquirer* has focused its cover and its articles on stars of TV, movies, and popular music. Dismissing *People* magazine as "too highbrow," Generoso Pope sharpened a style of journalism that had been pioneered in Hollywood's *Confidential* magazine: the journalism of embarrassment. Sometimes it features nice stories about celebrities, but mostly the *Enquirer* is known for its ruthless dish. "Prod, push, and probe the main characters in the story," Generoso Pope wrote in a 1973 memo to his staff. "Help them frame their answers. Ask leading questions like, 'Do you ever go in the corner and cry?'"

The *Enquirer*'s voracious hunger to dig, really dig, into people's private lives has sparked its reporters to rummage through garbage, fly over weddings and funerals in camera-equipped helicopters, and pay huge sums of money with what was described by *Rolling Stone* as "the fattest checkbook in journalism" to anonymous sources for spy photos, medical records, and other confidential information. This tactic hadn't changed since Mr. Pope acquired the magazine in the 1950s.

But for better or for worse, by the 1980s the *Enquirer* had clearly made itself a publication whose time had come. In earlier eras, there was news and there was gossip, and the two were treated differently by readers and by the press. News was considered important, whereas gossip was thought of as trivial and generally unworthy of intelligent people's attention. Some newspapers had gossip columnists, or possibly even a gossip page, but they were segregated from the rest of the paper; as for the *Enquirer*, which according to one critic "preyed on that which is most reprehensible in human nature," no one took it seriously. Now, although it has plenty of enemies and people who loathe it, the *Enquirer*

The Power of the Tabloids

- [99] **Dismissing:** rejecting; denying; ignoring

    People **magazine:** 1974年創刊の，写真をふんだんに使った――けっして highbrow（インテリ向け）ではない――セレブ雑誌
- [101] *Confidential* **magazine:** 1952–1978. スキャンダル暴露誌のパイオニアとされる．
- [102] **the journalism of embarrassment:** スターを embarrass させる（痛いところ，恥ずかしいところをつく）ジャーナリズムという意味．
- [104] **ruthless dish:** 情け容赦ないゴシップ

    Prod, push, and probe . . . :「突いて，押して，探れ」．P の頭韻に注目．
- [106] **Help them frame their answers. Ask leading questions . . . :** 答えをはめる枠を用意し，答えを誘導するような質問をしろ
- [109] **voracious hunger:** 飽くことをしらぬ貪欲さ

    really dig: ハンパじゃなく食らいつく
- [110] **sparked its reporters to . . . :**（火花が散るほどの勢いで）リポーターを〜に走らせた

    rummage through garbage:（証拠品を求めて）家から出たゴミをあさる
- [113] *Rolling Stone*: 1967年の若者文化が生んだ，元祖ロックジャーナル

    the fattest checkbook in journalism: ネタを買いあさるのに，他のどこよりもふんだんに金を使うこと．fat は "fat wallet"（札で膨れた財布）からの転用．
- [114] **to anonymous sources:**「匿名の情報源に」．動詞 pay からつづく
- [115] **confidential:** p. 113 参照
- [118] **for better or for worse:**「事の善し悪しはともかく」．for better or worse とも．
- [119] **whose time had come:**「それの時代がきた」とは，時代とマッチして大きく繁栄するに至ったということ．
- [125] **segregated:** separated; isolated; set apart
- [127] **preyed on that which is most reprehensible in human nature:** 人間性のなかでもっとも卑しい部分を食い物にした．reprehensible < reprehend: とがめる
- [129] **loathe it:** hate it; despise it; cannot stand it

has pretty well managed to shed its reputation as a freaky and essentially irrelevant sideshow; it has become a pop culture force to be reckoned with.

A change of climate has helped as well. By the end of the celebrity-crazed 1980s, even such apparently consequential periodicals as *Esquire* and *Vanity Fair* might just as easily be expected to run pictures and articles about Donald Trump or Nancy Reagan as about Henry Kissinger or Teddy Kennedy. Which was news and which was gossip? It has become increasingly difficult to know the difference, and so the *Enquirer*, which is nearly all unabashed gossip (verified 100 percent factual, its editor's guarantee), has been transformed into a deliverer of what is now considered news. If you doubt it, remember that it was the *Enquirer* that, in 1988, ran the career-destroying photo of Senator Gary Hart cavorting with girlfriend Donna Rice. Although it is still unapologetically scandalous and often utterly preposterous, it has become as mainstream-seeming (and as trivializing) as nearly any other popular periodical.

In a 1990 *New York Times* story about the increasing respectability of the *Enquirer* among the advertising community, one executive J. Walter Thompson said that forward-looking advertisers simply had to overcome their negative feelings about the tabloid. Staid old Proctor & Gamble had already bought ad space in the *Enquirer* and the *Star* (now owned by the same company) because P&G was eager to tap the buying power of the paper's readers, half of whom, according to demographic surveys, are women eighteen to thirty-four years old—a group of consumers with prodigious buying power. "The people who plunk down their money and read these publications," said the ad exec, "they don't think they're schlocky people."

The Power of the Tabloids

- [130] **has pretty well managed to shed its reputation as . . . :** 〜だという悪評を取り去ることにかなりの部分成功した
- [131] **irrelevant sideshow:** 現実とは関係しない見せ物小屋のショーのようなもの
  a pop culture force to be reckoned with: 無視できないポップ文化の力
- [134] **the celebrity-crazed 1980s:** セレブで盛り上がった 80 年代
  consequential periodicals: まともな意義や存在感のある雑誌
- [135] *Esquire*：1933 年に創刊された（高級志向の）男性向けマガジン
  Vanity Fair：戦前に廃刊になった有名雑誌の名を継いで，1981 年に出版開始．ポップカルチャーとファッションを中心に，政治・文化を広く扱う．
  might just as easily be expected to run 〈A〉 as 〈B〉: A も B も分け隔てなく掲載すると考えられる
- [136] **Donald Trump:** (1946–) 不動産からメディアまで多方面で活躍する億万長者．
- [137] **Nancy Reagan:** (1921–) 80 年代に大統領夫人として多くの話題をまいた．
  Henry Kissinger: (1923–) ニクソン政権 (1969–74) の国務長官として，中国との外交やベトナム戦争終結を牽引．
  Teddy Kennedy: (1932–2009) エドワード・ケネディ上院議員．二人の兄（大統領ジョン，司法長官ロバート）もそれぞれ Jack, Bobby と愛称で親しまれた．
- [140] **nearly all unabashed gossip :** 紙面全体が臆面もなくゴシップ
  verified 100 percent factual, its editor's guarantee: 100％ 事実間違いなし，編集長の保証付き
- [142] **what is now considered news:** *i.e.* what used to be considered gossip
- [144] **Senator Gary Hart:** コロラド選出のハート上院議員は，ヨット上の不倫写真がすっぱ抜かれ，1988 年の大統領候補選から撤退を余儀なくされた．
- [146] **unapologetically scandalous:** 堂々とスキャンダルを売り物にしている
  utterly preposterous: まったく常軌を逸している
- [147] **trivializing:**（物事を，世界を）卑小化する
- [151] **forward-looking:** 時代の変化に対して前向きの
- [152] **overcome their negative feelings:** 否定的な気持ちを克服する
- [153] **Staid old:** serious-minded; conventional; sober
  Proctor & Gamble: P&G のロゴで親しまれる，家庭用品の巨大企業．
- [155] **tap:** use; draw on; make use of
- [157] **demographic surveys:** 人口構成に関わる性別や年齢層別の調査
- [158] **prodigious:** huge; enormous; tremendous
- [159] **plunk down their money:** お金を（ポンと）出す
- [160] **the ad exec:** the advertisement executive. 広告担当の重役
  they don't think they're schlocky people: *National Enquirer* の読者は自分たちをケチな人間とは思っていない（彼ら相手にいい商売ができる）

[Session 11] Comprehension Check

Complete the sentences by choosing a or b.

1) The *National Enquirer* was founded in the [a. 1920s / b. 1950s] as the *New York Enquirer*, a tabloid newspaper published by the famous Hearst family.
2) It was not as [a. respectable / b. disgusting] as some other tabloids of the city like *Daily Mirror*.
3) Tabloids in those days competed with each other in their sensationalism to increase their [a. good reputation / b. circulation], and the rather old-fashioned *Enquirer* fell behind.
4) Under the new owner Generoso Pope, the *Enquirer* [a. took a relatively high road / b. reached a new level of success].
5) Pope had experience [a. in psychological warfare / b. as a fiction writer] and knew how the human mind worked.
6) He hired the cleverest writers to give [a. juicy melodrama / b. very accurate reports].
7) The *Enquirer* was famous for paying a handsome amount of money for articles and photos too [a. risky / b. expensive] for others.
8) In the late 1960s, Pope successfully changed the contents of his newspaper to be fit for [a. supermarket shoppers / b. newsstand buyers].
9) To be able to do this without [a. losing its soul / b. any changes at all] is said to be a miracle.
10) Ever since its move to Florida, the *Enquirer* has further emphasized its [a. soft-core sensationalism, focusing on stories that are extreme but uplifting / b. hunger for gossip, digging into the private lives of celebrities].

Editors' Note

　National Enquirer はエグかった．まさに血みどろトンデモ系情報のオンパレード．1960 年代，スーパーのレジの近くでは同じ号がこれでもか，とばかりに並んでおり，ギトギトの写真を載せた一面がこちらをじっと見つめていた．ケナゲな子供は目をそらす．とっても見たい．でも見てはいけない世界であることを知っていたからだ．

　それがいわゆるセレブリティのスキャンダル紙になり変わるのは，本セッションによれば 1970 年代のあたりから．さらに最近ではアンジェリーナ・ジョリーやブラッド・ピット，オプラ・ウィンフリーやパリス・ヒルトンらの「常連さん」ネタの合間を縫って，政界スキャンダルでも株を上げ，しっかり「ジャーナリズム」の一翼を担っているらしい．

　たとえば 2008 年，民主党内ではヒラリー・クリントン，バラク・オバマに次いでナンバー・スリーの大統領候補と目されていたジョン・エドワーズが，指名候補争いから撤退した．*Enquirer* が報道した不倫疑惑がきっかけである．エドワーズ夫人は乳ガンの再発に苦しんでおり，そんな中，不倫相手とのあいだには子供が生まれ……と同紙の報道はとどまるところを知らない．だが，このときほかの大手新聞や雑誌は遠巻きにしていた．君子危うきに近寄らず，あまりにも「タブロイド的な」内容だったので，あり得ないとでも思ったのだろう．

　ところがその後，エドワーズは選挙資金をスキャンダルもみ消しのために不正流用した疑いで連邦大陪審の取り調べを受け，2010 年，ついに不倫相手とのあいだに子供がいることを認めた．かくして *Enquirer* の一連の報道は，驚くべきことにピューリッツァー賞の候補にもエントリーしたらしい．

　ヒラリー・クリントンが異星人の赤ん坊を養子にする，なんておバカな記事はもはや同紙には期待できないのか．だとしたらちょっぴり残念である．

[Answer for the a/b Question]

[14] — a.

Session 12

The Monster Is Born

David J. Skal

Seventeen-year-old Mary Shelley wrote Frankenstein, or the Modern Prometheus *in 1816. The novel was published two years later and was repeatedly played on stage throughout the 19th century. It was the invention of the cinema, however, that brought the story of Dr. Frankenstein and his monster to international fame. The monster itself was a creation of machinery and electricity. Therefore, it is all the more natural that the story has strong affinities with the movie as a medium, which is also the child of technology. As early as 1910, Thomas Edison made a one-reel* Frankenstein, *but the classic of classics is the 1931 version, directed by James Whale, who had come to Hollywood prominence through various war pictures. Casting for the movie went smoothly enough, but the big question was who was going to play the most important part: the monster.*

Perfect Face for the Monster

"I spent ten years in Hollywood without causing the slightest stir," Boris Karloff recalled in later years. "Then one day I was sitting in the commissary at Universal, having lunch, when a man sent a note over to my table, asking if I'd like to audition for the part of a monster."

One of Whale's companions had suggested that he look at Boris Karloff, who had recently made a striking gangster

The Monster Is Born

[1]　*Mary Shelley*: (1797–1851) 父は社会思想家の William Godwin. メアリーは父の愛弟子であった詩人の Percy Shelly と駆け落ちし，いっしょに過ごしたスイスのレマン湖畔で *Frankenstein, or the Modern Prometheus* を執筆した．

[2]　**Prometheus** [prəmíːθiəs]: プロメーテウス，ギリシア神話の巨人神．天の火を盗んで人に与えたためゼウスに罰せられた．

[4]　*the invention of the cinema*: 諸説あるが一般的には1895年リュミエール兄弟がパリのグラン・カフェで開いた上映会が現在の映画の出発点といわれている．

　　brought ... to international fame: made ... world-famous

[7]　**all the more**: そのぶん益々．*She was wearing a flower in her hair, which made her all the more attractive.*

　　has strong affinities: is closely related．テクノロジーから生まれたモンスターの物語が，映画メディアというテクノロジーの申し子によって語られるところに「強い類縁性がある」．

[9]　*Thomas Edison made a one-reel* **Frankenstein**: レコードに続いて映画ビジネスにも進出したエジソン (1847–1931) が，Edison Studio で制作した *Frankenstein* は (当時の映画の例にもれず) 「一巻物」で，長さは12分少々だった．

[10]　*James Whale*: (1889–1957) イギリス演劇界で活躍後ハリウッドへ．『フランケンシュタイン』(1931) のほかに『透明人間』(*The Invisible Man*, 1933)，『フランケンシュタインの花嫁』(*The Bride of Frankenstein*, 1935) などを監督した．

[11]　*prominence*: fame; greatness; celebrity

[16]　**without causing the slightest stir**: 全く鳴かず飛ばずで．stir: commotion; sensation; excitement

[17]　*Boris Karloff*: (1887–1969) イギリスに生まれ育ち，カナダで役者デビュー．ハリウッドに来てからも無声映画の脇役時代が続いた．*Frankenstein* のヒットの翌年には『ミイラ男』(*The Mummy*) でも有名に．

[18]　**commissary**: 映画スタジオの食堂

　　Universal: ハリウッドの基礎を築いた実業家カール・レムリが，Universal Film Manufacturing Company を興したのは1912年のこと．Universal Pictures として現在に至る．

[20]　**audition**:「オーディションを受ける」という意味の動詞．

[22]　**made a striking gangster**: impressively played the role of a gangster

in *The Criminal Code*. Karloff sometimes drove a truck for a lumberyard between acting assignments. He had no illusions about the film industry owing him a livelihood, and no expectations whatsoever that his name would soon become a household word for horror. Whale thought Karloff's face had interesting possibilities. An amateur painter himself, the director sketched the actor, experimentally exaggerating the bony ridges of Karloff's head. He showed his ideas to Jack P. Pierce, head of Universal's makeup department since 1926.

Pierce was considered a genius by those who worked with him, although perhaps an egotistical one. He never publicly acknowledged Whale's part in developing the *Frankenstein* makeup. He said that he had spent three months of preliminary research in such areas as anatomy, surgery, criminology, and electrodynamics. The final monster design, he maintained, was a more or less logical result of these efforts.

Design in the Machine Age

In retrospect, it seems clear that Pierce, and Whale also, drew less consciously on design drafts than from the stylized machine-age aesthetic which, by 1931, had become a dominant force in the applied arts. Eclectically inspired by cubism, expressionism, and architectural theories of the Bauhaus, the zig-zagging style soon made its way into the worlds of advertising, decoration, and industrial design.

The movement had begun in 1925 in Paris, at the *Exposition Internationale des Arts Décoratifs et Industriels Modernes*, and the show's title gave birth to the two names used most often to describe the movement: *Art Deco* and *Art Moderne*. American designers further refined the aesthetic, and *Fortune* later recalled that Fifth Avenue shops soon filled their display windows with the "grotesque mannequins, the cub-

The Monster Is Born

[23] *The Criminal Code*: 邦題は『光に叛く者』. 1931年公開のギャング映画.
drove a truck for a lumberyard: 製材所に雇われてトラックの運転をしていた

[24] **had no illusions about the film industry owing him a livelihood:** 映画業界で食べていけると考えるほど甘くなかった. the film industry owing him a livelihood: the film industry having to support his living

[26] **no expectations whatsoever:**「これっぽっちの期待もしていない」. whatsoever は否定の強調.

[27] **a household word for horror:** ホラーといえば誰もが連想する名前

[29] **experimentally:** 実験的に, うまくいくかどうか試しに

[30] **exaggerating the bony ridges:** 骨張った隆起を誇張して

[37] **preliminary research:** 事前調査
anatomy, surgery, criminology, and electrodynamics: 解剖学, 外科医術, 犯罪学, そして電気力学

[39] **maintained:** claimed; asserted; declared

[42] **In retrospect:** 振り返ってみると

[43] **drew less consciously on ⟨A⟩ than ⟨B⟩:** 意識的に利用した度合いはBよりAの方が少ない; AよりもBを積極的に利用した
design drafts:（怪物の）デザインの下絵

[44] **the stylized machine-age aesthetic:**「様式化されたマシーン・エイジの美学」. 機械・速度・効率・進化などを連想させるイメージを誘惑的に用いる.

[45] **the applied arts:**「応用芸術」. 絵画・彫刻等の純粋芸術 (fine arts) に対して, 広告, 装飾, 工業デザインなどを指す.
Eclectically inspired: influenced by various ideas

[46] **cubism, expressionism, and architectural theories of the Bauhaus:** キュビズム（立体派の絵画），（絵画や映画における）表現主義, およびバウハウスの建築理論. Bauhaus は, 1919年にドイツで創設された学校. 建築を含む工業技術と芸術の統合をめざし, 合理主義・機能主義的なデザインを特徴とする.

[47] **the zig-zagging style:** ジグザグなどの直線模様を多用するスタイル
made its way into . . . : went into; spread into; was absorbed and used in

[50] **the *Exposition Internationale des Arts Décoratifs et Industriels Modernes*:** the International Exposition of Decorative and Modern Industrial Arts. 装飾芸術・現代産業芸術国際博覧会

[53] *Art Deco* and *Art Moderne*:「アール・デコ」と「アール・モデルヌ」

[54] *Fortune* **later recalled that . . . :** ビジネス誌『フォーチュン』は後の号で, 〜だったと振り返っている

[55] **Fifth Avenue shops:** ニューヨークの目抜き通り「五番街」に並ぶ高級店

[56] **the cubist props, the gaga designs:** キュビズム風の小道具や奇抜なデザイン

153

ist props, the gaga designs" that would define the style.

"Grotesque mannequin" well describes the Frankenstein monster, an amalgam of conventional bodies torn apart and reassembled according to new electromechanical principles. The square head—a common motif in advertising graphics of the time—powerfully evokes the difficulty of an old consciousness forced to occupy a new paradigm, a round brain bolted uneasily into a machine-tooled skull. As the movie script described its structure: "The top of its head has a curious flat ridge like the lid of a box. The hair is fairly short and quite obviously combed over the ridge to hide the defect of the joining where the brain was put in." The monster is a modernist designer's nightmare: the seams show, the clamps and bolts stick out. Form follows function, but just barely.

Beyond Whale and Pierce, various other designers in Universal's production and even in its promotion department had contributed visual concepts for the monster-in-development. Two recurring elements were especially notable: the protruding brow suggesting evolutionary regression, and the paradoxically futurist design of a completely mechanical man along the lines of "Televox," an automaton developed by Westinghouse Laboratories in the late 1920s. The most "mechanical" concept, by Universal's poster illustrator Karoly Grosz, first introduced the notion of

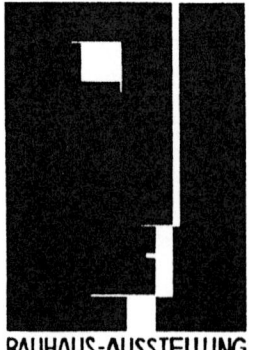

A Bauhaus postcard (1923) and an early concept for the *Frankenstein* makeup

The Monster Is Born

- [57] **define the style:** アール・デコやアール・モデルヌ様式の決定的な特徴を示す
- [59] **an amalgam of conventional bodies torn apart and reassembled according to new electromechanical principles:** 前時代的な身体を解体し，新時代の電気機械的原理によって組み替えたものの寄せ集め
- [62] **powerfully evokes:** 〜を強く感じさせる．evoke: to call forth; bring to mind
  the difficulty of an old consciousness forced to occupy a new paradigm: 「新しい世界の型に押し込められた旧式の意識（頭）の困難」．続く言い替えでは，a round brain が旧式の意識を，machine-tooled skull（工作機械で作った頭蓋骨）が新しいパラダイムを表している．
- [66] **has a curious flat ridge:** 奇妙に平べったくて（おでこに沿って）峰のように隆起している
- [68] **(the) defect of the joining:** 「接合の欠点」．縫い合わせが巧くいっていないところ．
- [69] **the seams show:** 縫い目が見えてしまっている
- [70] **the clamps and bolts:** 締め金やボルト
  Form follows function, but just barely: 「形体は機能に従うというが，そうとばかりは言いがたい」．機能がそのまま形をなしたようなものが最高のデザインだという金言も，モンスターにはなかなか当てはめがたい（かろうじて成り立つだけ）ということ．
- [74] **the monster-in-development:** 制作段階にある怪物
- [75] **recurring elements:** 繰り返し出てくる要素
- [76] **the protruding brow:** 突き出ている眉の骨
  evolutionary regression: 進化の退行
- [77] **the paradoxically futurist design:** 「（原始人への退行と）矛盾する未来主義的デザイン」．futurism は第一次世界大戦前夜のイタリアで始まった，現代テクノロジーの活力を礼賛する芸術運動．
- [78] **along the lines of "Televox":** 「〈テレヴォクス〉と同じような」．Televox (Mr. Herbert Televox) は 1927 年に作られた「しゃべる」ロボット (automaton).
- [79] **Westinghouse Latoratories:** 交流発電の事業化に成功した George Westinghouse が興したアメリカの大手電機企業の研究所．電球からラジオ放送，原子力発電まで，20 世紀の技術開発に広く貢献した．
- [80] **The most "mechanical" concept . . . first introduced . . . :** そのうちもっとも「機械的な」案は初めて〜を採り入れた
- [81] **Karoly Grosz:** カロリー・グロシュはホラー映画のポスター制作で有名．

155

a steel bolt through the neck, a detail that in itself would come to symbolize the total Frankenstein mythos.

Mechanical Man in Agony

The actual making of the monster was astonishing in itself. "We were all fascinated by the development of Karloff's face and head," recalled actress Mae Clarke, who was the heroine of the movie and had a ringside seat at the construction site. "White putty on the face was toned down to a corpse-like gray. Then there was a sudden inspiration to give the face a green tint. It awed us and gave Boris and the rest of us a different feeling about the whole concept." (Karloff himself is said to have suggested the heavily puttied eyelids, which added a dimension of pathos and incomprehension.) [85]

[90]

When the makeup was ready for a screen test—in black-and-white — Karloff had no idea how effective the finished product would be. Would it inspire horror... or laughter? "I was thinking this, practicing my walk, as I rounded a bend in the corridor and came face-to-face with this prop man. [95]

[100]

"He was the first man to see the monster. I watched to study his reaction. It was quick to come. He turned white, gurgled, and lunged out of sight down the corridor. Never

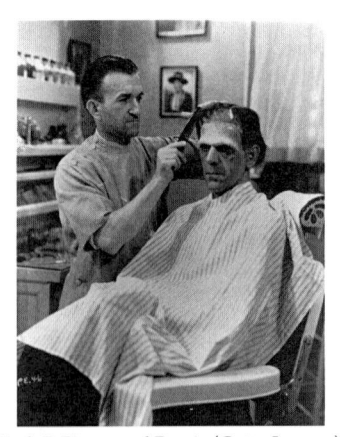

Jack P. Pierce and Borris (Getty Images)

The Monster Is Born

- [82] **a detail that in itself would . . . symbolize the total Frankenstein mythos:** それを見ただけで人々がフランケンシュタインの物語を思い出すほど，首にねじこまれた1本のボルトは象徴的なパーツだった．
- [88] **had a ringside seat at the construction site:**「建築現場でかぶりつきの席にいた」とは，怪物が develop していく（特殊メークによってだんだん造形が仕上がっていく）現場をつぶさに観察できたということ．
- [89] **putty:** パテ
  was toned down to a corpse-like gray: 色調を落として死体のような灰色になった
- [90] **there was a sudden inspiration to give the face a green tint:** 顔をやや緑っぽくしてみようというアイディアが突然ひらめいた．
- [91] **It awed us:**「それを見て私たちは畏敬の念を抱いた」．awe は畏敬と驚きと恐怖が混ざった感情を抱かせること．
- [92] **(a) different feeling about the whole concept:**「モンスターのコンセプト全体が違った感じになった」．単に客を怖がらせるための造形ではなくなった．
- [93] **the heavily puttied eyelids:** パテを厚く塗り重ねた瞼
- [94] **added a dimension of . . . :**（表情に）〜という面をつけ加えた
  incomprehension:（人間のようには世界を）理解できていないようす
- [97] **(the) finished product:** 完成品，つまりメイクが完成した怪物のこと．
- [98] **was thinking this:** "Would it inspire horror . . . or laughter?" と自問していた
- [99] **rounded a bend in the corridor:** 廊下の角を曲がった
- [100] **prop man:** 小道具の担当者
- [102] **It was quick to come:** *i.e.* He reacted right away.
  He turned white, gurgled: 顔面蒼白になってゲボゲボいった；言葉にならない音を発した
- [103] **lunged out of sight down the corridor:** 廊下を突っ走って消えて行った

saw him again. Poor chap, I would have liked to thank him. He was the audience that first made me feel like the monster."

Scenes to Remember, Innovations to Scare

There are various elements that contributed to the film's success. For one thing, the director did everything to frighten (or at least startle) the audience. His use of sound—various thuds, bangs, and assorted odd noises—pushed the limits of the time, and was exceptionally effective during the very early "talkie" era.

The opening scene contained what was, for 1931 audiences, a visceral jolt: the sound of earth crashing on the lid of a coffin at a cemetery. A microphone was placed in the casket, the better to magnify the reverberations. Whale also used visuals to unnerve audiences—lightning flashes, ominous shadows, even a grim reaper watching the proceedings in the cemetery.

Frankenstein's gleaming lightning-arc generators, created by electrical engineer Kenneth Strickfaden, were a wholly fanciful, high-wattage commentary on the machine age. "Electricity is life," he once told an interviewer. "We are just a bunch of sparks with various quantities of air." His sentiments reflected the distinctly reductionistic, mechanical-leaning tendencies of much cultural expression since the Great War. Untold millions had been left with the feeling that modern life—and death—was nothing but an anonymous, crushing assembly line.

Whale's film depicted a monster squarely in the grip of this confusion, a pathetic figure caught between humanism and mechanism. One of the most famous sequences of *Frankenstein* is one that was not seen in its entirety for almost fifty years. The monster encounters a little girl at the edge of a lake. Unfrightened, she leads him in a game of throwing flowers on the water to see them prettily afloat. The monster,

The Monster Is Born

[104]　**Poor chap:** Poor fellow（chap を使うのは，ボリスのイギリス人らしいところ）

[110]　**frighten (or at least startle) the audience:** frighten は心の底から恐怖すること．startle はかなり瞬間的で，怖がらせるよりもびっくりさせるニュアンス．

[111]　**thuds, bangs, and assorted odd noises:**「ズシンとかバーンとか，奇妙な音の取り合わせ」．thud は重量感のある鈍い音，bang は突然の激しい音．

[113]　**"talkie" era:** 1927 年公開の *Jazz Singer* とともに本格的な talking pictures の時代が始まったが，技術的な制約が依然多かった．1931 年に公開された *Frankenstein* では音そのものがアトラクションとなった．

[115]　**a visceral jolt:** 腹の底からぎょっとさせられる体験

[117]　**casket:** coffin と同じで「ひつぎ」

　　　　the better to magnify the reverberations: to magnify the reverberations even more: 反響をより強調するために

[118]　**unnerve:** 怖がらせる，落ちつきを失わせる (unsettle)

　　　　ominous: threatening; gloomy; dark. 名詞形 omen は「不吉な前兆」．

[119]　**a grim reaper watching the proceedings:** 経過（＝埋葬の様子）をじっと見ている死神

[121]　**gleaming:** ギラリと光る

　　　　arc generators:「アーク放電発生装置」．それによって「稲妻」を表現したので，lightning-arc generator と呼んだ．

[123]　**fanciful:** fantastic; unbelievable; brilliant

　　　　high-wattage commentary:「高電圧のコメンタリー」．稲妻さえも人工的に発生させてしまうこの装置こそ，マシンエイジとはどんな時代か雄弁に物語っている．

[124]　**We are just a bunch of sparks with various quantities of air:** 人間の生を放電にたとえた比喩．輝かしい人生も，つつましやかに光るだけの人生もその点は同じだということ．

[126]　**reductionistic, mechanical-leaning tendencies:** すべてを物質の現象に還元し，機械的に捉える思考傾向

[128]　**(the) Great War:** 第一次世界大戦

　　　　Untold millions: 膨大な数の人間．untold は「実数が把握できていない」

　　　　left with the feeling that . . . : 〜という気持ちにつきまとわれていた

[129]　**modern life . . . was nothing but an anonymous, crushing assembly line:** 現代人の人生を，単調にベルトコンベヤー上を進む製品製造過程にたとえたもの．anonymous [ənǽnəməs] は「顔（個性）がない」．映画 *Modern Times* (1936) ではチャップリンが，実際 assembly line で crush され（押しつぶされ）そうになる．

[131]　**squarely in the grip of . . . :** 〜にまともにはまってしまった

[132]　**pathetic:** pitiful; heart-breaking; poor

[134]　**one that was not seen in its entirety:** *i.e.* a sequence that had been edited out

159

carried away with delight, throws the girl in after the flowers, but unlike the daisies, she sinks and drowns. The scene ended up being radically cut.

Karloff insisted in later years that the scene didn't work because James Whale had insisted that he throw the child with a brutal, overhead motion, rather than set her gently on the water. Karloff, who had some back problems, was incapable of hurling the girl very far, and the resulting, compromised action looked buffoonish. Fortunately, just the idea of the child's death was sufficiently upsetting ("No little girl is going to drown in one of my pictures!" Carl Laemmle, Sr., the tycoon-father of the producer, is reported to have fumed to his secretary) so that the scene was cut for many engagements, ending with the monster reaching out for the child (and ironically, leaving some viewers with the impression that they had been spared the spectacle of some shocking molestation).

The drowning scene, found largely intact at the British Film Institute, was finally restored to a videodisc version of *Frankenstein* released by MCA in the 1980s, but still lacks close-ups of the child sinking, etc.—details the English censors marked for excision.

The Monster Is Born

- [138] **carried away with delight:** 歓びに我を忘れて
- [140] **ended up being radically cut:** 最終的には大幅にカットされた
- [141] **the scene didn't work:** シーンが「うまくいかない」とは，映画全体の意味や感動にそぐわないということ．
- [142] **throw the child with a brutal, overhead motion:** 荒々しく頭上に掲げてから少女を（湖に）投げ込む
- [144] **had some back problems:** 背中を痛めていた
  was incapable of hurling: was unable to throw
- [145] **the resulting, compromised action looked buffoonish:** その結果，中途半端な動作になってしまい，それが滑稽に見えた
- [146] **just the idea of the child's death was sufficiently upsetting:** 少女が死ぬというだけで十分に不穏だった
- [147] **No little girl is going to ... :** 「そんなことは絶対ゆるさん」という強い語調を伴う言い方．
- [148] **Carl Laemmle, Sr., the tycoon-father of the producer:** 『フランケンシュタイン』のプロデューサーはカール・レムリ Jr.，その父 (Sr.) がユニバーサル社の創設者．tycoon: ビジネス界の超大物（日本語の「大君」に由来）
- [149] **is reported to have fumed:** 「激怒したと伝えられている」．fume は頭から湯気をたてて怒るイメージ．
- [150] **for many engagements:** （契約上の支障など）いろいろなしがらみのために
- [152] **ironically:** 「皮肉にも」．逆効果になったことをいっている．
- [153] **they had been spared:** 〜を見ずに済んだ
  the spectacle of some shocking molestation: 何らかのショッキングな虐待シーン
- [155] **largely intact:** ほとんど無傷の状態で
  the British Film Institute: 英国映画協会．世界最大級の映画とテレビ番組のアーカイブを有する．
- [156] **was finally restored to a videodisc version:** ビデオディスク版のかたちで復元された
- [158] **details:** close-ups of the child sinking, etc. の言い替えで marked の目的語．
  censor(s): 検閲官
- [159] **marked for excision:** （印をつけて）削除を指示した

[Session 12] **Comprehension Check**

1. **Choose three reasons why Whale's *Frankenstein* became such a big success.**
   ( ) ( ) ( )
   a. The monster's make-up was very artistic and awe-inspiring.
   b. Boris Karloff had already starred in *The Criminal Code* and was able to attract a big audience.
   c. Its sound effects were very frightening for the audience who were not yet used to "talkie" movies.
   d. Its plot appealed to the people living in a mechanical world.
   e. Thomas Edison's early version of *Frankenstein* had made the story very popular.

2. **Match the features of the monster with the interpretation given in the text.**
   • the protruding brow: (   )
   • a steel bolt through the neck: (   )
   • a round brain tucked into a square head: (   )
      a. humans being displaced by the machine, or reshaped into something more machine-like
      b. the difficulty of an old consciousness forced to occupy a new paradigm
      c. evolutionary regression

3. **The following is an explanation of the movie's famous scene that was not found until the 1980s. Fill in the gaps with the most proper words.**
   The monster was caught between (   ) and mechanism. This was to be shown in a scene where the monster enjoys playing with a little girl. He thinks the girl is the same as a (   ) and throws her into the lake. In other words, he was able to feel happy, like a human, but could only think in a (   )-like way.

The Monster Is Born

Editors' Note

　アイディア勝負で人々をあっと驚かす．それがそもそもの映画の目的だった．そのためならば映画人は努力を惜しまず，ときにはとてもうさん臭いことをしでかしたりする．だが，映画の起源がヴォードヴィルやミンストレル・ショーなど，いかにも「庶民的」だったことを理解すれば，そのうさん臭さにも納得がいくだろう．

　たとえば最近，世間を賑わせている3D映画もかつてはその場かぎりのチープなからくりにすぎなかった．片方に赤，片方に青のフィルムが入った紙製のメガネをかけて映画を観た，そんな覚えのある方々もいるのではないか．一方，映画とともに臭いを出すアイディアなどは，早くも1906年からあったらしい．その着想の頂点は1960年に公開された『セント・オブ・ミステリー』だと言われている．30種類もの香りが映画体験をリアルなものにするばかりか，謎解きのプロットともうまく組み合わされる……はずだったが，臭いがきつすぎたり軽すぎたり，臭いを発する装置の音がうるさかったり，効果のほどは今ひとつだったようだ．

　我らが『フランケンシュタイン』を上映した映画館の主たちもあの手この手で観客の興味をかきたてている．たとえば看護婦を常駐させるとか，無料で気付け薬（要はお酒）を提供するとか，そんな宣伝が全米各地で派手に行われた．テキサスの映画館では，真っ暗な館内で最後まで一人で試写を見ることができたご婦人にはキャッシュが出る，と募集をかけ，85人もの応募者を出している．

　棺桶に振りかかる土の音，モンスターの土気色の顔，雷のとどろき．そんなホラーな仕掛けに加え，一人でも多くの観客を喜ばそう……というか怖がらせようとして，映画業界の人々は旺盛なサービス精神を発揮した．そんな手作り感が妙に愛おしい今日この頃である．

PART IV | Let's Face It

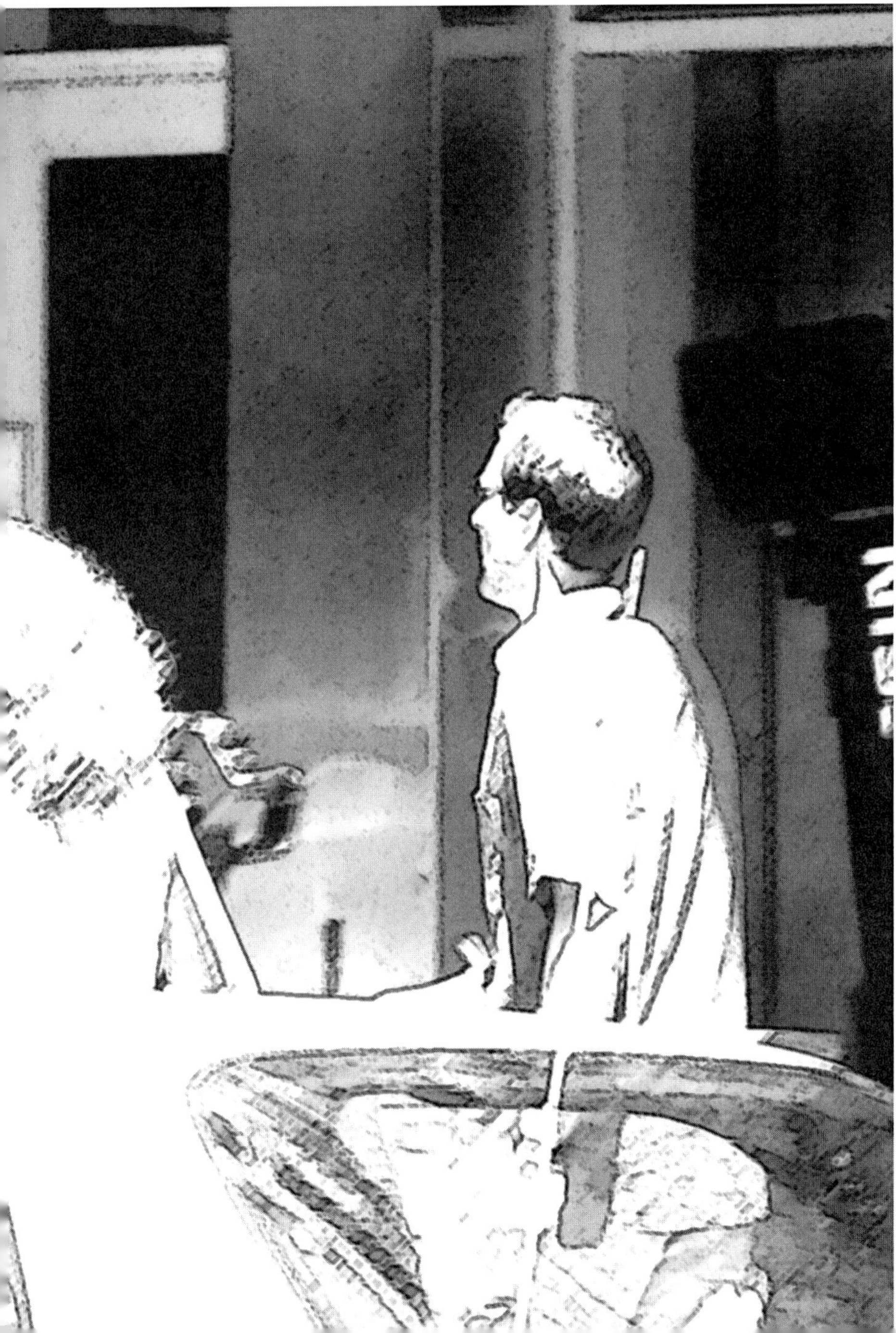

Introduction to Part IV

　夢も悪夢も大きなアメリカだからこそ，醒めた視線が重要視される．Let's face it.――というのは，グーグル検索で5,000万件ヒットする英語の頻出表現だ．「なに夢みたいなこと言ってるんの」「実際そういうことなんだから，しかたないだろ」というニュアンスをもつが，直訳すれば，しっかり顔を向けてよく見ろということだ．

　最終パートをこのような標題にしたのは，編者自身の自戒をこめてのことである．十数篇のつまみ食いによって「アメリカの宇宙」を描くなどという大それたことをしてきたわけだが，最後にちょっと，ハダカの現実らしきものにぶつかっておくべきかと思った．

　Session 13 は，本書でおそらく一番ストレートな語りだろう．フセイン政権崩壊後のイラクに，治安回復の名目で駐留したアメリカ軍の兵士が，ある日（2005年5月3日）恐怖に怯えて引き起こした事件．その痛ましさを書き綴った通訳兵ザカリ・スコット゠シングリーの文章がブログに載って話題となり，単行本（*The Best American Non-Required Reading, 2006*）に収録された．60代までが戦争を知らず，80歳以下の国民が戦地派遣を知らないという特別な国に住む私たちも，もっと知っていていい現実だ．

　平和な街の公営の乗り物にも，多様な現実がひしめいている．**Session 14** は変則的に，二つの異なるソースから取った．車椅子作家のシミ・リントンが『ニューヨーク・タイムズ』に寄稿した，公営バス・デビューの話．バリアフリー化される社会に，身体障害者の視点から face することもなかなか稀な経験ではないかと思って採用した．もうひとつは，編者がニューヨーク散策中に小さな書店で見つけた NY のサブウェイにまつわる短編集から．一時

に比べるとだいぶ「きれい」になったといわれる地下鉄だが，ホームレスを生みやすいアメリカ社会の構造は変わっていない．旅行者も遭遇しやすい出来事に，まずは作品で触れておくのもいいだろうと考えた．

　Session 1 はアメリカにファストフードが蔓延した話だったけれども，大手フランチャイズ企業による利潤追求の結果は，低所得者ほどよく太る，不健康な社会の出現だった．**Session 15** ではその現実に face する，ちょっとユニークなダイエット本の一節を読んでみよう．*The Philosopher's Diet* の著者リチャード・ワトソンは名の知れた哲学者．アメリカで健康に生きていくには，マーケットの論理に負けたらダメ．食のフィロソフィーが必要だ．堕落したみずからの味覚をどのように鍛え直していったらいいのか，デカルトの専門家からご意見をたまわろう．

　Session 16 で私たちが face するのは「現実」ではない．私たちの思考の形である．イギリスに生まれ育ったアラン・ワッツ（1915–1973）は，宗教学者として東洋の宗教思想を吸収した後，カリフォニアに居をかまえ，フリーランスの思索家として精力的なレクチャーと執筆活動を行った．"Nothing" と題したこの講演では，物理学のネタに「色即是空，空即是色」という仏教の教えを絡めている．アカデミックな厳密さに捉われることなく，宇宙大の類比の思考を大胆に進める小気味よさと，心を解放してくれるような話術ゆえ，没後も根強い人気を保った．そのワッツが「無」を語る．Let's face *nothing*.

Session

13

That Raid, That Boy

Zachary-Scott Singley

It was still dark. I got dressed in that darkness. [1]
When I was ready I grabbed an MRE (meal ready to eat) and got in the truck. I was going to go line the truck up in preparation for the raid we were about to go on. The targets were three houses where RPG attacks had come [5] from a few days prior. Sitting there in that darkness listening to the briefing on how we were to execute the mission, I let my mind wander from the briefing and said a prayer. "Just one more day God, let me live one more day and we will go from there . . . " It was the same prayer I said every [10] day because every day I did the same thing. I left the base. With a small team I would go out each day on different missions. I was their translator.

There were different people to meet each day. There were some who would kill you if they could. They would [15] look at you and you could see the hate in their eyes. I also met with people who would have given me everything they owned. People that were so thankful to us because we had rid them of Saddam. Well, this day was not really much different from all those other days so far. After the briefing we [20] all got into our assigned seats and convoyed out to the raid site. I was to go in directly after the military police that would clear the building.

The raid began without a hitch. Inside one of the court-

That Raid, That Boy

[1] **It was still dark:** 以下は 2005 年 5 月 3 日の出来事をつづったもの．
[3] **go line:** go and line
    line the truck up in preparation for . . . : get the truck ready to start for . . .
[4] **the raid we were about to go on:** the military attack we were heading for
[5] **RPG:** 旧ソ連が開発した携帯型対戦車兵器．なかでも安価簡便な肩掛け式の RPG-7 は，第三世界のゲリラ紛争地帯に広く出回っている．
[6] **a few days prior:** a few days ago
[7] **execute the mission:** 任務を遂行する
[8] **let my mind wander:** 「気持ちが離れてゆくに任せた」．つまり違うことを考えていた．
[9] **let me live one more day and we will go from there:** 「もう一日生きさせてもらったらそこからまた始めよう」．毎日が死と隣り合わせであることが伝わる一節．
[17] **would have given me everything they owned:** これだけでは言い足りないので，次に，どういう人たちか，補足説明がくる．
[19] **Saddam:** サダム・フセイン (1937–2006) は，1979 年イラク共和国第 5 代大統領に就任．1990 年クウェートに侵攻し，アメリカを中心とした多国籍軍に敗北するが，政権は延命．2003 年のイラク戦争で逮捕され，2006 年に処刑された．
[21] **convoyed out:** went out in convoy
[23] **clear the building:** *i.e.* rid the building of unwanted or possibly dangerous objects
[24] **The raid began without a hitch:** [a. Something / b. Nothing] went wrong with the raid at the beginning
    the courtyards: 中庭

169

yards of one of the houses, talking to an Iraqi woman checking to see if her story correlated with what the detained men had said, I heard gunfire. It was automatic gunfire. Ducking next to the stone wall I yelled at the woman to get inside her house, and when the gunfire stopped I peeked my head around the front gate. I saw a soldier amongst the others who was pulling rear security by our vehicles. This soldier I saw was still aiming his M249 (a fully automatic belt fed machine gun) at a black truck off in the distance. His was the weapon I had heard.

I ran up near his position and overheard the Captain in charge of the raid asking what had happened and why had this soldier opened fire. The soldier kept his weapon aimed and answered that he was sure he had seen a man holding an AK-47 in the back of the black truck. I was amongst the four (along with the soldier who had fired on the black truck) who had been selected to go and see what was up with that truck.

We were out of breath when we got to the gun-truck nearest to the black civilian truck (a gun-truck is a HMMWV or sometimes called a Hummer by civilians, with a .50 caliber machine gun on its roof). There was a group of four Iraqis walking towards us from the black truck. They were carrying a body. When I saw this I ran forward and began to speak (in Arabic) to the man holding the body but I couldn't say a word.

There right in front of me in the arms of one of the men I saw a small boy (no more than 3 years old). His head was cocked back at the wrong angle and there was blood. So much blood. How could all that blood be from that small boy? I heard crying too. All of the Iraqi men standing there were crying and sobbing and asking me WHY? Someone behind me started screaming for a medic. It was the young soldier (around my age) who had fired his weapon. He screamed and screamed for a medic until his voice was

- [26] **if her story correlated with . . . :** *i.e.* if she was basically saying the same thing (about the RPG attacks) as . . .
  detained: 拘留された
- [27] **Ducking:** bending down; dropping down; lowering the body
- [29] **peeked my head around the front gate:** こっそり頭を持ちあげて正門付近を見た
- [31] **pulling rear security . . . :** 後衛のガードを固める
- [32] **a fully automatic belt fed machine gun:** ベルト状に連なった弾が完全自動装塡されるマシンガン．
- [33] **His was the weapon I had heard:** It was his weapon that I had heard
- [35] **overheard the Captain in charge of the raid:** 今回の襲撃の責任者である大尉の声が聞こえた
- [37] **opened fire:** fired; shot; pulled the trigger
- [39] **an AK-47:** 1947 年にソ連軍が採用した歩兵用の銃で，第三世界の戦闘地域に広く出回り，現在でもテロリストの多くがこの型の銃（またはその非正規コピー製品）を使っている．
- [41] **what was up with that truck:** what the people in the truck were intending; what was going on in the truck
- [43] **the gun-truck:** the truck that belonged to [a. the US Army / b. the guerrilla]
- [45] **HMMWV:** high-mobility multi-purpose wheeled vehicle，発音は [hʌ́mvi]．（戦闘用）高機動多目的装輪車両
- [46] **a .50 caliber machine gun:** 50 口径（弾の直径が 0.50 インチ，fifty caliber と読む）のマシンガン
- [48] **a body:** a dead body; a corpse
- [52] **was cocked back at the wrong angle:** ありえない角度で後ろに傾いていた
- [54] **How could all that blood be from that small boy?:** It's surprising that such a small boy could be bleeding that much.
- [57] **a medic:** 衛生兵

AK–47

hoarse and a medic came just to tell us what I already knew. The boy was dead. I was so numb.

I stood there looking at that little child, someone's child (just like mine) and seeing how red the clean white shirt of the man holding the boy was turning. It was then that I realized that I had been speaking to them; speaking in a voice that sounded so very far away. I heard my voice telling them (in Arabic) how sorry we were. My mouth was saying this but all my mind could focus on was the hole in the child's head. The white shirt covered in bright red blood. Every color was so bright. There were other colors too. The glistening white pieces of the child's skull still splattered on that so very white shirt. I couldn't stop looking at them even as I continued telling them how sorry we were.

I can still see it all to this very day. The raid was over; there were no weapons to be found and we had accomplished nothing except killing a child of some unknowing mother. Not wanting to leave yet, I stayed as long as I could, talking to the man holding the child. I couldn't leave because I needed to know who they were. I wanted to remember. The man was the brother of the child's father. He was the boy's uncle, and he was watching him for his father who had gone to the market. They were carpenters and the soldier who had fired upon the truck had seen someone holding a piece of wood and standing in the truck bed.

Before I left to go back to our base I saw the young soldier who had killed the boy. His eyes were unfocused and he was just standing there, staring off into the distance. My hand went to my canteen and I took a drink of water. That soldier looked so lost, so I offered him a drink from my canteen. In a hoarse voice he quietly thanked me and then gave me such a thankful look; like I had given him gold.

Later that day those of us who had been selected to go inspect the black truck were filling reports out about what we had witnessed for the investigation. The Captain who

That Raid, That Boy

- [60] **hoarse:** rough; harsh; croaky (from too much shouting)
- [61] **numb:** without feeling; not able to respond
- [63] **how red the clean white shirt . . . was turning:** turn red で「赤に変わる」.
- [66] **I heard my voice telling them . . . :** 次でも my mouth was saying this と言っているように，自分の意識とは離れたところでしゃべっているようすを表現している．
- [68] **all my mind could focus on was . . . :** I couldn't think of anything but . . .
- [71] **glistening:** shining (because it was wet)

  still splattered on . . . : 飛び散って〜の上にまだ付いている
- [72] **even as . . . :** 〜している間も
- [74] **to this very day:** 今日になってもなお（"to this day" を very が強めている）
- [75] **accomplished nothing except . . . :**「〜以外に成果なし」．accomplish（成し遂げる）という言葉が，ここでは皮肉に使われている．
- [76] **a child of some unknowing mother:**「何も知らずにいる母親の子供」．some には「どういう人か知らないが」という気持がこもる．
- [79] **needed to know:**「知らずにはいられなかった」．need は切実さを表す．
- [84] **the truck bed:** トラックの荷台
- [88] **canteen:** 水筒
- [93] **filling reports out:** completing our reports
- [94] **the investigation:**（民間人を殺したことについての米軍側の）調査

had led the raid entered the room we were in and you could see that he was angry. He said, "Well this is just great! Now we have to go and give that family bags of money to shut them up . . . " I wanted to kill him. I sat there trembling with my rage. Some family had just lost their beautiful baby boy and this man, this COMMISSIONED OFFICER in the United States Army is worried about trying to pay off the family's grief and sorrow. He must not have been a father, otherwise he would know that money doesn't even come close . . . I wanted to use my bare hands to kill him, but instead I just sat there and waited until the investigating officer called me into his office.

To this day I still think about that raid, that family, that boy. I wonder if they are making attacks on us now. I would be. If someone took the life of my son or my daughter, nothing other than my own death would stop me from killing that person. I still cry too. I cry when the memory hits me. I cry when I think of how very far away I am from my family who needs me. I am not there just like the boy's father wasn't there. I pray every day for my family's safety and just that I was with them. I have served my time, I have my nightmares, I have enough blood on my hands. My contract with the Army has been involuntarily extended. I am not asking for medicine to help with the nightmares or for anything else, only that the Army would have held true to the contract I signed and let me be a father, a husband, a daddy again.

That Raid, That Boy

- [95] **and you could see . . . :** すぐに〜だとわかった；明らかに〜だった
- [96] **this is just great!:** まったくえらいことをしてくれた（反語）
- [97] **to shut them up:** so that they won't tell
- [98] **trembling with my rage:** 激しい怒りに体を震わせながら
- [100] **this COMMISSIONED OFFICER:** 兵卒 (soldier) や下士官 (noncommissioned officer) に対して，軍隊を指揮する立場にある「将校」．「そういう地位にある人間が……」という感情のたかぶりを反映して，大文字表記されている．
- [101] **is worried about trying to pay off the family's grief and sorrow:** 一家の嘆きと悲しみを金で払拭する試みがうまくいくかどうか心配している
- [103] **otherwise:** [a. if he were a father / b. if he had never been a father]
  money doesn't even come close: money is [a. no / b. a good enough] compensation for a lost child
- [104] **use my bare hands to kill him:**「素手で殴り殺す」．ちょっとやそっとでは収まりそうもない怒りの大きさを示している．
- [105] **the investigating officer:** 調査担当の士官
- [108] **I would be:** *i.e.* I would be making attacks if *my* child were killed like that.
- [109] **nothing other than my own death would stop me from killing that person:** I would be looking for the opportunity to kill that person as long as I live
- [114] **just that I was with them:**「一緒にいられる（＝家族のもとへ帰れる）こと」．動詞 pray から続く．
- [115] **I have served my time:**「もう任期は終えた」．serve one's time は「刑期をつとめる」ときにも使う表現．
  I have my nightmares:（米軍兵士としてイラクにいれば誰しも経験する）悪夢にもうなされている
- [116] **I have enough blood on my hands:** もう十分に自分の手を血で汚した
- [117] **has been involuntarily extended:** 私の意志と無関係に延長された
- [119] **only that:** I am only asking that
  the Army would have held true to the contract: *i.e.* the Army would have sent me back home because I have already served my time written in the contract

[Session 13] Comprehension Check

1. **The following is what the uncle recalls of May 3, 2005. Put the sentences in order. (Some of the sentences are already given.)**
   (a) → ( ) → ( ) → ( ) → ( ) → (b) → ( ) → ( ) → (c)
   a. My brother was going to the market, so I was looking over his small son that day.
   b. Another one of them spoke Arabic. He stayed longer and kept telling us how sorry they were. He asked questions about us.
   c. I still cry. We all still cry. We will never forget that day. How could we?
   d. There was also a young soldier standing close to him. I remember his eyes being unfocused, staring off into the distance.
   e. I took him in my arms and called his name but it was no use. We could not understand what had happened.
   f. We were driving through town when suddenly, there was gunfire.
   h. I later heard a rumor that he saw one of us standing on the truck, holding a piece of wood. He mistook it for a weapon.
   g. Four soldiers came up and one of them screamed for a doctor but there was nothing he could do.
   i. Everybody ducked but it was too late for my nephew. There was so much blood.

2. **Answer the questions in English.**
   1) What was the commissioned officer's reaction towards this sad incident?
   2) What did the author feel about the officer's reaction?
   3) What was the author's strongest wish when he was writing this journal?

Editors' Note

For a year as a foreign exchange student, I attended a private school in Virginia. The other day, as I was leafing through the yearbook of 40 years ago, my eyes fell on one particular face among the faces of the football team.

Tommy Chamoris. His eyes are cast down. Doesn't look proud being in the varsity team at all. He was in my French class. He wasn't doing too well academically. Perhaps he was trying to win a football scholarship to some college. But that didn't work. I later learned that he went to Base Quantico, the Marine Corp base that trains newcomers before shipping them to Vietnam. Anyone who's seen Stanley Kubric's *Full Metal Jacket* (1987) knows what it was like.

My year among the Southern upper-middle-class kids had little to do with the social turmoil that took place in the late 1960s. All I did was try to mingle with the American teenagers by being stupid enough to do the kind of things they used to do back then.

In early June, 1969, a few days after school was out, the boys "hit the beach." It was the last summer before each would head off for a different destination. They all knew which university they were going to—or that's what I thought.

Tommy was alone in the cottage when I walked in. I had been wandering on the beach, alone and almost penniless. He fixed me a fat sandwich, which he called a "Tommy Chamoris Special." What did we talk about? I don't remember. I was so ignorant. There he was, right in front of me, being drawn into the reality of America. What could have been my only connection to the Real America I had been so tactfully separated from was *there*, but I couldn't see it; nor did I care.

[Answers for the a/b Questions]

[24] — b., [43] — a., [103] — a.; a.

Session 14

Transported in NYC

"TRANSPORTED" by Simi Linton [1]

These days I find myself, regularly and happily, in the midst of the clutter of New Yorkers you find on the bus. I particularly savor the times when all of us, riders and driver, seem of one purpose: A woman [5] in a tailored suit and a man in slouchy pants stand together, commiserating about the traffic. Old and young, sitting side by side, laugh at a curbside quarrel between a spandex-clad Rollerblader and a delivery-man on a rusty bicycle. A young white man jumps up to give his seat to an elderly black [10] woman. It all seems so natural, like something that always was and always will be.

I take none of this—especially my own presence on the bus—for granted. I use a wheelchair, and only in the last few years have I been able to enjoy the convenience of public [15] transportation. I "went public" around 1998, when almost all of the New York buses had been outfitted with wheelchair lifts. I tried taking the bus in the mid-80's when the Metropolitan Transportation Authority began installing lifts, but even when a bus that had one showed up, the [20] driver sometimes couldn't find the key. Now the lifts are used more than 63,000 times a month. I account for about 40 of those.

[2]	**I find myself, regularly and happily in the midst of . . . :** *i.e.* I regularly enjoy being among . . . regularly は「定期的に」、つまり筆者は通勤にバスを使っている. in the midst of: in the middle of
[3]	**the clutter:** 雑多なものの集まり
[4]	**savor:** take delight in; enjoy fully
[5]	**seem of one purpose:** seem to be united in one purpose
[6]	**a tailored suit:** 注文で仕立てたスーツ **slouchy:** だぶだぶでだらしがない
[7]	**commiserating about the traffic:** 渋滞のひどさをグチっては互いに慰め合う **Old and young:** 通常は The old and (the) young となるところ.
[8]	**a curbside quarrel:**「道端の口ゲンカ」. curb は歩道の縁石のこと. **a spandex-clad Rollerblader:** a person wearing spandex and riding a Rollerblade
[9]	**a delivery-man:**（ピザかなにかを）配達中の男
[11]	**like something that always was and always will be:** これまでもそうだったし、これからもずっとそうであり続けることのように
[13]	**take none of this . . . for granted:** そのどれをも当たり前と思ったりはしない
[14]	**only in the last few years have I been able to enjoy the convenience of public transportation:** a few years ago, I [a. was / b. was not] able to use the bus service but now I [a. do / b. do not]
[16]	**"went public":**「公共の乗り物を使うようになった」ということだが、「秘密の、または私的な事柄がおおやけになる」という意味もかけられている.
[17]	**had been outfitted with wheelchair lifts:** 車イス用のリフトをつけ終えた
[19]	**Metropolitan Transportation Authority:** ニューヨークのバスと地下鉄を運営する組織. MTA の略称で親しまれている.
[20]	**had one:** *i.e.* had a lift
[22]	**I account for about 40 of those:** そのうちの 40 回くらいは私が乗ったぶんだ

A typical ride goes something like this: The driver sees me at the stop and steers the bus to the curb. The driver opens the door, and, using a key, activates the lift. It descends to the street, I back onto it, and it raises me up into the bus. It goes smoothly most of the time, and takes about two or three minutes. When the mechanism doesn't respond, it can take another couple of minutes. [25]

[30]

Still, the people inside, and those at the bus stop, must wait. It can delay their trip and I sometimes see irritation in their faces. I understand that feeling. New Yorkers don't take inconveniences without protest.

But the irritation is rarely expressed in words. There is nothing "wrong," per se, and people know that if they were to express annoyance, they would appear selfish and illiberal. This is all new, and we are all making up the rules and social protocols as we go. [35]

Now that I am a regular, I am particularly attuned to the drivers. They so often do their jobs with grace and good humor. One rainy day, I recall, the president was in town, sirens were wailing and Manhattan had become one big parking lot; yet the driver of the M104 shepherded us down [40]

- [24] **A typical ride goes something like this:** goes like this というと，is like this よりも動的なイメージが出て，コトが運ぶ感じがよく伝わる．
- [25] **steers the bus to the curb:**「歩道ぎわまでバスを近づける」．steer: ハンドル (steering wheel) を操作する
- [29] **When the mechanism doesn't respond:** When the machine doesn't work
- [30] **it can take another couple of minutes:** it might take two or three more minutes
- [32] **irritation:** イライラ感．[37] の "annoyance" も同じ感じ．
- [33] **don't take inconveniences without protest:** *i.e.* New Yorkers [a. do / b. do not] protest when someone causes inconveniences.
- [35] **the irritation is rarely expressed in words:** they [a. seldom / b. often] complain
- [36] **per se** [pərséi]: それ (= 車イスをバスに乗せるのに時間がかかること) 自体は
  if they were to express annoyance: うんざりした気持ちを外に表そうものなら
- [38] **illiberal:** 心が狭い (narrow-minded)
  we are all making up . . . as we go: 試行錯誤しながら私たちみんなで〜を作り上げている
- [39] **social protocols:** 社会の慣習 (rules of conduct; accepted behavior)
- [40] **I am particularly attuned to the drivers:**「バスの運転手たちにはことさら注意が向く」．attune は「心のチューニングをあわせる」という意味．*A politician must be well attuned to reality.*
- [43] **wailing:** wail は長く引き延ばされた鳴き声や叫び声をあげること．サイレンにもよく使う．
  become one big parking lot: Manhattan 一帯が大渋滞になったことの比喩表現．
- [44] **M104:** この循環バスは，マンハッタンの東側にある国連本部ビルから西へ向かい，ブロードウェイ沿いに北上して 125 ストリートでぐるりと周り，ほぼ同じルートで出発点にもどる．
  shepherded us:「(羊飼が羊を導くように) 私たちを連れて進んだ」．運転手の頼もしさが伝わる表現．

Broadway, paused to give clear directions to a befuddled tourist, and smiled encouragement at a child trying his hand at putting a MetroCard in the slot.

I've even gotten to know some of the drivers. One driver on the crosstown route always wears on his uniform jacket an array of red and gold apple pins, awards for exemplary service to the city. I nominated him for one a couple of years ago. There is an annual ceremony for drivers who have been recognized by disabled people for excellent service. Drivers bring their families, and there are speeches and a big breakfast spread. My nominee gave me a hug when I arrived, and now when he sees me at the bus stop, he says, "Hey girl, you riding with me today?"

On a summer night a while back, I met a driver I know only as Maria. When our bus pulled into my stop, she came to the rear door to activate the lift, but it jammed. After a few tries, she ushered the other passengers onto the next bus to arrive. Then Maria and I sat in the back of the darkened bus, with the doors open to let the warm night air in, and waited for the maintenance truck.

One rainy night, a truly collective effort was necessary to get me off the bus. When the lift descended to the street, the front lip on the platform would not go down. The driver jiggled the key, but it would not budge. I offered a solution—a trick I learned from another driver. I said that if everyone sitting on the right side of the bus moved to the left side, the plate would go down. Reluctantly, he and I asked the passengers if they would move their tired bodies.

It worked, and I rolled off toward home. The driver laughed at this very human solution, and he and the passengers standing behind him waved and bid me good night.

Transported in NYC

[45] **a befuddled tourist:**「混乱した観光客」．大統領が街にやってきたことでいろいろな規制が生じ，ガイドブックと全然違う事態に戸惑っているのだろう．

[46] **smiled encouragement at:**「微笑むことで子供を励ました」．smile はふつう自動詞だが，ここでは「激励を微笑みかける」という他動詞的用法になっている．
trying his hand at putting a MetroCard: try his hand at で「〜の腕試しをする」．trying to...に比べて，一生懸命になっている子供の手のおぼつかなさまでが目に浮かぶ．「メトロカード」は MTA 用のプリペイド・カード．

[48] **I've even gotten to know...:**「〜と知り合いにまでなった」．even がつくことで，仲良くなれたことを筆者がうれしく思っている感じが伝わる．

[49] **the crosstown route:** 街を東西に走る路線
wears...an array of red and gold apple pins:「赤と金のリンゴのピンをずらりとつけている」．ニューヨーク市の愛称は "The Big Apple."

[50] **awards for exemplary service to the city:** 街に模範的な貢献をした報償

[51] **nominated him for one:** recommended him for one of the awards

[53] **disabled people:** 身体障害者．Disabled doesn't mean unable.

[55] **breakfast spread:** 朝ご飯のご馳走．spread がつくことで料理がずらりと並ぶイメージが加わる．
My nominee: the driver I nominated

[58] **a while back:** a while ago. 口語的な言い方．
a driver I know only as Maria: マリアという名前以外なにも知らない運転手

[60] **jammed:** つっかかって動かなくなった

[61] **ushered the other passengers onto the next bus to arrive:** guided them to the next bus that was to arrive

[65] **a truly collective effort:** an effort done all together, with everybody

[67] **the front lip on the platform:** リフトの台座から段差をなくしてスムーズに歩道へと車イスが移動するためのパーツ．言われてみれば「唇」に似ている．

[68] **jiggled:** 小刻みに揺すった，ガチャガチャ動かした
would not budge: would not move at all

[71] **Reluctantly:** 及び腰で (unwillingly; hesitantly)

[73] **rolled off toward home:** 車イスを使わない健常者なら walked off...となるだろう．ここにも著者のユーモアが感じられる．

[75] **bid me good night:** said good night to me. bid はやや古めかしい言い方だが，エンディングの静かで落ち着いた雰囲気づくりに貢献している．

"TIRED" by Robert Dumont

His matted, tufted hair was filthy. So were his clothes—a loose fitting t-shirt that was more a grimy rag full of holes; a droopy pair of blue jeans that were several sizes too large in the waist and cinched with a piece of rope, and several sizes too long in the inseam, so that he just shuffled along like a seal with his bare feet lost somewhere up inside his pant legs. "PLEASE HELP ME" he keened. "I DON'T WANT TO BE OUT ON THE STREET! THEY THREW ME OUT OF THE SHELTER. I AM A VETERAN. I'VE LIVED IN THIS CITY ALL MY LIFE. I AM SO TIRED. WHAT DO I HAVE TO DO TO MAKE YOU UNDERSTAND?"

He worked his way slowly from one end of the car to the other. He was not one of these beggars who makes his pitch and passes the hat all between one stop and another and then scoots into the next car in order to maximize his target audience. This guy was oblivious as people came and went at each stop. His voice moaned like the wind. "PLEASE. PLEASE HELP ME SOMEONE! I AM SO TIRED. WON'T SOMEONE HELP ME?" When he reached the other end of the car he turned around and retraced his steps. Even now he wasn't thinking about getting off and working another car. He was sobbing almost. Walking even more

- [77] **His matted, tufted hair:** もつれて房になった髪
filthy: dirty はニュートラルに「汚い」から洗濯でもすれば済むが，filthy は嫌悪感をもよおす汚さ．
- [78] **that was more a grimy rag:**「アカで汚れたぼろ切れと言った方がいいような」．that was more like a grimy rag と言っても同じ．
- [79] **a droopy pair of blue jeans:** ぶかぶかでずり落ちそうなジーンズ
- [80] **cinched with a piece of rope:**（ベルト代わりに）ロープで締めてある
- [82] **shuffled along like a seal:** アザラシのように足をひきずって歩いた
with his bare feet lost somewhere up inside his pant legs: 裸足の足がズボンの中にすっぽりと覆われ
- [84] **keened:**「哀切な泣き声を立てた」．もともとは「死者を悼む嘆き声」のこと．数行あとには moaned like the wind と言い替えている．
- [85] **shelter:** ホームレスの人たちの保護施設
veteran: 復員軍人
- [89] **worked his way slowly:** ゆっくりと自分の窮状を訴えながら進んだ
- [90] **makes his pitch:** 口上を言う
- [91] **all between one stop and another：** 一つの駅から次の駅までのあいだずっと
- [92] **and then scoots into the next car:** それから次の車両へそそくさと移動する
maximize his target audience: 施しがもらえそうな聴衆（の数）をできるだけ多くする
- [93] **oblivious:** ぼんやりしている，まったく意に介さない
- [94] **His voice moaned like the wind:**「風のようにうめいた」"He moaned." というかわりに his voice を主語にすることで，生き物のように漂う声の不気味さが強調される．
- [97] **retraced his steps:** *i.e.* went back over to where he started
- [98] **working another car:** 別な車両で仕事（＝物乞い）をする．*cf. The hot-dog vendors work the streets of New York City.*

slowly, head down, withdrawn totally into his suffering. [100]
Every so often he dropped to his knees and folded his
hands as if this was all some sort of penance. This was just
too much for everyone. People don't mind giving a quarter
or a dollar to even the most repulsive looking character—
but for God's sake keep moving. Not this one though. The [105]
car was his own private beggar's corner, the full extent of
his territory. A franchise operation. He wasn't going anywhere. He didn't even hold out his hand or rattle a cup.

    Some guy with long dark hair and a beat-up, full-length
overcoat handed him a white paper bag before getting off [110]
the train. The beggar scarcely acknowledged him. He tore
open the bag and held up everyone to see: a half of a broiled
chicken. "Look at this!" His voice now had a raspy, angry
tone to it. "I can't eat this. I'm a vegetarian. It's all black on
the outside. They burnt it. You can get cancer eating burnt [115]
chicken!" He hurled the carcass against the door panel and
it splattered against the glass, leaving a big glob of grease.
When the door opened at the next stop he went over to the
heap of charred chicken flesh and broken chicken bones and
kicked it out onto the platform. "I CANNOT BE-LIEVE THE [120]
WAY THEY COOKED THAT FUCKING BIRD!" he shouted.

    And then, just like that, all of his anger had dissipated.
He reverted to his sad sack manner. He put his head on his
chest. He shuffled slowly along. As he embarked on his
third trip the length of the car, his voice reaching new [125]
heights of plaintiveness, on the faces of several passengers,
unavoidably, nervous smiles began to appear. Looks of commiseration were exchanged. And the next time he cried
"HELP ME! I AM SO TIRED," and resumed with his spiel,
there was nothing to be done—a sense of the absurd out- [130]
weighed any feelings of either pity or revulsion. Those who
could, laughed out loud. Those who couldn't, simply sat
there and shook their heads.

[101]　**Every so often:** Sometimes
[102]　**penance:** 罪の償い
　　　　This was just too much for everyone: *i.e.* everyone became uncomfortable
[104]　**repulsive:** おぞましくて嫌悪感をもよおすような
[105]　**for God's sake keep moving:**「頼むから消えてくれ」．for God's sake を使うことで感情的になっているようすが出ている．
　　　　Not this one though: But this homeless man would not move.
[106]　**his own private beggar's corner:** 物乞いのための縄張り，私有空間
　　　　the full extent of his territory: 彼の縄張りの全領域
[107]　**A franchise operation:** ここの営業権は俺様にある（と言わんばかりだ）
　　　　He wasn't going anywhere:「彼はどこにも行くつもりはなかった」．進行形はときに強い意志を表す
[108]　**rattle a cup:** コップに入った小銭をジャラジャラさせる
[109]　**beat-up:** よれよれの
[111]　**scarcely acknowledged him:** [a. almost completely ignored him / b. noticed and thanked him]
[112]　**held up everyone to see:** *i.e.* held it up for everyone to see
　　　　a half of a broiled chicken: 直火で焼いたチキンの半身
[113]　**a raspy, angry tone:** しわがれた怒りの口調
[116]　**hurled the carcass against the door panel:** 鳥の亡骸をドアのパネルに投げつけた．carcass という語が，「こんなもの！」という怒りを表現している．
[117]　**a big glob of grease:** 大きな脂の跡
[120]　**BE-LIEVE:** be- で一度ポーズを入れて，-lieve を特別に強調したことが分かる．
[122]　**just like that:** 一瞬のうちに
　　　　dissipated: disappeared と同じ意味だが，蒸気のように消える感じ．
[123]　**reverted:** went back
　　　　sad sack manner: のろまで悲しげな仕草，具体的には次に示される．
[124]　**embarked on his third trip the length of the car:** *i.e.* started to walk the length of the car (= walked from one end to the other end) for the third time. "the length" の用法に注意．*cf. a diamond the size of a walnut.*
[125]　**reaching new heights of plaintiveness:** 哀切口調にいっそう磨きがかかって
[127]　**Looks of commiseration were exchanged:**「哀れみの視線が交わされた」．お互い難儀なことですなぁ，と不思議な連帯感が生まれたのだろう．
[129]　**resumed with his spiel:** 口上を再び始めた
[130]　**a sense of the absurd outweighed any feelings of either pity or revulsion:** 不条理の感覚が，どんな同情や嫌悪の気持ちよりも勝った

[Session 14] Comprehension Check

1. Mark T for true, F for false.
1) It took more than 10 years for most of the New York buses to become equipped with wheelchair lifts. — (   )
2) On average, the author uses the bus twice a day, 5 days a week and she usually enjoys the ride. — (   )
3) A person on a wheelchair might take extra time to get on the bus, but the passengers are tolerant because of the social protocol. — (   )
4) Exemplary bus drivers are chosen by the disabled and are awarded with an apple pin and a big breakfast party. — (   )
5) When the wheelchair lift does not work, people must switch to another bus, and the driver waits for the maintenance truck to fix the problem. — (   )

2. Complete the summary by choosing a, b or c.

It was quite an unlucky day for the author. He hopped on a subway train and there was a beggar. He was filthy and annoying, [a. constantly moving from one car to another / b. asking for money from everyone in the car / c. staying in the car and just moaning out his misery].

A guy handed a paper bag to him, as he was getting off. The beggar tore open the bag, found a half of a chicken, but threw it against the door and kicked it away. He claimed that [a. it was too greasy / b. he was not supposed to eat it because he had cancer / c. he didn't like the way it was over-cooked and charred].

The passengers were not sure how to react. A certain bond of commiseration was formed. With the next cry of the beggar, some laughed out loud, others just shook their heads. [a. The situation seemed absurd, even to the point of being comical. / b. The sense of pity and repulsion grew stronger than ever. / c. The passengers were shocked at how the beggar had wasted the food.]

Editors' Note

マンハッタンといえば黄色いタクシーを思い浮かべる人が多い．でもこの街ではバスや地下鉄といった公共の交通手段が意外と発達している．これ自体，車社会アメリカでは非常に珍しい．そしてもう一つの特徴は"Transported"の冒頭にもあるとおり，こうした公共の乗り物を誰もが気軽に利用できることだ．当たり前じゃないか，と思うなかれ．全米には，区域や時間帯によっては危なっかしくてバスや地下鉄など乗れたものではない，という場所がたくさんある．マンハッタンもかつてはそうだったが，1990年代以降，市の政策により犯罪率は減少し，今ではバスや電車もすっかり快適になっている．

もちろん種々雑多な人々が一つの空間を共有するのだから，適度な緊張感は必要だ．日本と違って，地下鉄で居眠りをする人は誰もいない．また"Tired"の愛すべき（?）主人公のようなホームレスも多い．彼らにとって地下鉄は仕事場——口上を述べながら車両から車両へ移動して小銭を稼ぐその仕事ぶりはとても勤勉だ．乗客も心得たもので，口上のみごとさなど，彼らのパフォーマンスに見合ったお金をわたす．パッと取り出せるよう，小銭はいつでもポケットに用意している．

乗客が比較的少ない昼下がりが彼らの勤務時間のようだ．あるとき小学生から中学生と思しき数人の子供たちが隣の車両から移ってきた．一人がboomboxと呼ばれる大型ステレオラジカセをオンにするや，ラップのリズムが車内にとどろく．乗客は一気に緊張．が，音楽に合わせてナント！彼らは車中アクロバットを始めたではないか．乗客が座っていない空間をみごとに利用し，つり革や横棒からぶら下がり飛び移り，リズムをとりながら車両の端から端へ．しかも小柄な彼らは絶対に乗客の体をかすめたりせず，安全な距離を保っている．ラストのおじぎに，今や観客と化した乗客はやんやの喝采，年長とおぼしきおにいちゃんの帽子にはさまざまな額のお金が投げ込まれた．

そして電車が駅に止まる．人々の乗り降りにまぎれ，男の子たちは次の車両へと移っていった．

[Answers for the a/b Questions]
[14] — b; a., [33] — a., [35] — a., [111] — a.

Session 15

The Philosopher's Diet

Richard Watson

Philosophers sit and think a lot. I sat a long time in front of the typewriter trying to think if there is anything in the world that can give more lasting pleasure than good food. I think the answer is no. Descartes votes for friendship and conversation, but he always enjoyed them over a good meal. Freud says that our very dream of paradise stems from the enjoyment of sexual pleasure, and I would not deny it. Sex merits a chapter. But friendship and sexual pleasure would not last long if you didn't eat.

You may think I'm making a logical blunder here. "Is not food," one of my colleague asks, "merely fuel?" Being well-nourished is a necessary condition for enjoying the pleasures of friendship and sex, but it is not a sufficient condition. Am I not confusing the dance floor with the dance?

No. This is one place where logical analysis leads to a silly conclusion. Without good food, friendship languishes, and sex goes stale. Yet there are people like my colleague who think food is just fuel and who walk down the street and pick restaurants with such remarks as, "That place looks cheap, let's go there." Most Americans don't know any better. The heart of one of Henry Miller's best books, *Remember to Remember,* is an attack on white bread. For him white bread symbolizes America, a place so uncivilized that people would put something with the consistency of cotton

The Philosopher's Diet

Richard Watson, *The Philosopher's Diet* (1985)

[4] **the answer is no:** The author is saying that good food [a. is / b. isn't] the most pleasurable thing in the world.
Descartes: ルネ・デカルト (1596–1650) は『方法序説』で近代哲学の祖となったフランスの哲学者．

[5] **votes for . . . :** 〜に支持票を投じる

[6] **our very dream of paradise stems from the enjoyment of sexual pleasure:**「天国を夢見る思い自体が，性的快楽の充足に由来する」．人間精神の働きの根底に性衝動の充足（快楽原則）を置くのは，ジクムント・フロイト (1856–1939) が創始した精神分析学の基本．

[8] **Sex merits a chapter:** セックスは一章に値する（別の章を立てて論じるべき）

[10] **blunder:** mistake; error; misunderstanding
Is not food . . . merely fuel:「食べ物とは，しょせん燃料にすぎないのではないか？」Isn't . . . ? ではなく Is not . . . ? という疑問形に学者的な響きがある．

[12] **a necessary conditon:** 必要条件 ⇔ sufficient condition: 十分条件

[14] **confusing the dance floor with the dance:**「ダンスフロア」（活動を存立させる基盤）を「ダンス」（それ自体魅力的な存在）と混同する

[15] **No:** [a. I'm not mistaken. / b. The dance floor is not the dance.]
This is one place where logical analysis leads to a silly conclusion: これは論理的に分析していってもバカげた結論に通じてしまう思考領域のひとつだ

[16] **languish(es):** 生気を失う，だれる　（languid:「生気のない」）

[17] **go(es) stale:** 新鮮さを失う，しなびる　（stale ⇔ fresh）

[19] **with such remarks as . . . :** . . . のようなことを言いながら

[20] **don't know any better:**「そんな程度だ」．知力や感受性をさげすむ言い方．

[21] **Henry Miller:** ヘンリー・ミラー (1891–1980) は，性的なことを抑圧する傾向が強かったアメリカを離れ，『北回帰線』*The Tropic of Cancer* など赤裸々な人間性を追求する作品をパリで出版した．*Remember to Remember* (1947) の邦題は『追憶への追憶』．

[24] **something with the consistency of cotton and the taste of cardboard:**「綿のようにいつまでも口に残り，味はボール紙のようなもの」．堅焼きで中身が軽いフランスパンの香ばしさと比較して読むべきところ．

and the taste of cardboard into their mouths, masticate it into a dough ball, and swallow it. How can civilized human beings eat Wonder Bread? You and I were raised on it. We spread margarine and artificial grape jelly on it and smeared our faces. We didn't know any better.

I have to distinguish good food from bad. Your ordinary fat person does not eat good food. Oh, the fatties start with good ingredients: potatoes, chicken, apples, fresh vegetables. But if you chop up the potatoes and vegetables and fry them; smear a paste of dough on pieces of chicken and fry them; cut up the apples into a paste made of water, sugar, and cornstarch and bake that glop in a shell made of white flour and Crisco; salt the chicken and french fries heavily and dip them in tomato jam; put on your apple pie a big dip of ice cream made from air, sugar, vegetable oils, and stabilizers that never saw the inside of a cow—if you eat all that, then you have destroyed your appetite. And your palate.

Nobody denies that you like this food. You can eat other things, but you prefer meat and potatoes. In my childhood in Iowa, shrimp was a smelly mess the local butcher sold for catfish bait. Then french-fried shrimp swept the country. Now you can get chicken, ham, or shrimp in every small town in America. Even my mother will eat shrimp if she has to. Besides shrimp, I can remember the first time I ever tasted pizza. I gagged. So did my sister and brother. We learned to eat pizza. My mother still won't touch it, can't stand the smell.

Innovations in food can be survived. You can even learn to like most vegetables. Food habits are indeed strong, but they can be changed. Shrimp and pizza were pretty wild for country kids raised on ham, chicken, and minute steak, but we got our arms around them.

Just how was the move made from fried chicken to fried shrimp and pizza? Through salt and sugar. french-

The Philosopher's Diet

- [25] **masticate it into a dough ball:** 噛んで練り粉の球にする
- [27] **Wonder Bread:** 1920年代からアメリカの食卓に居すわり続けている食パンのビッグ・ブランド．最近都市部では「オーガニック」なパンに押され気味か．
  were raised on it: grew up eating it
- [28] **artificial grape jelly:** 粉末グレープをペプチンの粉と一緒に固めたゼラチン状の瓶詰め食品．これを塗った peanut butter and jelly sandwiches はアメリカの小学生に母親が持たせた定番ランチの一つ．
- [29] **smeared:** べったり汚した（ものだった）
- [30] **Your ordinary fat person:** まわりでよく見かける太った人
- [31] **the fatties** < fatty: おデブちゃん
- [34] **smear a paste of dough on pieces of chicken and fry them:** 鶏肉に練り粉を塗りたくって油で揚げる
- [35] **cut up the apples ... a shell made of white flour and Crisco:** フライドチキンに続いて，アップルパイの作り方を嫌悪感を込めて記述している．**glop:** べちゃっとしたもの．**Crisco:** ショートニング（小麦粉に混ぜる油脂）の商標
- [38] **tomato jam:** ketchup
- [40] **stabilizers:** 「安定剤」．アイスクリームの製造に欠かせない，氷の結晶の成長を抑えてクリーミーに保つ成分．
  never saw the inside of a cow: つまり「牛乳成分はまるで入っていない」
- [41] **appetite:** 食欲（おいしさを求める気持）
- [42] **palate** [pǽlət]: 味覚（ものをおいしく味わう能力）．前文 destroyed の目的語．
- [43] **Nobody denies that you like this food:** Nobody denies that は強調．You *really* like this food と同じ．
- [45] **a smelly mess:** 臭いを放つグチャグチャした存在
- [46] **catfish bait:** キャットフィッシュ（なまず）を釣るための餌
  swept the country: （揚げエビのフィーバーが）全米に広まった
- [50] **gagged:** （まずくて）喉を詰まらせた；むせかえった
- [53] **Innovations in food can be survived:** We can survive the new habit of eating. survive の他動詞としての用法に注意．*We all survived the storm.*
- [55] **pretty wild:** かなり過激な．**wild:** not tamed; unfamiliar; strange
- [56] **minute steak:** すぐ焼けるよう，小さめに切り売りされている牛肉
- [57] **got our arms around them:** （肩を組むほど）なじみの関係になった

fried shrimp taste much the same as french-fried potatoes if you forget the smell and dip them in sweet ketchup. People eat french fries for the salt, anyway, and if they eat something salty enough, they can even drink American beer. As for the pizza, the dough base reminds you of apple pie. Pizza is salt pie. Where I live some of it is also sweet because they mix sugar with the tomato sauce and the pastry shell. Even so, Americans were not easily converted to shrimp and pizza. Most still prefer hamburgers and french fries, with ketchup, of course.

Human beings will eat anything if you just put enough salt or sugar or both on it. Salt and sugar stimulate your appetite while destroying your taste for anything but salt and sugar.

When you cut out processed foods, don't use sugar, and go easy on the salt, all that fresh food tastes flat and bland at first. You will learn to eat and crave it, but it won't be as easy as learning to eat french-fried shrimp and pizza. Soon, however, your taste buds will recover from the heavy salt and sugar insult, and you will begin to taste other things. Some people never experience the variety of tastes in the foods of this world. The philosopher's diet opens a new world of taste.

It's punishing at first? Did Maurice Herzog complain about losing a few fingers and toes when he became the first person to climb Annapurna? He did not. Don't complain.

Let's consider an adult male 5'8" tall who weighs 170 pounds and wants to weigh 145. He has just started a 1200-calorie diet. Assuming that his maintenance diet is between 2,000 and 2,400 calories a day, how long will it take him to lose 25 pounds? Fat weighs in at 3,500 calories a pound. Thus, on 1,200 calories a day, our subject can probably lose a solid pound about every three days. At that rate, allow for two and a half months, seventy-five days, to lose 25 pounds.

The Philosopher's Diet

[62] **eat french fries for the salt, anyway:**「どのみち塩気を求めてフレンチフライを食べるのだ」．筆者の皮肉が炸裂しているところ．

[63] **can even drink American beer:** 返す刀で，今度は「水っぽい」アメリカのビールを皮肉っている．

[64] **the dough base reminds you of apple pie:**「ドウ（練り粉）を生地にするのでアップルパイに似ている」．the dough base は後出 the pastry shell と同じ．

[67] **Even so:** *i.e.* Even though our pizza looked and tasted like [a. traditional pie / b. real pizza]

[72] **destroying your taste for anything but salt and sugar:** 砂糖と塩以外の味覚はみな破壊されてしまう

[74] **cut out processed foods:** 調理済みの食品をやめる (= fresh food に転向する)

[75] **go easy on . . . :** 〜を控えめにする
tastes flat and bland: さっぱりしすぎて味気ない

[76] **learn to eat and crave it:** 慣れることで食べられるように，食べたくなるようになる

[78] **recover from the heavy salt and sugar insult:** 塩と砂糖による大々的なはずかしめから立ち直る

[81] **The philosopher's diet:**「賢者のダイエット」とは，著者がこの本のタイトルとしたキャッチフレーズ．副題が *How to Lose Weight & Change the World.*

[83] **punishing:** painful (as if you were being punished)
Maurice Herzog: モーリス・エルゾーグ (1919–) は，1950年に世界で初めて8,000メートル級の山（ヒマラヤのアンナプルナ）を征したフランスの登山家．

[86] **5′8″ tall:** 5 feet 8 inches tall（身長約 173 センチ）．ちなみに 170 pounds は約 77 kg.

[88] **Assuming that . . . :** 〜だと仮定すると

[90] **Fat weighs in at 3,500 calories a pound:**「3,500 カロリーに対して1ポンドという割合で脂肪はつく」．摂取カロリーが体内で脂肪に変換されるときの換算値をいっている．

[91] **our subject:** 私たちの被験者

[92] **lose a solid pound about every three days:**「3日ごとに丸々1ポンドずつ減っていく」．現状維持 (maintenance) に1日 2400 カロリー必要なところ，1,200 カロリーの摂取では，3日間で 3,600 カロリー（脂肪1ポンド相当）不足になる．

[93] **allow for . . . :** 〜の期間をみてください（それだけかかると考えよう）

Don't you believe it for a minute. You have to go to dinner with friends. If you don't have a drink when you go on a business lunch, your client may think you are some kind of kook. You honestly forget and have your usual coffee and sweet roll when the wagon comes around. Monday night: football, beer.

What to do? Bear with it. Keep track of the calories, and when you go over one day, cut down to less than 1,200 calories the next day. It won't hurt you—if you are a normal, healthy adult—to go one or even two or three days without any food at all. Fasting makes you feel weak and gives you a headache? It sure does. I don't recommend it. But it is an interesting experience for someone who is obsessed with food and has always had enough to eat. Dick Gregory says that after a week or so you lose all your appetite, and then it is easy to continue the fast. Perhaps. But unless you are on a hunger strike for a very good cause, forget fasting for more than a day at a time.

Let's eat; after all, that's what God put us here for, isn't it? Try to stay off processed foods, and try to stay on 1,200 calories a day. Unless you go into hibernation, it is not going to take two and a half months to lose 25 pounds. It may take a year. Slow loss is better for you, anyway. Only if you are impatient enough to crash it can you do it in two and a half months. If you do crash, it will then be harder to keep your weight down than if you took a year to get there, because crashers bounce.

If you keep at it, eventually, *eventually*, you will begin to be able to handle the diet. It is hard to turn down desserts, but people do and you can. The worst thing may be that nobody particularly notices your heroism.

Determine in the depths of your being that no matter the setbacks or relapses, you will reach your weight goal and stay there.

The Philosopher's Diet

- [95] **Don't you believe it for a minute:**「(そんな計算上の日数は) 一瞬たりとも信じてはだめ」．否定の命令文で Don't のあとの you は，念を押す気持ちを伝える．
- [98] **kook:** a strange person; an oddball; a geek
  honestly forget:（ズルで忘れたふりをするのでなく）マジに忘れる
- [99] **sweet roll:**（しばしばナッツやレーズンやシナモン入りの）甘いロール・パン．コーヒー・タイムによく出るので，coffee roll とも呼ばれる．
- [99] **when the wagon comes around:** アメリカの大手企業のオフィスでは，新幹線の車内販売よろしく，軽食や飲み物をのせたワゴンが回ってくる．
  Monday night: football, beer: 1970 年以来，初秋から厳冬にかけての月曜夜は，"Monday Night Football" のライブ放映を見ながら，缶ビールをたくさん飲むというのが，アメリカ庶民の典型的オヤジ道だった．
- [101] **Keep track:**（記録をつけて）把握せよ
- [104] **go . . . without any food at all:** まるっきり食べずにいる
- [108] **Dick Gregory:** (1932–) 社会風刺に活躍した先駆的アフリカ系コメディアン．1981 年に 70 日間に及ぶ断食 (fasting) の実験を行った．
- [111] **a very good cause:** とても重要な大義；社会的意義の大きな目的
  forget fasting for more than a day at a time: your fasting should be [a. longer / b. shorter] than one day each time.
- [113] **after all, that's what God put us here for:** なんだかんだ言っても，やはりわれわれは食べるために創世主によって作り出された存在だ
- [115] **hibernation:** 冬眠
- [117] **Only if . . . can you do it:**「～という場合にのみ可能だ」．Only で始まった文の後半は，ここでの can you のようにしばしば主語と動詞の順番が入れ替わる．
- [118] **impatient enough to crash it:**「我慢が足りず体に無理をかける」．"crash it"（激しくぶつける）は「急にやる」ということ．*cf. crash course*（速成講座）
- [120] **than if you took a year to get there:** 1 年かけてたどりついた場合より．there = your weight goal
- [121] **crashers bounce:** 急なダイエットに走ると必ずリバウンドがくる．
- [122] **keep at . . . :** ～を根気よく続ける
  eventually:「最終的には」．もう一度はっきりと，イタリックスで強調して繰り返したのは「なかなかそこまではいかないけど」と警告する意図．
- [124] **The worst thing may be that . . . :** 悪くてもせいぜい～くらいだろう
- [125] **your heroism:** あなたの英雄的なガンバリ
- [126] **the depths of your being:** being という単語を使ったのは，空腹や習慣に打ち勝つには，単に mind で決心しただけではダメ，という含み．
  no matter the setbacks or relapses: どんな挫折や逆戻りに見舞われようと

This is an existential choice, by the way. Sartre says that each of us is responsible for what he or she is. If you are some kind of pervert, it is self-deceptive to blame it on your parents or society. What about being fat? Did you choose to be fat?

Spinoza states the extreme opposite of the existentialist's total freedom and responsibility. Spinoza says that everything you do is absolutely determined, and that freedom consists in assenting to what you must do and then you're responsible for being what you couldn't avoid being. That's called double-think.

Descartes, as usual, counsels prudent realism. The father of modern philosophy says that you should change your opinions and desires to fit the world only when you cannot change the world to fit your desires and opinions. It would appear that you can lose 20 pounds and then maintain the weight you reach, by responsible, free choice.

Can't you?

- [129] **an existential choice:** 実存主義的選択．実存主義哲学 (existentialism *cf.* p. 47, [21]) は，個人が虚空としての世界に向かい合っているという感覚からスタートし，このパラグラフにあるように，個人の絶対自由／絶対責任を説く．
  Sartre: ジャン＝ポール・サルトル (1905–80) はフランスの哲学者．小説，戯曲，評論も執筆し，第二次世界大戦後，実存主義哲学の世界的隆盛をリードした．
- [130] **If you are some kind of pervert, it is self-deceptive to blame it on your parents or society:** たとえ性格に異常なところがあったとしても，（それも自分の責任だから）親や社会のせいにするのは，自分をだます（自分についての真実から目をそらす）ことである．
- [134] **Spinoza:** スピノザ (1632–1677) はオランダの哲学者．偶然や自由意思を認めない決定論者として知られる．
  states the extreme opposite: その対極，正反対の考えを述べている
- [137] **consist(s) in . . . :** （その本質が）〜にある．*Health consists in harmony with nature.*
  assenting to what you must do: 「あらかじめやると決まっていることに同意する」．スピノザ流の逆説的な「自由」の定義．
- [138] **responsible for being what you couldn't avoid being:** それ以外なりようのないものであることに対して責任をもつ
- [139] **double-think:** ジョージ・オーウェルの小説『1984年』の暗い「未来社会」で権力が押しつける「二重思考」．小説中の定義を引用すると——"the power of holding two contradictory beliefs in one's mind simultaneously, and accepting both of them."
- [140] **counsel(s):** （専門家の意見として）勧める
  prudent realism: つつましやかな現実路線
- [141] **change your opinions and desires to fit the world:** [a. be flexible / b. be willful]
- [143] **change the world to fit your desires and opinions:** [a. control / b. give in to] the world
  It would appear that . . . : 〜のようですね．（柔らかな主張表現）
- [145] **by responsible, free choice:** 「現実に対応した自由選択によって」．非哲学風に言い換えれば「無理をしない範囲でのがんばりによって」．

[Session 15] Comprehension Check

1. **Complete the sentences that express the author's view by choosing a, b or c.**
   1) Friendship [a. is sustained by / b. is more important than / c. often spoils] good food.
   2) Food is [a. merely / b. not / c. more than] fuel.
   3) Henry Miller implies that Americans who eat Wonder Bread ought to be [a. proud / b. healthy / c. ashamed].
   4) Changing your food habits is [a. almost impossible / b. sometimes worth the effort / c. not good for your health].
   5) Processed foods are [a. nice and handy / b. very nutritious / c. not good for you].
   6) Too much sugar and salt damages your [a. sense of taste / b. appetite / c. fasting].
   7) Dieting is a matter of how [a. patient / b. daring / c. rigid] you are in carrying out your plans.

2. **Match each idea with one of the four philosophers given below.**
   1) (   ): "There's no such thing as free will."
   2) (   ): "You are responsible for what you are."
   3) (   ): "Sexual pleasure is basic to all our pleasures."
   4) (   ): "Know what you can do, and do what you can."

Freud   Descartes   Spinoza   Sartre

The Philosopher's Diet

Editors' Note

　壮絶なダイエットを実践したとして紹介された Dick Gregory (1932–) の本業はコメディアン．公民権運動の時代，差別された黒人として，Malcolm X に匹敵する毒舌で白人社会をコケにして，それでアメリカを笑わせていた．その功績は，日本でももっと知られていいと思う．

　英語版 Wikipedia の彼のページに紹介されているジョークのひとつ．"Last time I was down South I walked into this restaurant and this white waitress came up to me and said, 'We don't serve colored people here." I said, "That's all right. I don't eat colored people. Bring me a whole fried chicken."

　おわかりだろうか．日本語には「に」と「を」の区別がある．英語にはそれがないから「お出しする人」と「お出しする物」の混同が起こりうる．そこをついたブラック・ジョークなのだけれど，a whole fried chicken と続けることで，「黒人の黒焼き」のようなものが目の前に浮かんでくるところが痛烈である．

　だが冗談ではないのだ．アフリカ系のアメリカ人は，リンチされ，木に吊され，文字通り黒焼きにされた過去をもつ．

　南部にも黒人に「理解を示す」人たちはいた．その人たちを皮肉る Dick のギャグ——"You know the definition of a Southern moderate? That's a cat that'll lynch you from a low tree."

　「五十歩百歩」というのは中国の故事だったが，3 メートルの木に吊したからって，10 メートルの木に吊したのより罪が軽くなるわけではないのだ（なお "cat" とは人間のこと）．

　TV パーソナリティにして活動家という Dick Gregory は，1968 年の大統領選に出馬して黒いジョークを振りまいた．これらのエピソードは，グレゴリーの人間性（彼はいまではすっかり穏やかな老人だ）というよりむしろ，1960 年代という時代について多くを語っているというべきだろう．

[Answers for the a/b Questions]
[4] — a., [15] — a., [67] — a., [111] — b., [141] — a., [143] — a.

Session 16

Nothing

Alan Watts

When I consider the weirdest of all things I can think of, do you know what it is? *Nothing*. We have a saying in Latin, *Ex nihilo nihil fit*, which means, "Out of nothing comes nothing." In other words, you can't get something out of nothing. It's occurred to me that this is a fallacy of tremendous proportions.

Imagine nothing but space, space, space, space with nothing in it, forever. But there you are imagining it and you're something in it. The whole idea of there being only space, and nothing else at all, is not only inconceivable but perfectly meaningless, because we always know what we mean by contrast.

We know what we mean by white in comparison with black. We know life in comparison with death. We know pleasure in comparison with pain, up in comparison with down. But all these things must come into being together. You don't have first something and then nothing or first nothing and then something. Something and nothing are two sides of the same coin; they are inseparable, they go together. The nothing is the force whereby the something can be manifested.

We think that matter is basic to the physical world. And matter has various shapes. We think of tables as made of

Nothing

Alan Watts (1915–1973)

[1] **weirdest** < weird [wiərd]: mysteriously strange
[3] **a saying in Latin:**「ラテン語の諺」．ローマ帝国崩壊後，ラテン語は各地域でイタリア語，フランス語，スペイン語等へ変化していくが，学問の共通語として使われ続け，ヨーロッパ文化圏の古典教育で重要な位置を占め続けた．
[4] **Out of nothing comes nothing:** 主語は最後の nothing で，普通の語順に直すと Nothing comes out of nothing.
you can't get something out of nothing: Judging from this paragraph, the author himself [a. supports / b. does not support] this view.
[5] **It's occurred to me . . . :** It appears to me . . . ; I've found . . .
[6] **a fallacy of tremendous proportions:** 途方もなく大きな規模の誤り
[9] **The whole idea of there being only space:**「無の空間しか存在しないなどという考え」whole は強調．*The whole idea of us getting married next week is absurd.*（来週結婚しようだなんて，ほんと，バカげてるわ．）
[10] **inconceivable:** 心に抱くことができない (unthinkable)
[16] **all these things:** より的確に言えば all these opposite pairs．この文章は講演の言葉をそのまま拾っているので口語的な言い方が多い．
come into being: 生じる
[17] **You don't have . . . :** この文は，"first something and then nothing" という状況，および "first nothing and then something" という状況は「ない」と否定している．you は読者も話者も含む「人一般」．
[20] **The nothing is the force whereby the something can be manifested:** *i.e.* The nothing is what makes the something stand out before our eyes.
[22] **matter is basic to the physical world:**「物理的世界の基本は物質である」．以後この考えを否定する議論が続く．

wood as we think of pots as made of clay. There is, in the back of our mind, the notion, as a root of common sense, that everything in the world is made of some kind of basic *stuff*. Physicists, through centuries, have wanted to know what that was. Indeed, physics began as a quest to discover the basic stuff out of which the world is made. And with all our advances in physics we've never found it. What we have found is not stuff but form. We have found shapes. We have found structures. When you turn up the microscope and look at things expecting to see some sort of stuff, you find the shape of crystals. Beyond that you find molecules, atoms, electrons and other subatomic particles. And between particles there are vast spaces. We can't decide whether electrons and positrons are waves or particles and so we call them wavicles.

What we will come up with will never be stuff. We never get to any stuff for the simple reason there isn't any. Actually, stuff is when you see something unclearly or out of focus, fuzzy. When we look at it with the naked eye it looks just like goo. We can't make out any significant shape to it. But when you put it under the microscope, you suddenly see shapes. It comes into clear focus as shape.

And you can go on and on, looking into the nature of the world and you will never find anything except form. Think of stuff; basic substance. You wouldn't know how to talk about it. You couldn't say anything about a structure in it, you couldn't say anything about a pattern or a process in it, because it would be absolute, primordial goo.

What else is there besides form in the world? Obviously, between the significant shapes of any form there is space. And space and form go together as the fundamental things we're dealing with in this universe. The whole of Buddhism is based on a saying, "That which is void is precisely form, and that which is form is precisely void." Let me illustrate

Nothing

- [26] **some kind of basic *stuff*:** 世界をつくる素材．「何だか分からないがそういうものがある」という気持ちを some kind of が表している．
- [27] **Physicist(s):** 物理学者．*cf. chemist, biologist, psychologist*
- [28] **a quest:** a search; an exploration; a mission
- [29] **with all our advances:** これだけ進歩しても
- [32] **turn up the microscope:** 顕微鏡の倍率を上げる
- [34] **crystal(s):** 結晶

    molecules, atoms, electrons and other subatomic particles: *Molecules*（分子）are made of *atoms*（原子）, which in turn are made of *subatomic particles*（素粒子）such as *electrons*（電子）, *protons*（陽子）and *neutrons*（中性子）．
- [36] **vast spaces:** たとえば水素原子 (a hydrogen atom) のモデルは，1個の陽子からなる核のまわりを1個の電子がまわっているというものだが，原子の大きさ（電子が取りうる最も外の軌道の直径）を100メートルと見なすと，核の大きさはたった1ミリほど．それほど「スカスカ」な存在なのだ．
- [37] **positrons:**「陽電子」．電子と同じ質量で電子と逆にプラスの電荷を持つ．
- [39] **What we will come up with:**（考えた結果）答えとして出てくるもの．　*cf. He came up with a marvelous idea while walking in the park.*
- [40] **for the simple reason there isn't any:** because there simply isn't any (basic) stuff in the world
- [41] **stuff is when you see something unclearly:** 何かをクリアでなく見るときに stuff というものが現れる

    out of focus, fuzzy: 焦点を合わさずに，ぼんやりしたものとして
- [43] **goo:** 形なく，べちゃっとしたもの

    make out: 見定める，判別する
- [46] **you can go on and on . . . and you will never . . . :** どこまで〜し続けても絶対に〜できない
- [49] **You couldn't say anything about a structure in it:** 単に You couldn't talk about its structure というのに比べだいぶ強い言い方．
- [51] **because it would be absolute, primordial goo:**「だって，絶対の，原初のドロドロなんだから」．ちなみに聖書創世記のはじまりは，"In the beginning God created the heaven and the earth. And the earth was without form, and void."
- [54] **space and form go together as the fundamental things:** 空間と形は基本的なモノとして組になっている
- [56] **That which is void is precisely form:** 空なるものこそ形なり．「空即是色」を訳した英文．本文 [67] では簡潔に "void is form" といっている．
- [57] **illustrate:** 図解する，具体例で示す

this to you in an extremely simple way. When you use the word *clarity*, what do you mean? It might mean a perfectly polished lens, or mirror, or a clear day when there's no smog and the air is perfectly transparent like space.

What's the next thing *clarity* makes you think of? You think of form in clear focus, all the details articulate and perfect. So the one word *clarity* suggests to you these two apparently completely different things: the clarity of the lens or the mirror, and the clarity of articulate form. In this sense, we can take the saying "Form is void, void is form" and instead of saying *is*, say *implies*, or the word that I invented: *goeswith*. Form always *goeswith* void. And there really isn't, in this whole universe, any substance.

Form, indeed, is inseparable from the idea of energy, and form, especially when it's moving in a very circumscribed area, appears to us as solid. For example, when you spin an electric fan the empty spaces between the blades sort of disappear into a blur, and you can't push a pencil, much less your finger, through the fan. So in the same way, you can't push your finger through the floor because the floor's going too fast. Basically, what you have down there is nothing and form in motion.

Most forms of energy are vibration, pulsation. In the case of very fast light, very strong light, even with alternating current you don't notice the discontinuity because your retina retains the impression of the *on* pulse and you can't notice the *off* pulse except in very slow light like an arc lamp. It's exactly the same thing with sound. A high note seems more continuous because the vibrations are faster than a low note. In the low note you hear a kind of graininess because of the slower alternations of on and off.

All wave motion is this process, and when we think of waves, we think about crests. The crests stand out from the underlying, uniform bed of water. These crests are perceived as the things, the forms, the waves. But you cannot

[63] **articulate:** くっきりしている，際立っている

[68] **instead of saying *is*, say *implies*, or the word that I invented: *goeswith*:**「空は色〈である〉という代わりに，空は色の〈含みをもつ〉とか，これはわたしの造語だが〈ともゆく〉とかいったほうがいい」．be 動詞を使って世界のありさまを固定的に捉えるのでなく，対照的な者同士が相互に連れ合い，規定し合うような思考が大切だということ．

[72] **moving in a very circumscribed area:**「非常に限られた領域を動き回っている」．ここで著者は，物質の根底をなす素粒子レベルで起こっていることを念頭に置いている．

[77] **you can't . . . because the floor's going too fast:** このあたりは，話の勢いがついて比喩が先走り，ナンセンスでユーモラスな味わいが出ているところ．

[80] **pulsation:**「波動，拍動」．扇風機が回るというケースも，羽―空―羽―空の波動と見なされる．

[81] **very fast light:** この fast は fast-pulsating の意味．光を波として見た場合，その振動が速いこととエネルギーが高いことは等しいので，very strong light と言い替えている．

even with alternating current: 交流の電流では，電子の流れる方向が 1 秒間に数十回ほどのサイクルで逆転する．光の振動はその約 10 兆倍速い（数百テラヘルツ）．

[82] **the discontinuity:** 電流の切り替わり

your retina retains the impression of . . . : 網膜には〜の残像が残る

[84] **very slow light like an arc lamp:** ここでいう「遅さ」は光自体の波動ではなく，ライトの明滅．水銀灯などアーク放電による灯りは，1 秒当たりの放電回数がさほど多くないのでチラチラして見える．

[85] **A high note:** ピッチの高い音

[87] **graininess:** ざらざらした感じ

[88] **the slower alternations of on and off:** オンとオフのゆっくりした切り替え

[89] **and when we think of waves, we think about crests:** and *yet*, when we think of waves, we think *only* about crests (and forget about the whole pulsating process).

have the emphasis called a crest, the convex, without the de-emphasis, or concave, called the trough. So to have anything standing out, there must be something standing down or standing back. We must realize that if you had this part alone, the up part, that would not excite your senses because there would be no contrast.

The same thing is true of all life together. We shouldn't really contrast existence with nonexistence, because actually, existence is the alternation of now-you-see-it / now-you-don't, now-you-see-it / now-you-don't. It is that contrast that presents the sensation of there being anything at all.

But there are other circumstances in which the waves are extraordinarily slow, as in the alternation of day and night, and the much vaster alternations of life and death. But these alternations are just as necessary to the being of the universe as in the very fast motions of light and sound, and in the sense of solid contact when it's going so rapidly that we notice only continuity or the *is* side. We ignore the intervention of the *isn't* side, but it's there just the same, just as there are vast spaces within the very heart of the atom.

So, don't be afraid of nothing. I could say, "There's nothing in nothing to be afraid of." But people in our culture are terrified of nothing. They're terrified of death. They have a lurking fear in the back of their minds that the universe is eventually going to run down and end in nothing, and it will all be forgotten, buried and dead. But this is a completely unreasonable fear, because it is just precisely this nothing which is always the source of something.

One final thing that I would like you to consider is this. When you observe the world, there is always a blank spot, and that's your observing self. You can't look at your eyes with your eyes. You can't observe yourself in the act of observing. You can't touch the tip of a finger with the tip

Nothing

- [93] **convex:** でっぱり
- [94] **concave:**「へっこみ」．de-emphasis を言いかえたもの．さらに crest（波頭）と対照の関係にあるものとして trough（波くぼ）が続く．
- [97] **excite your senses:**「諸感覚を刺激する」すなわち「知覚される」

  because there would be no contrast: ここで著者は，知覚とはコントラストへの反応であるという考えに基づいている．たとえば明滅するものが目立つのは，視野における明暗の「違い」が，ニューロンを活性化させるから．
- [100] **contrast existence with nonexistence:** 存在と非在を対照づける（反対のものとして考える）
- [101] **now-you-see-it / now-you-don't:** もともとは「いないいないばあ」をするときの決まり文句．
- [103] **the sensation of there being anything at all:** そもそもそこに何かが存在するという感覚
- [106] **much vaster:**「もっとずっと広大な」．the much vaster alternations of life and death といういい方で著者は個人の生死だけでなく，文明の盛衰や星の誕生と死滅など，宇宙的な規模の出来事をイメージしているのだろう．
- [107] **these alternations are just as necessary to the being of the universe as in ⟨A⟩ and in ⟨B⟩:** これらの（非常にゆったりとした）交代（対立項の入れ替わり）も，AやBの場合と同じで，宇宙のありようにとって必然的な現象なのだ
- [108] **the very fast motions of light and sound:** 光や音の非常に高速な波動
- [109] **the sense of solid contact:**「固体物質を触ったときの感触」．このときもニューロンのレベルでは，非常に短いサイクルで，刺激が流れる／流れないの「交代」が続いている．
- [110] **intervention:** 介入，干渉
- [113] **There's nothing in . . . to be afraid of:** 〜には恐れるところなどない
- [116] **(a) lurking fear:** 奥深くに潜んでいる恐怖心

  the universe is eventually going to run down: 宇宙はいずれ（ネジの巻きがゆるんだ機械のように）静止していく
- [117] **end in nothing:** 無に帰す
- [119] **just precisely this nothing:** まさにこの無なるもの
- [120] **the source of something:** 有のみなもと，存在の起点
- [123] **that's your observing self:** それ（the blank spot）は観察している自分自身だ
- [124] **observe yourself in the act of observing:** 観察しているさなかの自分を観察する

of the same finger no matter how hard you try. That's unknown.

We always get this division of experience into one-half known, one-half unknown. What I'm suggesting is that the blank side of experience has the same relationship to the conscious side as the *off* principle of vibration has to the *on* principle. There's a fundamental division. The Chinese call them the *yang*, the positive side, and the *yin*, the negative side. [130]

All that side of life which you call unconscious, unknown, impenetrable, *is* unconscious, unknown, impenetrable because it's really you. In other words, the deepest you is the nothing side, is the side which you don't know. [135]

Think once again of the image of clarity, crystal clear. *Nothing* is what brings *something* into focus. This nothing, symbolized by the crystal, is your own eyeball, your own consciousness. [140]

Nothing

- [126] **That's unknown:** それ (= 観察の主体) は知られざるものなり
- [128] **this division of experience into one-half known, one-half unknown:** 経験の全体が，認識される側とされない側に二分されること．
- [129] **What I'm suggesting is that ⟨A⟩ has the same relationship to ⟨B⟩ as ⟨C⟩ has to ⟨D⟩:** AとBとの関係はCとDとの関係と同じなのではないだろうかと私は言っているのである
- [132] **There's a fundamental division:**「そこに宇宙を深く二分する原理がある」．nothing を something のソースであると述べたところから，著者は陰陽 (yin and yang) の思想にもとづいて語っている．「陰陽」は一般に，陰が陽を，陽が陰を生み出しつつある「巴」の姿で図示される．
- [132] **call them the *yang* ... and the *yin*:** これら (このような対照をなす二者) を「陽」と「陰」と呼んでいる
- [136] **impenetrable:** 進入を許さない，考えることができない (= not to be penetrated)

ying and *yang*

[Session 16] Comprehension Check

1. **Mark T if the statement is Watts' own, F if it contradicts him.**
   1) The old saying "out of nothing comes nothing" is indeed correct. — (   )
   2) In order to better understand the world, we should look at one thing at a time, rather than two for comparison. — (   )
   3) Through centuries of investigation, physicists have identified the basic stuff the world is made of. — (   )
   4) The word "clear" implies nothingness; it also suggests sharply focused vision. — (   )
   5) The world around us may appear solid, but in fact it isn't. — (   )
   6) The world can be understood as waves, or alternation of opposites. — (   )
   7) Even when we hear a tone that sounds smooth, what we are really experiencing is the cycle of now-we-hear-it/now-we-don't. — (   )
   8) Part of the universe is unknowable for a very fundamental reason. — (   )

2. **What did you think of Watt's lecture? Try to use any of the given adjectives and form your opinion.**

abstract	brilliant	fundamental	groundless
liberating	stimulating	ambiguous	illogical

Editors' Note

ロックの世界に，British Invasion という言葉がある．もともとアメリカ南部の「下層の」音楽伝統がポップな形で売り出されたのが rock 'n' roll だったわけだが，それを音楽的に磨いていって世界のポピュラー音楽にしていったのは，The Beatles ら，イギリス人のアーティストだった．

ロックの興隆は，音楽を専門家の支配から解放し，感性豊かな一般人の手に享楽に委ねる出来事だったといえる．実は，人文心理系の学問でも，それに似た「非専門家の歓びのための解放」の運動が，同時代，アメリカを中心に起こっている．50年代の禅の浸透に始まり，70年代に "New Age" という呼び名のもとにまとめられていく思想の展開．これに，イギリス生まれの3人が強く絡んでいることを記しておこう．

まず小説家 Aldous Huxley (1894–1963)．目を患った彼は治療のために渡米し，1937年以降，南カリフォルニア等で暮らした．その頃から神秘主義への接近の度合いを強め，メスカリン体験記『知覚の扉』(1954) などを書きながら，最終的にユートピア小説『島』を著した．

オックスフォード大学に落ち，独学で宗教研究を続けていた Alan Watts がアメリカに渡ってきたのは23歳，1938年のことだった．後年はサンフランシスコ湾のボートハウスに住み，バークリーの大学ラジオ局でレギュラーの教養番組を担当した．alanwatts.com を訪ねてみると，死後40年近くを経てなお強い人気を保っているようすが見られて面白い．

p. 208 [97] に「コントラストが感覚を刺激する」とある．認知科学的にも認識論的にも，深い言葉だ．こういうことを，誰よりもきちんと考え，20世紀後半の諸学の展開に大きな影を落とした Gregory Bateson (1904–1980) がアメリカに渡ってきたのは1940年のこと．Watts の自伝にも，Bateson との出会いから受けた影響について記されている．アメリカで興隆した文化人類学と精神医学に，最大級の British Invasion をもたらした Bateson も，後年はカリフォルニアで暮らしていた．

[Answer for the a/b Question]

[4] — b.

Answer Keys for Comprehension Check

[Session 1] 1. (d)→(a)→(c)→(b)
2. c, d, a, b
[Session 2] 1. (b), (c), (f), (h)
2. corner, supper, matter のあとに (☺).
笑い上戸の人は別.
[Session 3] a, c, c, b, b, b
[Session 4] 1. 1) combustible 2) enduring 3) harsh
4) accepting
2. 1) T 2) T 3) T 4) F 5) T 6) F
[Session 5] 1. (a)→(d)→(e)→(b)→(f)→(c)
2. 1) c 2) c 3) b 4) c 5) a
[Session 6] A) 1. b 2. c 3. a 4. d
B) 1. c 2. b 3. a 4. d 5. e
[Session 7] 1. (b), (f) 2. (a), (b), (d)
[Session 8] 1. 1) F 2) F 3) T 4) T
2. 1) a 2) c 3) b 4) b 5) a 6) c
[Session 9] 1. 1) T 2) F 3) T 4) F
2. bad, good/cool, good, bad/cool, cool/bad 3. (c)
[Session 10] 1. (b), (d) 2. (d), (b), (e), (a), (c)
3. (a), (d)
[Session 11] 1) a 2) b 3) b 4) b 5) a 6) a 7) a 8) a
9) a 10) b
[Session 12] 1. (a), (c), (d) 2. (c), (a), (b)
3. humanism, flower, machine
[Session 13] 1. (a)→(f)→(i)→(e)→(g)→(b)→(d)→(h)→(c)
[Session 14] 1. 1) T 2) T 3) T 4) T 5) F
2. c, c, a
[Session 15] 1. 1) a 2) c 3) c 4) b 5) c 6) a 7) a
2. 1) Spinoza 2) Sartre 3) Freud 4) Descartes
[Session 16] 1. 1) F 2) F 3) F 4) T 5) T 6) T 7) T 8) T

214

Index

Aberdeen, Idaho	4
absurd	186
acceptance	54
accomplishment	130, 172
activism	52
Adams, James Truslow	32
addicts	88
adrenaline	126
adverbs	22–26
advertising (campaign)	8, 86, 90, 146
affection	134
affluent	36
Afghanistan	126, 130
afraid	22, 28, 208
afterlife	100
Age of Dinosaurs, the	32
Age of Innocence, the	32
AK-47	170
alchemy	48
aliens	102, 122, 142
alienation	46
Anaheim, California	112
ancestors (human)	72, 76, 80
anger	52, 54, 174, 186
annoyance	180
anonymous	144, 158
anthropologists	72
apartment houses	36–38
appeal, (un)appealing	10, 50, 90, 100
appetite	192–96
apple pie	192–94
Arkansas	92
Army, U.S.	126–32, 168–74
Art Deco	152
Art Moderne	152
assembly lines	4, 158
Astor, Mrs. William	34
attitude, a bad-girl	116
audiences	50, 114, 120, 158, 184
authority	20, 134
auto accidents	140
awards	182
awesome	114
baby boomers	90
Babylonians, the ancient	100
Baccarat crystal	40
ballrooms	34, 40
banquets	32
barbed wire	102
barking	74–76
Barry, Dave	114, 120
baseball	54, 92
bas-relief	40
Bauhaus	152
Bay Area, the	112
beer	194, 196
Beetle Bailey	52
bills	66, 126, 132
beggers	184
bioelectric	100
bizarre	140
black marketeers	88
blood	102, 170, 172, 174
blue jeans	14, 184
bonds	130
boots	14, 116
boredom	50
brain	96–100, 104, 154
brand loyalty	92
brevity	18
Buddhism	204
bus drivers	180–82
business	6, 22, 38, 42, 98, 116, 140, 196
cadavers	96–100, 104
canines	74–76
carbonation	84
calories	90, 192–94
celebrities (stars)	30, 140, 144, 146
cellar clubs	50
censorship	140, 160
Charlie Brown	46
Cheese Whiz	8
Cherry Coke	92
chicken, broiled	186
Chicken-of-Tomorrow	8
childhood	48–50
children	46–50, 160, 172
Christianity	52, 114
CIA	140
circulation	92, 138–40, 144
clarity	206, 210
class secretary	118
Clark, Edward	36–40
Clarke, Mae	156
cliché	24
cognitive science	78
Cokeaholics	84, 88
Columbia Pictures	92

215

comic strips	46–54
commissioned officers	174
commodities brokers	6
common sense	204
condition, necessary/sufficient	190
convenience/inconvenience	178, 180
Confidential magazine	144
Conroy, Frank	46
consumers/consumption	12, 80, 90, 146
context	22
contrasts	202, 208
cool	18
corpses	96–100, 104, 138,156
corruption	114
Crisco	192
cruelty	48, 50
crying	54, 142, 170–72
cubism	152
curious	90, 154
Daily News, the	138
dairy products	12
Dakota, the	38–42
"dandelions"	24, 26, 28
day care	128
dead/death	20, 96–104, 158, 160, 172, 200, 206, 208
Declo, Idaho	6
Denver, Colorado	12
deployments	126–134
depression	46
Depression-era	8
Descartes, René	190, 198
desperate	84, 88, 126
determined	90, 92, 196–98
determinism	198
dialogue attribution	24–28
Dick Tracy	52
Diet Coke	90, 92
dieting	194–96
disadvantaged	114
discipline	132
distressing	84
disturbing	128
divergence	76
domestication	78
double-think	198
dough	192, 194
down town	4
drawing rooms	40
dress shirts	118
drive-in restaurants	10
Dubuque, Iowa	6
Dumbo	28
Dunlap, Ray	10

duties	28, 128, 132
Dyson, Brian	86
dystopia	50
eating habits	12, 192
Edison, Thomas	150
Edsel	84
Egyptians, the ancient	100
Eisenhower-era	4, 46
electric/electricity	98, 138, 150, 158
electromechanical	154
embarrassment	144
emotion(al)	22, 28, 46, 92, 104
empire	6, 14
empty	68, 206
endurance	50–54
England	20, 34
enlisted men	128
Enrico, Roger	84, 90
environmental contamination	74
ESP (extrasensory perception)	142
Etch-a-Sketch	102
etiquette	36
Everyman	52, 54
evidence	72, 78
evolution	76–80
excited	132
executives	14, 92, 146
existence	80, 208
existentialism	46, 198
explosives	128, 130
expressionism	152
extravagance	38
fallacy	202
family	104, 114, 120, 126, 128, 174
fast food industry	12
fasting	196
fat	192, 194, 198
father	6, 172–74
fear	22, 28, 46, 126, 208
FedEx	88
Fifth Avenue, the	152
flash-freezing	4
flavoring formulas	86, 90
flexibility	78, 80
focused/unfocused	172, 204–06, 210
football	196
forceful	22
fortitude	52
Fortune magazine	152
45s	116
foxes	74
franchise (chains)	12, 186
Frankenstein's monster	150–58

Index

freedom	48, 114, 198
freight cars	4
french fries	4–12, 194
Freud, Sigmund	190
friendship	190
frozen food	4–12
fuel	190
fury	52
f-words	114
gamble(r)	6, 90
garage parties	116
garbage	72, 144
geyser	102
God	88, 100, 168, 196
Goizueta, Roberto	92
Goldmark, Kathi Karmen	112
goo	204
gossip	144–46
Graham, Billy	142
grace	180
grape jelly	192
Gregory, Dick	196
groceries	128
Groening, Matt	114
Grosz, Karoly	154
gunfire	170
gurneys	96, 102
hamburger stands	4, 10–12
happy/unhappy	46–48
hate	15, 115–16, 126, 168
Hart, Gary	146
Hearst Corporation, the	140
heart (as an organ)	96–104
heartless	104
heroism	196
Herzog, Maurice	194
hibernation	196
highbrow	144
hogs	6
Hollywood	88, 116, 144, 150
homesteaders	6
horror	50, 152, 156
how-to books	36
human	46, 52, 100, 140, 142, 144, 158, 182
humor	48, 50, 180
hunting	72, 78, 80
ice cream	192
ice cubes	84
imagining	202
immigrants	114
independent	42
industries	4, 6, 12, 90, 152

inferiority	46, 76
ingredients	192
innovations	8, 158, 192
insult	48, 194
intellectual	42, 50
intelligence/intelligent	42, 100, 144
inventions	6, 32, 150
Iowa	192
Iraq	126, 132
Iraqui people	168–72
irrigation	6
irritation	64, 180
Jefferson, Thomas	10
Jewish	50
Jell-O	8
Jet-Puffed Marshmallows	8
Joe Palooka	52
ka	100
Karloff, Boris	150–60
Kennedy, Edward	146
Keough, Donald R.	92
ketchup	194
kidney	98, 102, 104
killing	132, 174
King, Stephen	18–28, 114, 120, 122
Kingsolver, Barbara	114
Kissinger, Henry	146
kitchen appliances	8
koans	46
Kona, Hawaii	114
Kooper, Al	116
Korea	132
Kroc, Ray	12
labor costs	12
labor-saving	10
Laemmle, Carl (Sr.)	160
land	6, 14
Lantana, Florida	142
laptops	120
larynx	76–78
laundry	132
lauging off	86
laughter	48, 52, 64, 66, 156, 182, 186
lawyers' torts	20
license plates	14
Lieberman, Phillip	78
lightning (bolts, flashes)	66, 158
Li'l Abner	52
Lincoln Continental, a	14
lipsticks, white	118
Little League	142
liver (as organ)	98–102

217

lizards	66
logical analysis	190
Lucy (*Peanuts*)	46
ludicrous	24, 112
lust	66
M249	170
mechanical	32, 154–58
machine guns	32, 74, 170
magic	48
Main Street	4
mainstream	50, 146
makeup	120, 152, 156
mannequins	152–54
manuals	18, 20
Marcus, Greil	116
market/marketing	36, 84, 86, 90, 92
marriage	50, 66, 126, 132–34
Marsh, Dave	116, 120
mass production	10
maturity	50
maximization	92
McAlister, Ward	34
McDoland's	12–14, 132
McDonald, Mauric (Mac)	10
McDonald, Richard (Dick)	10
McMurtry, Larry	28
melodramas	138, 140
mental health	130–32
MetroCards	182
Miller, Henry	190
Minnesota	46
minute steak	192
Miracle Whip	8
MIT	140
model trains	54
molecules	204
money	32–36, 128, 144–46, 174
Montreal	88
morgues	102
Morse code	102
Mount Rushmore	90
MTA	178
muggles	20
multibillionaires	14
murders	136, 140
Murdock, Rupert	142
Mustang, a	126
muzzles	78
mysteries	92
nail polish	118
National Enquirer, the	138–146
national headquarters	88
NCOs (noncommissioned officers)	130

Neanderthal man	76–80
nervous	186
New Coke	84–92
New York City	
society 32–36; appartments 36–42;	
buses 178–82; subway 182–84	
New York Daily Graphic, the	40
New York Times, the	142
New York Tribune, the	32
New Yorker, the	50
New Yorkers	34, 36, 42, 178, 180
news	144–46
newspapers	28, 32, 46, 50, 140–44
newsstands	138, 142
Newsweek	126, 134
nightmares	174
9/11	132, 134
nostalgia	90
notorious	138
obsessed	196
Onassis, Jacqueline	142
organ transplant surgeries	100–04
Outback Steakhouse	130
pain	48–50, 98
palates	84, 192
panic	64
paper bags	66
paper cups	66
paperback originals	26
Paris	10, 152
particles	204
partnership	80
pastry	194
patriotism	92
Patty (*Peanuts*)	48
Pearson, Ridley	114
peeves	18
Pemberton, Dr. John	84
People magazine	144
Pepsi Challenge, the	86
Pepsi Cola	84, 86, 88, 90
Ph.D.	118
philosophers	190, 194, 198
physics	204
Pierce, Jack P.	152
pinups	140
pizza	192–94
plastic jugs	84
pleasure (pleased)	28, 64, 190
plumber/plumbing	26, 36
pommes frites	10
Pontiac, a	102
Pope, Generoso	140–144

Index

popular	10, 34, 90, 116, 144, 146
postcards	66–68, 122
potatoes (boiled, mashed, baked)	10, 12
praying	168, 174
preachers	114
preposterous	36, 146
pretensions	14, 34
primitive	72, 76, 78, 120
privacy	40
processed foods	8, 194, 196
Proctor & Gamble	146
Progresso, Il	140
prom queen	116
Pryor, David	92
psychics	142
PTSD	130–32
public sanitation	74
public transportation	178
publicity	112
pulp fiction	26
punchbowls	118
puppies	48, 134
Queen Victoria	20
quintessential	92
radio broadcasts	52
rage	174
raids	168–74
railroad tracks	4
Reader's Digest, the	142
Reagan, Nancy	146
real	14, 44
realism	198
reality	120
recipes	10, 90
relationship (business)	6
relationship (man-dog)	72, 80
relationship (*yin-yang*)	210
religion	14
reptiles	64
repulsive	142, 186
respectable	32, 36, 146
responsibility	198
rewards	114
rifles	6
rituals	42, 84
road kills	122
Rock Bottom Remainders, the	114–22
rock 'n' roll	112, 114, 122
Rollerbladers	178
Rolling Stone magazine	144
Roosevelt, Theodore	88
rotting	72, 74, 104
Russet Burbank potatoes	6, 10
ruthless	144
Saddam (Hussein)	168
salt	192–94
sarcasm	40
Sartre, Jean-Paul	198
SAT (Scholastic Assessment Test)	28
scent	80
Schulz, Charles M.	46–54
school dances	118–20
seat-of-the-soul debate	100
security	76, 170
selective breeding	76
self, the	100, 208
self-congratulation	50
self-deception	198
self-pity	50, 54
senators	92, 146
sensationalism	138, 142
sense of humor	40, 64
senses	208
serious	22, 80, 144
service	182
7-Up	116
seven cardinal virtues	52
sexual pleasure	190
shame	28, 114
Shane	28
Shelley, Mary	150
shelter	184
Shermy (*Peanuts*)	54
shipping	8, 88
shoulders	20, 66
shrimp	192–94
Simplot, J. R.	4–12
Sinatra, Nancy	116
Sing-Sing (prison)	138
singing	112–14, 120
sinners	28
skeletons	78
small towns	6, 90, 142, 192
smoking	120
Snyder, Ruth	138
social protocols	180
society (high)	32–36
South Pacific, the	72
space-age	8
spaghetti	66
speculations	18, 78, 80
Spiegelman, Art	48
spirit	4, 98–102
spoken language	78–80
spouses	120
squatters	36
stabilizers	192

stage actresses	32	town houses	38
Stanford University	114	tracking	80
Star, the	142, 146	triumphs	44, 142
starch	10, 192	trucker paraphernalia	122
steel mills	32	Trump, Donald	146
steroids	26	TV dinner	8
stomping	112		
strangers	76, 96, 104, 132	UFOs	142
strategic	54, 120	uncanny	140
structure	80, 154, 204	uniformity	12
Strunk, William	18	Union Square	34
stuff, basic	204	unique	24, 84, 96
stupid	118	Universal Pictures, the	150–54
Stuyvesant, Rutherford	36–38	universe, the	208
suburbs	50	US Army, the	128–132, 174
subversive	50		
success(ful)	10, 14, 38, 80, 86, 90, 92, 140, 142, 158	*Vanity Fair* magazine	146
		variations	76
suffering	130, 186	verbs, active and passive	18
sugar/nonsugar	90, 192, 194	vertebrae	68
suicides	134	veterans	10, 184
sunlight	66, 128	Victor Appleton II	26
supermarkets	8, 86, 142	*Village Voice*, the	50
surgeons	98, 104	violence	52, 140
survival	54, 78–80	vocal tracts	78
sweet rolls	196	vodka	116
symptoms	130–32	void	206
		volcanic soil	6
tactics	144		
Taiwan	114	war zones	128, 130
Taliban militants	126	warehouses	6–8
talkie	158	*Weekly World News*, the	122
Tan, Amy	114–22	weight	194–198
taste (flavor)	10–12, 84–92, 192–94	weird	78, 142, 202
taste (refinement)	34	Westinghouse Laboratories	154
taste buds	194	Whale, James	150–54, 158
taste-tests	86, 92	wheat flour	12
tears	48, 54, 134	wheelchair	178–82
technology	4, 8, 150	Wild West	40
teenagers	26, 50, 90	willing	4, 18
television	32, 46, 100, 132, 144	wolves	74
Televox	154	Wonder Bread	192
thankful	168, 172	World War I / the Great War	10, 158
Tiffany, Charles L.	34	wounds	48
timid	18–22, 28	wrongness	48
Tom Swift	24–26		
tomato jam	192	Yellowstone	6

Morsels of the Universe

テキスト本文から，英語的思考のなかで非常によく使われる小さな「部品」を並べてみた．これ以上は砕かずに，むしろもっと大きく成長させる方向で吸収してほしい．これらに馴染んでから本文を読むと，英語を英語のまま読んでいる感覚が得られ，リーディングがそのまま，書くこと，話すことの学習につながるはず．（表示は行番号）

Session 1

smells like (someone's doing . . .)	8
turn (potatoes) into (fries)	10
by industry standards	11
check (the fries) for (imperfections)	17
(obtain land) for free	30
rebell against (his father)	33
drop out of school	33
at the age of (fifteen)	34
(was) just getting started	45
the nearest available (place)	54
head down to (some place)	59
⟨A⟩ gave way to ⟨B⟩.	73
make (them) seem better	74
come with (something)	77
(they) might want to (do . . .)	79
have (enormous) potential	81
more (fries) than ever before	82
(eat) behind the wheel	94
learn (it) the hard way	98
based as much on ⟨A⟩ as ⟨B⟩	112
all the more (important)	121
The idea of . . . appealed to (someone)	123
despite being . . .	151
more (potatoes) than any other (food) except	140
have little patience for (that)	155
didn't sell out	165
just hang on	166

Session 2

find room to (discuss . . .)	2
be sent to bed without supper	10
for that matter	11
get (it) off (my) chest	12
before we move along	13
come in (two) types	14
just let it happen	17
put it this way	31
there's no place for (it)	37
(he) ends up somewhere else	38
a fair way to put this	40
just about any (thing) ever (done)	47

not to mention (that one)	48
make me want to (scream)	49
with (that) in mind	63
get the point across	69
by no means (bad)	71
ask yourself if . . .	73, 121
see them for [the . . .] they (really) are	87
know what (we're) talking about	93
the best of the lot	108
debate whether or not to . . .	119
put (it) into practice	113
urge you to (read . . .)	133
need only look . . . to know (it)	141
just another (ordinary . . .)	142
be pretty good about (it)	143
(had) my share of . . .	144
never fall so low as . . .	146
won't understand me if I don't	149
with the help of . . .	155
feel the urge to (do it)	156

Session 3

never before been imagined	4
worth as much as . . .	7
all manner of (things) from . . . to . . .	15
(there was) emphasis on . . .	18
nor (were) there any . . .	22
more than (that) was involved	49
a matter of great importance	53
in the far reaches of (the place)	55
For one thing,	72
easily the most (expensive . . .)	74
in a respectable neighborhood	75
had not gone far before (you did . . .)	89
(spend) yet another (million)	90
might just as well be doing	98
to make the most of it	101
x feet wide and y feet long	114
set ⟨A⟩ apart from ⟨B⟩	138
It has been assumed that . . .	146

Session 4

This was something new (in . . .)	10

221

don't feel the way (I'm) supposed to	15
come and go in a flash	48
Nobody was saying (this)	56
strike at the heart of . . .	64
life as we know it	65
could not have been more (different)	66
get stuck in (a marriage)	70
push (them) to the breaking point	79
What is more (delightful) than . . .	86
kick (it) clear out of (the room)	88
get good and mad	95
what it is to be human	97
(a fighter) in terms of (endurance)	106
how well he handles (it)	111
unaware of (his) presence	117
There is no (anger), just (acceptance).	125
the moment (he) became . . .	126

Session 5

could hardly stand (her)	6
(which) helped for a second	11
had nothing else to do	12
(was) in an utter panic	22
not one bit	24
What sort of decent human being could possibly (do it)?	24
You're the one (doing it)	28
about this, about that	38
Guess who (was there).	50
did not like the way . . . were so (broad)	55
could spot (it) across an ocean	64
hit me in a bolt of lightning	72
What makes you so sure . . .	75
Why would I consider (doing it)?	76
have a bite of (some food)	80
make faces at (him)	84
like he thought she might	94
during the time it took to (do that)	97
have to watch out for	99
before you even realize . . .	100

Session 6

It is most likely the case that . . .	4
grab a quick bite	19
dispose of the garbage	27
This has led to the suggestion that . . .	27
if needed	41
we are not talking about . . .	44
over a half-minute period	57
in the same time period when doing . . .	60
(was) disposed of as being useless	70
(This) seems to explain (it).	71
(not) physically equipped for it	77
This leaves room for (them to . . .)	82

ends up in a (weird) position	101
an advantage over (dogs) in terms of . . .	108
for far longer than (we) have imagined	122
It is possible that . . .	123
It is well established that . . .	128
never got along with (dogs)	131
ultimately died out	131
have (dogs) to do the (tracking)	142
no longer need (them)	143
In other words	147
It may well be the case that . . .	161
owes its very existence to . . .	162

Session 7

certainly none of those . . .	4
all too soon	13
way back in (1886)	21
closing in (fast) on (the day)	22
a better than two to one margin	25
in danger of becoming . . .	28
Even worse,	35
greater than the sum of its parts	41
the way we quench our thirst	48
explore the possibility of . . .	49
beat (the opponent) by as much as . . .	56
Next week, they'll be doing . . .	82
unlike almost every other . . .	89
One thing it never was (was)	90
(are) curious about the next thing	106
(You) could have done it without . . .	114
want more out of life	106
Perhaps he went too far.	130
get caught up in	131
What (you) fail to realize it that . . .	135
there is more to (it) than . . .	136
the quintessential representation of . . .	138
You cannot . . . any more than you can . . .	149

Session 8

(She is) unique in that . . .	5
what is known as . . .	7
alive and well everywhere but (her brain)	8
There was no such (thing)	9
breathe on (its) own	10
for a matter of days	12
like your own	17
one at a time	25
has a (joyous) ring to it	29
(doesn't) make sense to (her)	37
play tricks on (her)	40

Morsels of the Universe

the things that happened to (them)	42
behind (their) back	43
without (their) noticing	43
All that remains is . . .	49
(have) long been considered	50
couldn't tell for sure whether . . .	52
having trouble hearing it.	53
grounded in a belief that . . .	60
(That) take some getting used to.	63
It must be noted that . . .	63
started out as . . .	65
find it hard to imagine . . .	78
If I were . . . I guess I might	84
You can tell by (something) that . . .	111
(chooses it) out of habit	122
appears no different from . . .	129
on a (rational/emotional) level	141
have a hard time accepting it	143
(. . . is) the last thing you'd call her	149

Session 9

yet another (request)	3
for the better half of (the year)	4
As I can best recall	8
said something to (this) effect	8
Could there possibly be anything more . . . ?	14
Amend that to . . .	18
for the benefit of (the disadvantaged)	28
sing (my) heart out	30
come within earshot of (me)	32
bring shame on (your family)	39
be only too happy to (do it)	44
second only to . . .	52
none other than . . .	61
break things to (me)	67
have (the boys) fall all over you	74
vying to be (prom queen)	82
I must confess . . .	86
hate myself for being perceived as	90
Neither . . . had any effect on . . .	105
can (do it) only so many times before . . .	108
make up another reason why . . .	109
That would show them.	116
not in a million years	119
When's it going to be *my* turn?	130
the best part about being (it) was . . .	134
swear on an oath of death	144

Session 10

would rather be (there) than . . .	1
(show) what's what	16
do whatever you want	18
love it above all else	23

There's something disturbing about . . .	25
get the groceries	30
Where is the line between . . . ?	31
a tiny fraction of . . .	34
whether (you) like it or not	42
No one is authorized to (do it).	63
The way I see it,	64
I can just tell.	69
(I've) learned not to . . .	70
I don't look at it like that.	73
in a hostile setting	76
(do it) in ways that others don't	83
in worst-case scenarios	93
(That) can be lethal.	94
what bugs (him) about	107
It's a hassle for (him).	112
always have been (a bit) that way	114
drop out of high school	116
kick (him) out of the house	116
could use the discipline	118
missed out on (it)	131
(He's) emotionally closed.	138
let down his (tough-guy) guard	141

Session 11

hadn't been always so (bad)	13
give (them) the reputation for . . .	22
known as much for its ⟨A⟩ as for ⟨B⟩	23
(was) well prepared to (do . . .)	29
already had experience in . . .	30
Word went out that . . .	53
every bit as (repulsive) as	61
To make matters worse,	62
make (it) fit for . . .	66
cut out ⟨A⟩ in favor of ⟨B⟩	68
Most of the stories were about . . .	78
was . . . still no competition for . . .	82
doesn't really interest most people	84
the first of the . . . to . . .	89
Circulation was up to *x* copies.	95
for better of (for) worse	118
unworthy (someone's) attention	123
segregated from the rest of . . .	125
No one took it seriously.	128
force to be reckoned with	132
easily be expected to (do it)	135
has become increasingly difficult . . .	138
overcome your negative feelings about . . .	152

Session 12

The big question is (who . . .)	13
no expectations (whatsoever)	26
a house hold word for . . .	27

never publicly acknowledged (it)	34
become a dominant force in	44
made its way into the world of . . .	47
⟨A⟩ is ⟨B⟩'s nightmare.	68
(It does,) but just barely.	70
It awed us.	91
had no idea how . . . would be	96
came face-to-face with (him)	99
would have liked to (thank him)	104
make me feel like (the monster)	105
elements that contributed to . . .	108
left with the feeling that . . .	128
caught between ⟨A⟩ and ⟨B⟩	132
(not) seen in its entirety	134
carried away with (delight)	138
insisted that he throw (the child)	142
No (one) is going to . . .	147
is reported to have (done it)	149

Session 13

(the briefing) on how we are (to do . . .)	7
let my mind wander from . . .	8
would kill you if (they) could	15
rid them of (Saddam)	19
without a hitch	24
checking to see if . . .	25
(is) still aiming (his gun) at . . .	32
see what's up with . . .	41
couldn't say a word	50
there right in front of me	51
How could all that blood be from . . . ?	54
screamed and screamed until . . .	59
can still see it all to this very day	74
There were no (weapons) to be found.	75
look so lost	89
pay off the family's grief	101
He must not have been (a father).	102
doesn't even come close	103
Nothing other than . . . would stop me.	109
have served (my) time	115
hold true to the contract	119

Session 14

something that always was and always will be	11
take (none of this) for granted	13
go something like this	24
can take another couple of minutes	30
see irritation in their faces	32
don't take inconveniences without	33
we are all making up . . . as we go	38
Now that I am . . .	40
be recognized for excellent service	53
(The key) would not budge.	68
asked them if they would	72
bid (me) good night	75
several sizes too large	81
works his way from one end to the other	89
withdrawn totally into	100
(This is) just too much for (me.)	102
Not this one though.	105
can get cancer eating . . .	115
cannot believe the way they cooked . . .	120
There was nothing to be done.	130

Session 15

(conversation) over a good meal	6
I would not deny it.	7
would not last long if . . .	9
make a logical blunder	10
don't know any better	20
(We) were raised on it.	27
(shrimp) swept the country	46
will eat (it) if she has to	48
the first time I ever (did it)	49
got (our) arms around them	57
taste much the same as . . .	60
not easily converted to . . .	67
will eat anything if you just put enough . . . on it	70
go easy on . . .	75
Assuming that . . .	88
lose a solid pound every three days	92
Allow for (two months).	93
Don't you believe it for a minute.	95
Bear with it.	101
It won't hurt you.	103
go (days) without any . . . at all	104
makes you feel weak	105
That's what God put us here for.	113
but people do and you can	124
The worst thing may be that . . .	124
responsible for what he or she is	130
blame it on (your parents)	131
choose to be fat	132
the extreme opposite of . . .	134
Freedom consists in . . .	136

Session 16

of all things I can think of	1
of tremendous proportions	6
the whole idea of there being only (space)	9
two sides of the same coin	19
in the back of our mind	24
with all our advances in (physics)	29
what we will come up with	39

Morsels of the Universe

can't make out any significant shape to it	43
come into clear focus	45
"can go on and on and will never . . . "	46
What else is there besides . . .?	52
Let me illustrate this to you.	57
You can't do ⟨A⟩, much less ⟨B⟩	75
It's exactly the same thing with . . .	85
You cannot have ⟨A⟩ without ⟨B⟩	92
The same thing is true of . . .	99
(The Universe) ends in nothing.	117

[編者紹介]

佐藤良明 (さとう・よしあき)

1960年代にかぶったロックとアメリカの対抗文化の影響を引きずったまま現在に至る．アメリカ文学・メディア文化・ポピュラー音楽に関する論考多数．東大教授時代は，*The Universe of English* シリーズと自主制作のビデオ教材を通じて駒場（東京大学教養学部）の英語改革をリードした．早期退職後も，うたとことばの研究を通して，英語の心を伝える仕事を続けてきた．NHKテレビ『ジュークボックス英会話』『リトル・チャロ』講師．放送大学では歌うエクササイズに重きを置いた『ビートルズ de 英文法』を制作．主著に『定本 ラバーソウルの弾みかた』『ニッポンのうたはどのように変わったか』『英文法を哲学する』，主訳書にベイトソン『精神の生態学へ』，ピンチョン『重力の虹』，ディラン『The Lyrics』．

栩木玲子 (とちぎ・れいこ)

サンフランシスコに生まれ育つ．映画やテレビ番組の吹き替え翻訳を起点として，アメリカ文化の心を伝える仕事に長く関わってきた．法政大学教授時代には二つの母語で映像や文化に関する講義を担当しつつ，ウィリアム・T・ヴォルマン，コラム・マッキャン，アンナ・バーンズ，ジョイス・キャロル・オーツなど，現代の英語小説を翻訳・紹介．小説以外にも思想家ティモシー・リアリー，音楽家ビョーク，希代の女装俳優ディヴァインら，20世紀の先端文化に関わる人物たちのノン・フィクション翻訳も多い．NHKの総合英語教育企画『リトル・チャロ』では，コロンビア大学大学院で参加した脚本コースでの経験を生かして英文シナリオ制作に携わり，ラジオ番組の講師をつとめる．

The American Universe of English
アメリカの心と交わるリーディング

2010 年 4 月 28 日　初　版
2025 年 7 月 1 日　第 2 刷

［検印廃止］

編者──────佐藤良明・栩木玲子

発行所─────一般財団法人　東京大学出版会

　　　　　代表者　中島隆博

　　　　　153-0041　東京都目黒区駒場 4-5-29

　　　　　電話　03-6407-1069　FAX　03-6407-1991

　　　　　振替　00160-6-59964

印刷・製本──大日本法令印刷株式会社

© 2010 Yoshiaki SATO and
Reiko TOCHIGI, editors

ISBN 978-4-13-082141-4 Printed in Japan

JCOPY〈出版者著作権管理機構　委託出版物〉
本書の無断複写は著作権法上での例外を除き禁じられています．複写される場合は，そのつど事前に，出版者著作権管理機構（電話 03-5244-5088，FAX 03-5244-5089, e-mail: info@jcopy.or.jp）の許諾を得てください．